HARPERS' JOY
by
Bert Goolsby

Copyright © 2005, 2008, and 2018 by C. Tolbert Goolsby, Jr.

All rights reserved,
including the right of reproduction
in whole or in part in any form.

Artwork by Sara Jones

This book is a work of fiction. All the events, places, and characters are products of the author's imagination or used fictitiously. Any resemblance to actual events or locales or persons, living or dead, is purely coincidental.

Printed in the United States of America.
Third Edition

ISBN-13:978-1717106230
ISBN-10:1717106234

For Rachel, Jessica, and Anna Layne

Harpers' Joy

Today

    Many years ago, a dirt road, known to the locals as The Narrow Road, intersected State Highway 231 eight miles west of Tekoa, the seat of Semmes County. A traveler turning left onto the road and following its deep ruts all the way to the end would have seen a church and, behind the church, a cemetery dominated by its first grave marker, a large, eroded cross fashioned from Tennessee marble. The surrounding area, the traveler might have discovered, took its name from the last two words inscribed on the cross.

THE HARPERS
Buried here in this common grave are the remains of
William and Nancy Harper and their son John Robert,
Whom a Whirlwind lifted to the Arms of Jesus on May 13, 1815.
In the blink
Of an eye,
The souls of
The Harpers and
Their little boy
From the grave,
To Glory Land
They did fly.
Friend, do not grieve,
But believe
'Tis the Harpers' joy!

Saturday, September 7, 1946

Candle Reid squirmed, causing the chair to creak and grate. His distress came not so much from the throttling temperature in the courtroom of the Semmes County Courthouse as it did from the heat generated by the answers his wife gave to the questions asked by her divorce attorney.

"And how often would you say your husband drank to excess?" J. Hopson Fleming asked, his baritone voice rebounding off the once white but now dingy gray plaster walls of the courtroom.

Paula Gachet Reid patted both eyes with her fingertips. "Practically every night, if not every night. I can't think of one he didn't, come to think of it."

"And would the children see this? Your two daughters?"

"Yes, sir."

"What would be the effect on them, please ma'am?"

"They would cry. Get upset. I couldn't get them to do their homework. Because of that, their grades have suffered."

Fleming, who also served as the judicial district's solicitor or prosecutor, retrieved a document from a file folder that lay on his counsel table. "Mrs. Reid, by this petition for divorce *a mensa et thoro*, which I filed the other day, you express your intention to press for a legal separation against your husband, is that correct?"

Paula lowered her head. "Yes, sir."

"And that's because of his drinking, is that right?"

"Yes."

Fleming withdrew a handkerchief from his rear pocket and blotted his face. "His habitual drinking?"

"Yes, sir."

"Why don't you seek an outright divorce—a divorce *a vinculo matrimonii*?" Fleming held the last syllable of his last spoken word like an opera singer holding a note.

"I'm a Roman Catholic. We don't believe in divorce."

He turned toward Candle. "Is your husband a Catholic?"

For the first time since the hearing began, Paula looked at Candle. Her eyes imparted deep sorrow. "No," she muttered, "I don't know what he is. I don't think he's anything."

Fleming, still facing Candle, nodded. "I see. I see." After a moment, he turned back to Paula. "Have you sat down and tried to figure out how much you and the children will need each month to get by on? You got a figure?"

"Well, if we can keep the car and the house—"

"Excuse me, ma'am, are they paid for? The car and the house?"

"No," Paula said, shaking her head. "Together, the payments run close to one hundred dollars a month."

"So, how much do you feel you and the children require each month?"

"I've tried to be reasonable about this. I know he's got to live, too, and he'll need a place to stay at. I think we could get by on maybe two hundred and twenty-five dollars a month. Although, to be honest, it'll cost us closer to three hundred. Then there are some things you don't ordinarily think about. Goodness, I've thought about three or four things just sitting here. There's the children's—"

"Thank you, Mrs. Reid," Fleming said with a slight bow.

"Any cross-examination, Mr. Blumberg?" the Honorable L. Malcolm Pryde asked, fanning himself with a legal pad.

Bernard Blumberg, a Phi Beta Kappa key hanging from a watch chain across his vest, pulled himself up from his chair. "Just a couple of questions, if Your Honor please." He stepped toward the bench and smiled at the pretty, dark-haired woman on the witness stand. "You really feel you need two hundred and twenty-five dollars a month, Paula?"

Judge Pryde bolted forward. "Excuse me, Counselor, but let's not get familiar here. I know Mrs. Reid's the wife of your law partner. But she's also a party in a separation action. You will refer to her as 'Mrs. Reid.' Got that?"

Blumberg turned his head to one side. "Yes, sir. I'm sorry, Your Honor. Habit, I suppose."

"I didn't ask for an explanation or an apology. Get on with it, but hurry," he said with a wave of the hand. "It's as hot as blue blazes in here and I've got all this sweat dripping down and messing up my seeing glasses." He removed his black, horn-rimmed spectacles and wiped them with a sleeve of his robe.

Blumberg continued. "Mrs. Reid, do you need two hundred and twenty-five dollars a month? Do you honestly?"

"At a minimum."

"You know, of course, how much your husband makes annually; rather, has been making annually?"

"Yes."

"Being married to a lawyer—for what ten years?—you know that a lawyer's income is not at all predictable, is it?"

"He wasn't a lawyer when I married him, Mr. Blumberg. Except for when he was in law school, Candle's income has gone up every year we've been married. Thanks to your generosity."

Blumberg tilted his head and smiled. "So, if you are awarded two hundred and twenty-five dollars a month in temporary support, do you know how much that would leave him with to pay rent and to buy groceries and so forth?"

"He'll have enough, Mr. Blumberg, especially if he'd quit drinking," Paula said, now on the attack.

Blumberg crossed the courtroom to his counsel table and began sifting through a file folder as though he had all day to find whatever he was looking for. While he searched, a stillness settled over the courtroom, producing a silence that seemed to solidify.

Candle, embarrassed by the delay and sweating from every pore, pulled at Blumberg's arm, intending to offer him assistance so that he might him hurry along.

Before Candle could speak, Judge Pryde broke the silence. He did not sound happy. "Mr. Blumberg, let me tell you something. There's no need for you to beat a dead horse. I've seen the financial statements you and Solicitor Fleming have provided. And, you know, I have some personal familiarity with Mr. Reid. I'm ready to rule."

"If it please the Court," Blumberg said, "I still have some questions I'd like to ask Mrs. Reid."

Judge Pryde shifted his shoulders around and fanned his round, bald head. "Well, you can ask them if you want to, but they're not going to make any difference. I've already told you I'm ready to rule. I've heard enough. And I've got other things to do. I'm supposed to go play golf. As a matter of fact, it's with a couple of your clients, Mr. Blumberg. The Mayfields—the old man and Lester Junior. I'm looking for them any minute. We're supposed to go meet Dr. Kittredge at Ravenwood at eleven." He pointed to his wristwatch. "Look at what time it is now. You and Solicitor Fleming, both of y'all said this wouldn't take but a half hour at the most. Y'all've taken—what? Hour and fifteen minutes?"

Blumberg took a deep breath. "Yes, sir."

"Another thing," Judge Pryde went on, "the probate judge says he needs to use the courtroom at ten-thirty. He's got a marriage ceremony to do."

Blumberg bowed. "All right, sir. Thank you, Mrs. Reid. I've no more questions."

"I hope you don't have anything further, Solicitor," Judge Pryde said, shaking his head and using an irritating tone.

Fleming stood, glancing at Paula. "No, sir."

Blumberg, still standing, gestured toward Candle. "Your Honor, don't you wish to hear from the respondent?"

Judge Pryde sighed. "For what? I told you I've got his financial statement. Will he testify to anything differently than what he's already sworn to?"

"No, Your Honor, it's not about that."

"Then I don't need to listen to him, now do I?"

"Well, I would like for him to respond to Paula's—Mrs. Reid's testimony about his drinking."

"This is not a hearing on the merits, Mr. Blumberg. I'll hear from him about that all in due course. Anything else?"

Blumberg glanced at Candle and frowned. "I guess not. No, sir."

Judge Pryde grinned and pushed back the sleeves of his robe. He reminded Candle of a card shark with a winning hand, preparing to sweep the table of all its chips. "You may step down, Mrs. Reid."

Judge Pryde waited until Paula seated herself next to Fleming before saying more. "Gentlemen, by agreement, temporary custody of the parties' two children, Rose Mary and Margaret Ann, remains with Mrs. Reid. I'll get y'all a written order out the first of next week. But you're not going to like it, Mr. Blumberg, and Mr. Reid won't either. I'm gonna put in there he can't visit the children without some kind of proof he's sober at the time. Now if Mr. Reid wants to appeal, I'll tell you what. I've got a map out there in my car that'll show y'all exactly how to get to the Court of Appeals—or as I've heard it called, the Forum of the Mystic Oracles. He needs to get all his things completely out of the house today. Got that? I'm kinda inclined to give her exclusive possession of it. We stand adjourned."

With a bang of his gavel, Judge Pryde fled the courtroom. His flight reminded Candle of a vulture—a plump, well-fed one—taking wing from carrion upon the approach of a car.

***

Dewey Coltraine opened the massive oak door of the courtroom to admit his bride-to-be, Nellie Grace Prevatt, a seventeen-year-old, two years his junior. Before he could usher her inside, two men in seersucker suits stepped from the courtroom and eased past them into the hallway. One man, who carried a briefcase and who appeared the older of the two, smiled at Dewey and nodded toward Nellie while the other man neither spoke to nor looked at them. Dewey watched the men, whom he assumed to be lawyers, disappear down a flight of stairs.

Once inside the sweltering courtroom, Dewey removed a marriage license from his coat pocket and displayed it to Nellie. "You know what? You know what I think I'm gonna do with this right here once we get us a place to live at? I'm gonna frame it and put it up on the wall in our bedroom."

Nellie shifted a bouquet of violets from one hand to the other and reached for the back of Dewey's neck. "Don't be silly," she said, pulling his head down toward hers and pecking his cheek with a kiss that left a red, oval mark. "Nobody frames their marriage license."

Dewey touched where Nellie's lips had been and grinned. "You know, Nellie, what's just now dawned on me? After seein' them two fellas with their coats and ties on and everything, I'm not sure I'm dressed right for no weddin'."

Nellie's face brightened. "Oh, who cares what you've got on? I mean, look at me. Penny loafers, white socks, a skirt, and an old worn-out sweater. Do I look like a bride?"

"You do to me. And they don't come no prettier. Shoot, you'd look pretty even if you were wearin' an old croker sack."

Right at ten-thirty, Probate Judge Graham Anderson sailed into the courtroom with two giggling girls in tow. He invited Dewey and Nellie to join him inside the well of the courtroom. The two girls continued to giggle as Dewey and Nellie presented themselves to the judge. Dewey overheard one of the girls say, "Look there how she's shaking."

"You got the license, son?" Judge Anderson asked, casting a frown toward the girls—without effect.

Dewey handed the judge the license. He felt guilty doing it. He knew Nellie had lied about her age to avoid having to obtain parental consent to the marriage, a marriage her parents had no knowledge of and would not have approved of had they been asked.

The judge read over the license, pausing every now and then to glance up at the bride and groom. Each time the judge looked his way, Dewey dropped his head. He could not look the judge in the eye, knowing what he did.

"Okay," the judge said, laying the license on a nearby desk, "everything looks in order. I'll sign it after we get done here. Are y'all ready?"

Dewey's voice caught when he answered the judge. This prompted a fit of laughter from the two girls.

The judge pointed at the girls, his face glowing red. "Miss Prevatt. Mr. Coltraine, these two hyenas are my granddaughters. Please don't pay them any mind. They're just at that silly stage. There's no cure for it. Not as far as I know, there isn't."

Each of the girls looked at the other, covered her mouth, and burst into more laughter, leaving the judge to close his eyes and shake his head.

Dewey glanced at Nellie. He noticed she no longer seemed happy and gay but appeared as though she might break down and cry at any moment. He figured her change in mood had more to do with the behavior of the judge's granddaughters than with anything else—such as Nellie's not telling her parents what she and he planned to do that morning. The girls had managed to turn what was supposed to be a sweet, tender, serious affair into something to be made light of, to be laughed at. In the short time he had known and courted Nellie, Dewey had come to realize how fragile her emotional state could be. She wanted things to be just right and she would sometimes go to pieces when they weren't.

Judge Anderson wasted no time in administering Nellie and Dewey their vows, pronouncing them husband and wife, signing the license, pocketing the ten dollars that Dewey palmed him, and wishing them good luck and a "passel of young'uns." The granddaughters never stopped laughing and poking each other during the brief ceremony. Their grandfather's occasional scowls served only to encourage them to misbehave all the more.

When Dewey and Nellie exited the courtroom, Nellie broke down. "Dewey, those little girls, they . . . they just ruined everything. That judge, he just let them make fun of us. Did you hear them? He could've made them leave, if he'd wanted to. It wasn't anything like I expected."

The whole experience had also unnerved Dewey, so much so he felt an urgent need to use the toilet.

After Nellie's crying waned into sniffles and while she waited in the hallway, Dewey headed for a nearby men's room, a place of graffiti-filled walls and an overpowering stench. Too shy to use an open urinal unless he had to, he entered a stall and shut its door. Moments later, he heard footsteps and then voices. They seem to come from the vicinity of the urinals.

"Dad, did you see that?"

"See what?" the other voice said.

"That out there in the hall. With the flower bouquet."

"No, huh-uh."

"You didn't see that? Why, Helen Keller could've seen that."

"I thought you were married. What you looking at other women for?"

"Man-o-man, how I'd like to—"

The other man chuckled. "Now, now, son. We haven't got time for you to go messing around with some gal you just happened to see standing outside a latrine. We're late now. By the time we pick up the judge and get out to the golf course, we'll be lucky to make our tee time."

"'The judge'? What a joke. 'The judge.' If he's a judge, I'm Clark Gable."

"Well, regardless of what you may think, he's still our kind of judge, if you know what I mean."

Dewey heard a urinal flush.

"Wonder who that girl is anyway? She's the best-looking thing I've seen since I got out of the service, I'll tell you that. And I bet she's as pure as the driven snow. Bet you anything, she is."

"Son, you want my advice? I think you best leave that and anything like it alone."

"Look who's talking."

Another urinal flushed.

Dewey waited until the two men left before he vacated the stall. He knew they could only have been talking about Nellie. He felt nauseated, hearing them talk about her like they did. He also felt guilty for not confronting them and defending Nellie's honor. After all, she was his wife now. She was his to protect. Was this the way it would be from now on—other men wanting his wife? He felt relieved he had not seen the men or knew who they were. Somehow, not seeing them made it easier for him to try and put behind him what had occurred.

When Dewey rejoined Nellie in the hallway, he found her crying again. He rushed to her side and put his arm around her. He felt her trembling. "What's the matter, Nellie, honey? Somethin' wrong? Is it them little girls again?"

Nellie shook her head and wiped her eyes. "Did you see those two men who came out of the restroom right before you did?"

"No, why?"

"One of them about scared me half to death."

"He did? Did he touch you?"

"No. Not with his hands. I felt like his eyes did, though. He just . . . he just looked at me . . . in a real, real dirty way. I can't describe it exactly."

"What'd he look like?"

"I don't know, other than he had this golf hat on. Kinda young, but older than us. When he looked at me like he did, I . . . I turned the other way, he scared me so bad."

"What'd he do when you did that?"

"He just laughed, and him and the other man, they went on down the hall."

Dewey held his new wife close until she stopped crying. He wished he could do something about what had happened, but he didn't know of anything he could do; even assuming he could find the man. Besides, the man hadn't touched Nellie and he hadn't spoken to her. He'd only looked at her, and he'd laughed.

Harpers' Joy

Tuesday, November 5, 1946

Candle Reid stood nude in front of a three-member panel of laughing and pointing appellate judges. He attempted to hide his nakedness, front and back, with pages yanked from a legal pad, but the effort only provoked more laughter from the black-robed jurists. All at once, the presiding judge, a man with the face of a Boston Terrier, stopped laughing and scooted backwards in his chair. The judge reached down and, using both hands, lifted from the floor a gavel the size of a sledgehammer. Then he stood and began to pound the top of the bench, swinging the gavel like he was a gandy dancer.

"Mr. Reid! Mr. Reid!" the judge bellowed as he banged away at the bench top.

Candle opened his eyes at the mention of his name and found himself clothed in pajamas and buried deep below a stack of warm, musty, handmade quilts. Everything about his dream had vanished—everything, that is, but the banging noise. It continued.

"Mr. Reid! Mr. Reid!" his landlady called. Her voice sounded loud and urgent. "It's close to seven-thirty. Okay?" When Candle did not answer, she knocked again on the door, this time harder. "You awake? You said you didn't wanna be late for work."

He brought his head out from under the covers, blinking his eyes. "Thank you, Mrs. Blankenship. I hear you," he said with a heavy sigh.

"Better grab your umbrella when you get ready to leave. It's raining out. A regular toad-strangler."

"Yes, ma'am."

Candle, his tongue pasty and his throat dry, flung back the bed covers. He swung his skinny legs out from the bed and onto the cold floor. The second his bare feet touched it, sharp pains shot up his legs and spine and knifed their way through his shoulders to his arms and hands. Hopping on the sides of his feet and exclaiming "Ooh! Ooh! Ooh!" as he went, Candle bounded across the room toward an unlit, gas space-heater.

After an extended search, during which he alternated standing on his right foot and then on his left, he found a book of matches on the mantelpiece. He bent down to light the heater, thankful he had extinguished its flames the night before. The task, as with any other he undertook, required more effort than he expected. He spent three matches in the process.

With the heater lit and the room smelling of new heat, Candle hurried back to bed. He disappeared beneath the pile of quilts, but not before grabbing a glass off his bedside table and guzzling its contents: the watery remains of a bourbon-on-the-rocks.

Candle kept himself covered until he sensed the temperature in the room would permit at least his head to venture out. He turned onto his right side and gazed at the linoleum rug that covered most of the dust-laden floor. Embraced within the red border of the rug was a large, faded, white print of the United States of America, its states outlined in blue. The print, however, no longer depicted the forty-eight states. Florida no longer formed part of the Union. It had worn away.

The missing state reminded Candle of how ripped apart his life had become in the two months since Paula, his wife of ten years, had turned him out of their two-story home and initiated divorce proceedings in which she accused him of alcoholism. Paula's discovery one weekend of a quarter-filled bottle of bourbon hidden in the tank of a commode had been the last straw.

In addition to being awarded their much-mortgaged house, Paula had been given custody of their only automobile, a new 1946 Ford, and of Rose Mary and Margaret Ann, their two daughters—nice, pretty girls, but given to much whining and, like their mother, to expensive tastes. As Candle had anticipated, the district judge, the Honorable L. Malcolm Pryde—or Meng the Merciful, as Candle and other lawyers in Semmes County called Pryde because of his remarkable resemblance to The Buddha and his inclination to give a woman anything she prayed for in a divorce case—had clobbered him with temporary alimony and child support. The amount Pryde had ordered Candle to pay left him just enough each month to maintain a close relationship with his favorite bottled companion, Johnny Gray.

Candle missed his wife and his dog—but at that moment, not necessarily in that order. He missed his neighbors. He missed his house. He missed his car. And he missed his bed. But most of all, he missed his daughters.

The afternoon of the hearing on his wife's request for temporary support, both girls had wrapped their slender arms about his neck and shoulders and wailed like mourners at a funeral, telling him over and over how much they loved him and wanted him with them. After the hearing, Candle, accompanied by a deputy sheriff, had been allowed back in the house to collect some of his clothing and other personal items. Not only had his daughters cried, they had begged their mother to let them live with Candle so he would have someone to look after him when he came home from work each day. His wife had dismissed the idea with an order that the children march to their rooms and do their homework.

It had been difficult for Candle that afternoon to make his daughters break their hold of him. Indeed, their distress and his longing to remain encircled by their warm little arms had moved Candle to resolve to quit drinking altogether. If complete sobriety was all it would take for his wife to permit him to return home and make the family whole again, he decided he would make that concession.

Nor did Candle have any doubt that he could do it. His conviction stemmed from the fact that he did not see himself as an alcoholic. He realized he sometimes drank too much, but that, he reasoned, did not make him an alcoholic. He knew a lot of people who drank more than he did and more often, and he never heard anyone accuse them of being alcoholics. Also, he had never missed a day of work because of his drinking. And he knew this about himself: he never drank before five in the afternoon, or what he referred to as "bull-bat time."

But Candle's resolve to give up alcohol proved short-lived. It died moments after he brought his things in from his house and found himself alone in his new abode: two furnished rooms close by his downtown law office. The lure of a bottle, still in its brown paper bag and sitting on the kitchen table next to his stuffed, black-leather briefcase, had proved too powerful for Candle to resist, especially considering all the work the briefcase contained—work that he dreaded to do.

Bert Goolsby

As he lay in bed staring at the floor, Candle debated which of the two rooms was the more depressing—the bedroom, with its linoleum rug and its framed print of a rail-thin wolf standing beneath a darkening sky on a snow-covered hilltop, or the kitchen, with its two curtainless windows and its bare walls and floors.

Candle decided a small, black-and-white photograph that he had placed on the mantelpiece the day that he moved in probably gave the edge to the bedroom, though he had thought the photograph would brighten the room as well as his spirits. The photograph, a snapshot of Candle with his wife and daughters, had been taken on Easter morning seven months before. The four of them stood in front of their home in Forest Hills, one of Tekoa's more desirable subdivisions.

Both daughters wore black, patent-leather shoes and carried an Easter basket. His wife gripped a large, white purse with both hands. Candle, droopy-eyed and dressed in a dark suit that predated the late war, stood behind his daughters and to the right of his petite wife, his scissors-like left hand hidden, as usual, in a coat pocket. Everyone but Candle was smiling. His thin face carried a dazed and drained expression. And for good reason. Candle's thoughts that Easter morning, as he recalled each time he viewed the photograph, were not on the price Jesus paid at Calvary for the sins of man but on the price Candle had paid at Tanenbaum's for the new outfits worn by his wife and daughters.

The bathroom was also a dreadful, cheerless place. And it was not just the fixtures—the toilet that ran nonstop and always, always demanded two flushes; the free-standing sink that consumed anything dropped into its basin; and the rust-stained, slow-draining bathtub that defied every known cleaning agent—that gave the bathroom its dismal atmosphere. Rather, it was the *Watchtower* and *Awake!* magazines that his landlady, a Jehovah's Witness, left scattered all about in a none-too-subtle effort to convert Candle to her faith.

Although the magazines did not have their desired effect—for he refused to read them—their covers and illustrations, in particular those that pictured a Coming-Again Jesus or an avenging angel, made Candle uneasy and fed his always-present feeling of impending doom.

Not that he lacked good reason to believe that doom was imminent, even aside from Paula's recent actions and Judge Pryde's temporary support order, a veritable road map to instant poverty. Bernard Blumberg, his law partner for all of the seven years Candle had been a lawyer and their firm's managing partner, principal trial lawyer, and main breadwinner, now lay in a coma in DeBusk-Inman Hospital.

Blumberg had suffered a massive stroke several days before while arguing a motion before Judge Pryde. To add insult to injury, Judge Pryde sent word to Candle right afterward that Blumberg had lost. But Blumberg always lost in front of Judge Pryde, no matter the merits of his case, if another Semmes County lawyer represented the other side. There was one exception to the latter rule: if the State Bank and Trust Company of Tekoa, a major client of Blumberg & Reid, was a party to the action, the State Bank and Trust Company would always win.

Candle heard the toilet flush and, after a minute or so, flush again. "Mr. Reid," came Louise Blankenship's coarse voice from inside the bathroom, "it's all yours. And don't forget to wash the tub out when you're done." Then came the sound of his bathroom door being unlatched, followed by the opening, shutting, and latching of the door to her side of the house.

Candle eased himself out of bed, stretched, and yawned. How he dreaded the next nine and one-half hours.

***

A sweep of the windshield wiper on the green-and-yellow Swizzle-Kola truck gave Dewey Coltraine a glimpse of Vasil Franklin's Grocery. A rusted, black and white "See Rock City" sign covered the top of the store, a gray, weathered building that tilted to the right. It was one of the many almost-everything-behind-the-counter stores on his soft-drink route.

Dewey knew the challenge he faced in selling Swizzle-Kola to Vasil Franklin and other storekeepers would be almost hopeless that day as hard as it was raining. The weather was also very cold, uncommonly so for that time of the year. Few people went to the store to buy soft drinks in that type of weather. Too, most folks on the Harpers' Joy leg of his Tuesday route drank Pepsi or Coca-Cola, not Swizzle, a lemon-lime, minted cola promoted more for its medicinal qualities than its taste. "Don't Fizzle, Drink Swizzle," read the stenciled yellow letters that arched above the Swizzle-Kola label on the back of his green jacket.

Aside from the rain, the cold, and the competition, Dewey knew he was not a good salesman. But he was willing to give selling soft drinks a try. So far, nothing else had worked out for him since the Army had discharged him in the spring. Also, jobs were becoming harder to find as more and more returning servicemen entered the work force. For the most part, he had worked here and there at odd jobs, mainly on construction sites or in filling stations. Two regular, full-time jobs had initially held promise, one at a meat packing plant and the other at a peanut oil mill; but he did not last long at either place because each one required lifting heavy weights that his small, bony frame simply could not handle.

The job at Swizzle-Kola had been a godsend, coming as it did soon after his marriage. He had landed the job as a result of a chance encounter with Troy Hammond, the owner of the Swizzle-Kola Bottling Company. While walking and thumbing his way down the road early one morning to Tekoa to seek work, Dewey had happened across the soft-drink bottler as he grappled with a flat tire in a bad location. Dewey had stopped and helped. Hammond had not only given him a ride into town that day, he had also given him a job.

Dewey turned into the store's puddle-filled drive, stopped next to the overhang out front, and switched off the ignition. The motor, seemingly gifted with the right of free choice, continued to run until it choked down.

With the cold rain stinging his face, Dewey made a dash for the front door. Once inside, he went straight to where Vasil Franklin and another man stood next to a small, trash-burner stove. "Mornin', Mr. Franklin," he said, his teeth chattering and body shaking.

The storekeeper did not return his greeting. He simply nudged the other man's shoulder, edging him over to make room for Dewey.

"Who that is, Mr. Vasil?" the other man asked.

Franklin, a pale, narrow-shouldered man, turned his head and spit at the hot surface of the stove. The spit hit its mark, rolled up into a little white ball, sizzled and vaporized. "Ain't nobody," he said to his blind companion. "Just the Swizzle man."

As all three men crowded around the stove, their backsides toward its red glow, Dewey recalled what Hammond had told him about Franklin the first time Hammond had shown Dewey the route. Hammond had said Franklin probably would never buy anything, but Dewey would have to stop and make the attempt anyway. Hammond said he believed in "always keeping on keeping on," a notion Dewey did not share.

To him, a hurdle was not a barrier to jump over but to go around—if you could. If you couldn't, then you were to stop and wait for the barrier to disappear or turn around and go back the way you came.

Dewey turned and faced the rough-breathing storekeeper and the other man. "Mr. Franklin, I don't reckon you wanna buy no Swizzles from me this mornin', huh?"

Franklin laughed. "Boy," he said, his thumbs stretching the faded, red braces that held up his grimy, gray britches, "I ain't bought nothin' from you since you done took over this route. And I didn't buy nothin' from the fella what had it 'fore you did neither. Y'all ought to only sell that stuff at the drug store. It tastes awful. Taste like somethin' my mama used to give me for the croup when I was a little boy. You ever taste it, Moses?"

"Taste what, Mr. Vasil?" the other man asked, his unseeing eyes drifting and bobbing about.

"Swizzle. Swizzle-Kola."

"No, sir," Moses said.

"Well, you ain't missed nothin', I'll tell you that."

Franklin walked over to the soft-drink cooler a few feet away. "Let me ask you somethin', boy. How much you done sold this mornin' already?"

"How many cases, you mean? A case of Swizzles and one root beer," Dewey said as Franklin marked the number with his fingers. "A strawberry. And a mixed crate of orange and grape." He paused, noting the four fingers Franklin held up. "But you're just my second stop."

Franklin lowered his hand to his side and snickered. "Four

crates? That all? That ain't much."

Dewey lowered his head. "No, sir. It ain't."

Franklin, running his tongue over his lips, lifted the stainless-steel lid to the cooler and peered inside. "Boy," he said, "come over here a second. I wanna show you somethin' other."

Dewey joined Franklin at the cooler, a rusting white box with red lettering that advertised Coca-Cola. Franklin, holding the lid with one hand, pointed with his other to the twenty or so bottles immersed up to their necks in the cooler's cold, turbid water. "Look down in there and tell me what you don't see."

Dewey studied the insides of the cooler for a moment. With his head held to one side and his mouth open, he looked at Franklin. "Sir?" he said.

"I asked you to tell me what you **don't** see."

Dewey looked again and laughed a nervous laugh, still not sure of what he should not be seeing. "Well, Mr. Franklin, I don't see a lotta things."

Franklin let go the lid, causing Moses to jump and cry "Hup!" when it hit the top of the cooler.

Franklin chortled and, still looking at Dewey, nodded in Moses' direction and chortled again. Dewey did not respond in kind. He was still thinking about Franklin's question.

Franklin walked behind the counter that paralleled the left-inside wall of the store. He picked up a small Blue Horse tablet, opened it, and tore a clean, blue-line page free from the binder coil. "Boy, that was a good answer. A real good'un. Wasn't it, Moses?"

"Sir?" Moses asked, turning toward Franklin, a hand to his ear.

Dewey remained by the drink box, going over in his mind about why his answer had been a good one. Franklin, his lips puckered and eyes half closed, twice ran a finger back and forth along the surface of the counter. He wet the dull point of a pencil with his long tongue and wrote something down on the page from the tablet. "You married, ain't you?" he said, lifting his head and pointing to Dewey's wedding band.

Dewey lifted his left hand and bent his ring finger. "Yes, sir, I am," he said, his chest swelling. "Her name's Nellie."

Franklin raised up and rubbed his chin. "Where y'all live at, you and your wife?"

"Up near Gladstone right now. There with her folks."

"Her folks?"

"Yes, sir. Me and Nellie, we can't afford to rent us no place. Not right now, we can't. Not 'til I get this route built up some," Dewey said, returning to the stove.

"Well, boy, if you ask me, that might be a long, long time." Franklin smiled, exposing teeth that would soon leave open spaces unless attended to. "Let me ask you this. What'd you do 'fore you hired on with Swizzle?"

"Well, after I got outta the Army in March, I worked here and yonder. I tried workin' at—"

"You mean the Army took a little bitty skinny fella like you?" Franklin said.

"Yes, sir. I was in for near 'bout two years. From '44 to the first part of this year."

"What you make of that, Moses?" Franklin asked.

"Make of what, Mr. Vasil?" Moses said, turning his head toward Franklin's voice.

"Near the end of the war, the Army started draftin' the runts," Franklin said, using a disparaging tone.

"I wasn't drafted," Dewey interjected. "I joined up. Did it soon as I turned seventeen. That's how come I dropped outta school my junior year."

Franklin laughed. "What'd you do in the Army? I know you wasn't in no infantry. You sho' don't look like no fightin' man. Not to me, you don't."

"Drove a truck."

Franklin slapped his thigh. "See there!" he exclaimed, breaking into a big smile. "I sho' can call 'em. Didn't I say you wasn't no fightin' man? Yes, sir. I sho' can call 'em." He bent over the counter, resting his elbows on its top. "You go overseas?" he asked.

"No, sir. We stayed right here. My outfit—we was supposed to go to Japan, though. Least, that's what somebody said. Then the war ended, and we didn't have to go. I sure was glad. I didn't—"

"You ever been in any kinda trouble? With the law, I mean?" Franklin said, interrupting and looking squint-eyed at Dewey.

"No, sir."

Franklin grinned. "You know what? I do believe you the one. Yessiree. Don't you, Moses?"

Moses raised his head. "Yes, sir. If you says so."

"There's this fella what comes in here sometime," Franklin said, his smile broadening into a grin. "Rich fella. He owns a coupla hundred acres up the road a piece, there in Harpers' Joy. He uses it for huntin' and fishin' and such." Franklin chuckled and winked at Dewey. "Tell you somethin', though," he whispered. "I seen him ride by here a coupla times on his way up yonder, and both times he's had him a—" Franklin caught himself and did not complete his sentence.

"Let's just say it's his gitaway and leave it at that," he said, speaking louder. "Besides, it ain't nobody's business what he does up there noways. That's one thing what's wrong with this world today." Franklin now talked with his hands in motion. "Folks, they don't mind their own business. Ain't that right, Moses?"

"Yes, sir. Right. They don't. Ain't nobody do it," Moses replied. "Least, nobody I knows do."

Franklin glanced at Moses out of the corner of his eye and then continued. "Anyhow, the fella, he was in the store here just the other day and told me he needs him somebody to kinda watch over his place when he ain't up there. Says he's done bought one of them Stout foldin' houses and had 'em tow it in up there. He's done sunk a well, put in electricity—everything. The person, he could live in it, in the foldin' house for nothin'. Says he lookin' for him somebody what wouldn't be one what'd steal or nothin'. Fella told me he'd give me ten dollars iffen I'd help him find somebody like that. 'Bout the only ones come to mind was you and the Bamby Bread man. You know him, don't you, boy? Sissy-talkin' fella. Name's Yandle."

"Yes, sir. I've seen him a time or two."

Franklin's tongue darted out and licked at his lips and his cheeks twitched in and out as he stood staring at Dewey. "But ain't no need for me to talk to him 'bout it 'cause I do believe you it," he said, nodding.

Dewey stepped away from the stove and brushed the seat of his trousers with the back of his hands. "Me? How come me?" he asked.

"Well, you need you a place, don't you? Mr. Troy Hammond, he give you a job, didn't he? That tells me he must think you're all right. Plus, you done been in the Army and all. Main thing, though, is you got yourself a wife. The Bamby Bread man, I know he don't. With a wife livin' there with you, that'd mean there'd just 'bout always be somebody watchin' the place when you'd be off at work or gone somewhere or other. The fella what owns the place, he'd like somebody like that better, I'd 'spect. I know I would."

Franklin nodded toward Moses. "Also, he don't want nobody but white folks livin' on his place neither."

For the first time, it registered with Dewey that the color of the third man in the store differed from his. Franklin's reference to color embarrassed Dewey and caused his face to feel warm.

"Whatcha face all red for, boy?" Franklin said.

Dewey looked at Moses, relieved Moses could not see him.

Franklin laughed. "Come on, boy, don't you worry none 'bout him," he said. "He knows he ain't white. Don't you, Moses?"

"If you says so, Mr. Vasil," Moses said. "I can't say I rightly knows what color is."

Franklin aimed a long finger with a yellow nail at Dewey. "One other thing. Fella said whoever lives there, he can't be nosey. Your wife, she can't be neither. You and her, y'all'd have to mind your own beeswax."

The qualifications confused Dewey. "He wants somebody to watch his place, but they can't be nosey?" he asked.

"When it comes to **him**, dang it all!" Franklin exclaimed. "They can't be nosey when it comes to him," he said, using a less excited tone. "Anybody else, they'll need to find out exactly what they're doin' there and who they are and all. Understand?"

"Yes, sir. Don't be nosey when it comes to him but be that way with everybody else."

"The fella's name is Lester Mayfield, Jr. Him and his daddy, they own the State Bank and Trust in town and a whole lotta other things." Franklin held out the paper that he had torn from the tablet. "Here, put this in your pocket," he said as Dewey reached for it, "and sometime today, when you git a chance, you give him a call there at the bank. I done wrote down his name for you and the phone number he left with me." Franklin pointed to the counter top. "He told me he don't usually go home 'til 'round six-thirty or so."

"Yes, sir."

"Now when you talk to him, you tell him I the one told you to git in touch with him. That's important. Real important." Franklin's tongue again made a sweep of his lips. "You hear me good, don't you, boy?"

"Yes, sir." Dewey nodded. "I'll tell him you the one told me."

Dewey did not know whether to believe Franklin or not about the possibility of having a free place for him and Nellie to live. Hammond, his boss, had told him that Franklin was known to play tricks on route salesmen and he did them most times out of meanness rather than for fun. Still, he wondered if what Franklin had told him could be true. He knew this much: trick or no, the first chance he got he would try to get in touch with the man. He didn't see where he had anything to lose. He had endured tricks many times in the past and they had not hurt him any—at most, they had only embarrassed him. Besides, he thought, if he could get the place, it would be such a wonderful surprise for Nellie.

Excited, he put the note Franklin gave him into the shirt pocket of his green, yellow-striped Swizzle-Kola uniform. "I'm much obliged, Mr. Franklin," he said, buttoning his pocket and patting it.

"Ain't no need to thank me. Just so I git my ten dollars."

"Yes, sir," Dewey said.

"And one other thing."

"Yes, sir," Dewey replied, thinking Franklin had more advice to impart.

"I still don't need no Swizzles."

Dewey didn't care. He figured he'd come away with something better than the sale of a couple of cases of drinks. He'd got a lead on a place where he and his pretty bride could live for free, a place far removed from his in-laws. Everything seemed to be looking up.

***

Lester Mayfield, Jr., vice-president and loan officer for the State Bank and Trust Company of Tekoa, smirked at the two faces staring down at him from the other side of his oversized, mahogany desk. His chair groaned as he sat back, his lips together and his arms crossed. "We'll give you until Friday afternoon, Lucas. That's three more days." He uncrossed his arms. "If you haven't made your payment by five o'clock that afternoon, then you can just kiss your place goodbye because that's when we'll just turn it all over to our lawyers. Understand me?"

Colin Lucas nodded. The child by his side, her mouth held open, twisted her neck and gawked at him.

Mayfield pitched forward in his chair. "Lucas, let me hear you say it. 'Five o'clock Friday afternoon.' "

"Yes, sir. I got me till Friday, five o'clock." Lucas stood staring at Mayfield for three or four seconds and then slapped his hat against his thigh. "I'm much obliged, Mr. Mayfield." He took the child by her bent wrist. "Come on, honey. Tell Mr. Mayfield so long."

The child, her head jerking about, mumbled something to Mayfield that sounded to him like "yo yo."

Mayfield studied the child for a few seconds, scowled, and glanced down at some papers on his desk. Without looking up or speaking, he waved Lucas away. The trembling man, saying nothing more and, followed by the limping, jerking little girl, withdrew from Mayfield's office, his bare head held low.

After they left, Mayfield stood and peeked out through the Venetian blind behind his desk. He saw the rain had slackened. He felt he just had to get out of there. He hated working in the bank. It was not the job; it was the place. The bank gave him chills each time he walked inside. It reminded him of a crypt, with its somber sandstone exterior and its cold marbled interior. And then there were the caged employees, most of whom appeared old as Scottish ghosts and moved about like zombies.

The job itself, however, brought him much satisfaction, particularly when he made borrowers honor their solemn obligations—borrowers like Colin Lucas. Were it not for people like he himself, he believed, people like Lucas would ruin life for everyone else and chaos would hold sway.

His brief association with the Japanese had convinced him—if he had needed convincing, which he didn't—that there was value in having a class of warrior nobility to enforce society's rules. Indeed, he considered himself a samurai, albeit an economic one. When he became a banking executive, the responsibility fell to him for enforcing the rules of commerce that society imposed upon itself. And for his efforts, society conferred upon him certain privileges. These privileges, as he viewed them, allowed him to do pretty much as he pleased.

Mayfield turned around and switched on the intercom that connected him with the secretary he shared with his father, the president of the State Bank and Trust Company of Tekoa. "Miss Thacker, is my old man still here?"

Flossie Thacker's snippy voice responded but not quick enough to suit Mayfield. "You mean **Mr. Mayfield**?"

He cursed to himself. He hated the woman, but he understood why his father kept her on the bank's payroll. As the elder Mayfield explained it one afternoon over several whiskey sours at the country club, "Son, one night—it was before you were born, probably about thirty years ago—I took that woman to bed. The way I figure it, that little indiscretion has cost the State Bank and Trust Company about fifty thousand dollars thus far." Mayfield shuddered at the mental picture that revelation produced each time that he thought about it.

"You **know** who I'm talking about," Mayfield said, through clenched teeth. "Is he here?"

This time there was a definite, obvious, deliberate wait. "He's with someone," she said at last.

Mayfield cursed to himself again. "Tell him I'm leaving, and I'll call him tonight. I'll call him after I get out of the Vestry meeting," he said, using the same tone as before and remembering his early evening appointment at St. John's Episcopal Church. He did not relish attending the meeting; however, he understood Southern society expected its banking executives to participate fully in all aspects of community life, from the courthouse to the schoolhouse and from the clubhouse to the church house and he did his part. Mayfield held leadership positions in almost every organization to which he belonged and almost always volunteered to direct fund-raising campaigns, whether to fight disease or pursue some other notable objective.

"And what should I tell your wife should she call, Mr. Mayfield, hmmmmm?" Miss Thacker asked.

Mayfield recoiled at the thought of his wife, a quarrelsome, beefy woman. When he last saw her that morning, she had waddled naked from the bathroom into the hallway, her thick thighs scraping against each other and her colossal breasts covered over by arms that reminded Mayfield of fresh hams. He blinked away the image. "Just tell her I'll see her later," he said, grimacing as he spoke.

Mayfield left his office and hurried behind the bank to the parking lot where he had parked his Packard, a polished, black four-door sedan with whitewall tires. He stood beneath his brass-handled umbrella, gazing at the front of the car for a moment and admiring the chromed grille extensions that wrapped around the bottom of the two front fenders. Mayfield likened the five curved, silvery bands of each extension to a music staff. Each one, the right as well as the left, gave the automobile the look of a love tune.

He had been the first person in Tekoa to get one of the Clipper Deluxe Eights after the Packard Motor Car Company resumed automobile production. His father gave him the car following his discharge in New Orleans from the United States Navy. His father also made him vice-president of the bank and gave him a twenty-five per cent share of the bank's stock.

Mayfield tossed the umbrella behind the front seat onto the carpeted floor and leaned into the car. As light rain pelted his back, he ran a hand across the front seat, caressing its soft leather. Once settled behind the steering wheel, he shut the door and sat still for a moment, savoring the new-car smell that still graced the interior of the automobile and thinking about how relieved he felt to be away from his desk.

A degree in history from Sutcliffe College had not prepared Mayfield for a career in banking. Although he enjoyed the power and prestige of being a banker, he had intended to become a lawyer. But the war, as it did for so many others, intervened and he entered the Navy in 1942 after graduating from college and marrying Georgia Ann Hascall, his high school sweetheart.

Mayfield served as a communications officer aboard the USS Hansford, an attack transport ship. Although he saw no combat, he traveled seas prowled by Japanese submarines and he was in Tokyo Bay when the Japanese representatives signed the surrender documents aboard the battleship Missouri. Mayfield left the Navy nine months later, having attained the rank of lieutenant.

Mayfield unbuttoned his vest, freeing his ballooning belly, and loosened his tie before starting the car and shifting into reverse. As he adjusted the rearview mirror, he glimpsed the top of his head and swore. Although only twenty-five, he was already bald as a schoolboy's marble. He blamed his baldness on the head coverings that the Navy had made him wear, especially the steel helmets.

Pulling out of the parking lot, Mayfield turned left and drove up Main Street. He circled the courthouse square at the end of the block, racing past the law offices opposite the courthouse, running red lights and daring any policeman to stop him. After all, his father was the county chairman of the Democratic Party and his father-in-law, the Honorable Robert William Hascall, was the municipal judge.

***

Candle Reid stood in the wind and rain outside the courthouse, waiting to cross the street while gripping a file folder with one hand and pressing down his hat with his other. When at last the light changed, he stepped from the concrete sidewalk down onto the slick, brick street. Suddenly, out of the corner of his eye, Candle spotted a fast-approaching dark object. He leapt backwards for the safety of the curb as a large Packard automobile sped by. "You're going to kill somebody one of these days, you stupid idiot!" he shouted at the receding car.

"Wonder why that big ol' Packard ain't stopped for you, Mr. Reid?" a vendor of parched peanuts asked Candle, who stood beside him thoroughly shaken. "He tryin' to kill you or somethin'?"

"Why don't you 'ask the man who owns one'?" Candle answered, repeating the Packard Motor Car Company's popular slogan, his voice quivering. "The sorry devil. Those Mayfields, they think—" He did not finish the sentence but looked around to determine if anyone other than Shorty, the peanut vendor, had heard him. He felt relieved when he saw no one else in earshot.

His heart pulsating, Candle reached the opposite curb. He made his way to the blue awning of the *Tekoa New Dealer*, pausing there until he recovered from the close call. He then walked to a stairway next door to the newspaper office. The stairway led up to the second-floor law offices of Blumberg & Reid, a defense firm in a judicial district whose ill-tempered judge often bragged, even in open court, about being "a plaintiff's judge."

Candle shook his head. It was always something. Always. It had all started the day he entered this world—before that, even. His poor mama died at his birth, but not before, so his aunts had reminded him often enough, she saw he had only two fingers on his left hand. They always believed she had died of a broken heart. And then somebody, his daddy or the doctor who delivered him or some clerk at the courthouse, went and screwed up his name on the birth certificate. His name should have been "Candell," not "Candle."

Candle wondered while he stood in front of the newspaper offices what else could happen to him that had not already happened. "Yes, sir. It's always something," Candle said aloud as he opened the door to the stairway and began the long trip up to his office, the file under his arm.

Exhausted by the climb, he entered the firm's outer office, an area that doubled as a waiting room and as a secretary's office. Almost immediately, Judy Claire, the firm's only secretary, stood and handed him a note from across the divider that separated her desk from the waiting area. "He wanted you to call him just as soon as you got in," she said, pointing to the paper. "I'm sorry."

Candle nodded while throwing the file onto Judy's desk. The file hit an empty flower vase, knocking it to the bare wooden floor. The vase broke, as glass splinters flew in every direction. Judy winced. So did Candle.

"Aw durn. Now, why'd I go and do that? I swear," he said, removing his hat. "Anything about Mr. Blumberg?"

"No, sir," she answered, bending to pick up the broken glass.

"When you get done with that," he said, nodding toward the floor and grimacing, "how about calling the hospital while I return this." He waved the note and headed down the hallway toward his office.

The instant Candle switched on the light and saw everything atop his desk—scattered files, unanswered mail, unpaid bills, and old *Look* and *Life* magazines—a nauseous feeling swept over him. "Lord, have mercy," he said, his chest heaving, "just look at all that crap. Just look at it!"

He searched his desk for the telephone but did not see it anywhere. He found it only when he went behind his desk and followed the phone line from the wall to where the line entered the bottom, left drawer of his desk. The telephone sat next to a half-filled bottle of Johnny Gray. Candle considered the telephone, especially why he would put it in a desk drawer. He tried to think, but he could not remember.

He retrieved the phone from the drawer and felt tempted to pick up the bottle of Johnny Gray too, but he put that devil behind him—for right then. He lifted the handset.

"Number, please," the operator asked.

He held the note at arm's length. "Seven, one, one, three, five."

After two rings, a female answered. Her voice reminded him of the sound rusted hinges made when a door opened.

"Put me through to Mr. Mayfield, please, Miss Thacker," he told her. "This is Candle Reid returning his call."

"Junior or senior?" she inquired. "Because if you're calling—"

"Senior," Candle said, cutting her off.

He waited, cradling the telephone between his chin and shoulder as he lit a cigarette. Mayfield greeted Candle as he inhaled a deep draw. Candle choked as he tried to respond.

"I'm fine," Candle said, coughing.

"Doesn't sound like it," Mayfield retorted.

Candle pounded his chest. "Just my cigarette. What can I do for you, Mr. Mayfield?"

"How's Bernie? Y'all heard anything different? Last I heard, things didn't look too good for him."

Candle sighed, relieved Mayfield had not asked about the *Brazeale* case, a complicated foreclosure action he had neglected to file for the State Bank and Trust Company. The bank had given him the file over three months before. "I've got Judy calling right now on our other line. I'll let you know if his condition's changed any."

Judy appeared in the doorway just as he spoke her name. She shook her head. "Judy just came in here. Mr. Blumberg hasn't changed."

Judy nodded.

"Well, keep me posted," Mayfield said. "The other thing I was calling you about was that *Brazeale* property."

Candle started thinking up excuses for not having filed suit. "Yes, sir."

"Have you done anything on it yet?" Mayfield asked.

"Well, yes," Candle lied. "But I—"

"Have you served the summons and complaint yet?"

"No, sir. I haven't. I needed to—"

"You haven't?" Mayfield asked. "Good. Excellent, in fact. Don't do it."

"Don't do it?" Candle asked, not believing. "Don't do it, you say?"

"Yeah. They've contracted to sell the property to Smuggy Parker. You know, runs Parker's Recapping and Vulcanizing. Smuggy's thinking about putting a Western Auto Store there. He's got a franchise all lined up and everything."

Candle jumped from his chair, thrilled beyond measure at the news.

"And Candle?"

"Yes, sir?"

"Next time you talk to Mrs. Blumberg, tell her I called and asked about Bernie. Would you do that for me?" Mayfield hung up before Candle could respond.

"Maybe I will and maybe I won't," Candle said to a dead phone line, wondering why Mayfield could not just call Mrs. Blumberg himself and express his concern for her husband.

"Sir?" Judy asked.

"Oh, nothing," he said. "Nothing."

When Judy left to return to her desk, Candle sat thinking about his law partner and what he was going to do if, as expected, he died. Candle had always felt like he was in way over his head. But Mr. Blumberg had always been there to help him. Always. He eyed the bottle of Johnny Gray, wishing it was "bull-bat time."

***

Five miles out of town, Lester Mayfield, Jr. spotted Vasil Franklin's store. He drove beneath the overhang and blew the horn. No one appeared. He blew again, this time longer. Still, no one came out.

Mayfield switched off the engine and stormed out of the car, turning his coat collar up against his neck as he ran. Cursing, he flew up the loose, rickety steps that led to the front entrance of the store. When Mayfield got to the top step, he yanked open a shredded screen door and lunged for the sign-plastered front door. Before he could push it open, however, the door gave way, causing him to stumble forward.

Vasil Franklin, who stood on the other side of the door, his mouth wide open, caught Mayfield before he could fall to the floor. "Mr. Mayfield, sir!" Franklin exclaimed, his voice marked by nervous laughter. "Whoa there! I got you! I got you!"

"Let go of me!" Mayfield yelled, shifting his shoulders about. Franklin dropped his hands from Mayfield's upper arms. "How many times has somebody got to blow his horn to get some service around here?"

"Sorry, Mr. Mayfield, sir. I come as fast I could, sir. Had to grab myself a jacket." Franklin put on a pleasant, appeasing face. "You need somethin' other, sir?"

"No, I don't need anything. I was just out for a nice little walk in the rain and thought I'd drop in and see how you were getting along," Mayfield responded, his face angry and tense. "Of course, I need something, you old fool. Why you think I stopped?"

"Yes, sir. Yes, sir. 'Course you want somethin'. Sorry, sir," Franklin said. "What can I do you for, sir?"

"Fill it up and be quick about it," he said, gesturing from the doorway.

"Yes, sir. I'll git right on it. Yes, sir."

Franklin hurried past Mayfield and hopped down to the ground, stopping behind the long, black vehicle. Franklin glanced up at Mayfield and made a hand motion. "Go on back there to where the stove is, Mr. Mayfield, sir, and warm yourself up some while I do this. You want me to check under that hood for you too, don't you, sir?"

"No, I don't. I don't want you touching a blessed thing. You just do like I told you. Fill it up." He pointed to a gas pump. "I want the Ethyl."

Mayfield stepped backward into the store as Franklin uncoupled the nozzle of the gasoline pump. He swung around and saw the man Franklin called Moses sitting in a cane-bottom chair and huddled next to the stove. Mayfield remembered him from other visits to the store. The man's chin rested against his chest and his mouth lay open.

"You stay here all the time, uncle?" Mayfield asked.

The blind man's body shook, and his head flew up. "Sir?" he said, his eyes twirling.

Mayfield walked closer to the old man. "I said, old man, do you stay here all the time?"

Moses, smiling toward the sound of the voice, labored to stand. "No, sir. Not all the time, I don't. But most time, I do."

"What you waste time in here for anyway?" Mayfield said, looking all around and grimacing.

"What's time to me, sir? It just be somethin' else I can't see."

"Is that right, old man?" Mayfield responded.

"Time, it ain't nothin'. No, sir. Time, it ain't nothin'. Just like us, it be all gone one of these here days."

"Time ain't nothing, huh? Well, it's something to those who need it, uncle," Mayfield said, sneering.

Mayfield walked behind the store counter, toward Franklin's display of cigarettes and other tobacco products. Looking around at the blind man and back again at the cigarette display, he removed two packs of Camels from off the shelf and slipped them inside his coat. He came out from behind the counter and waited for Franklin to finish up outside.

In a few minutes, Franklin returned, shivering as he entered the store. He headed straight for the stove, his hands outstretched. "Iffen you'll just give me a second or two, Mr. Mayfield, sir, to warm up these old hands, I'll be right with you. It'll be two dollar and fifteen cent, sir."

"You sell beer?" Mayfield asked.

"No, sir. I ain't got no license to do that."

Mayfield reached for his wallet, withdrew two one-dollar bills, and dug for the change in his pocket. He slapped the bills and a dime and five pennies onto the counter. "Here," he said and walked toward the door, preparing to leave. "You ought to close this sorry place up if you can't afford to sell beer."

Franklin, rubbing his hands together, turned and walked behind the counter. "Before you go, Mr. Mayfield, sir, you recollect tellin' me you needed you a white fella to watch after your place?"

Mayfield stopped at the door and wheeled around. "Yeah. What about it?"

"And you said you'd give me ten dollar iffen I found somebody for you?" Franklin turned his head sideways. "Remember you tellin' me that, sir?" Franklin asked, his voice dropping.

"Well, what? You found somebody?"

Franklin smiled. "I think I did, sir. Yes, sir. 'Course, that'd be for you to say, sir." He reported his conversation with Dewey Coltraine, the Swizzle-Kola man, emphasizing Coltraine's marital status. "You'd probably find him somewheres up the road a piece, sir. He's probably on the other side of Harpers' Joy by now, iffen you wanna talk to him, sir. But I done give him the phone number you left with me, iffen you don't wanna go try and find him, sir."

"What's this Coltraine fellow like?" Mayfield asked.

"He's a clean-cut, little fella. Polite," Franklin said. "You know, respectful actin', sir. One thing I noticed ever' time he come in. He's always smilin'. I dunno why come 'cause I ain't never bought nothin' from him."

Mayfield shook his head in disgust. "Will you tell me what that's got to do with anything—whether you've bought something from him or not?"

"Yes, sir. I—"

"Does he strike you as dependable?" Mayfield growled.

Franklin directed his eyes toward the ceiling and put his thumbs in his pants waist. "Well, sir. I reckon so, sir. He ain't missed comin' by here since Mr. Hammond give him the route. The tater-chip man, he missed me three weeks runnin' last summer. Didn't he, Moses?"

"Yes, sir. Right. Three weeks he don't come in," Moses affirmed.

Mayfield, sighing and aggravated, turned, opened the door, and stepped back. A gust of cold wind whistled in, picking up small, brown paper sacks stacked on the counter and scattering them all over the floor. Mayfield slammed the door shut but did not offer to help Franklin recover the sacks. "So you think he might be on the other side of Harpers' Joy by now?"

Franklin nodded as he joined Mayfield at the door.

"Well, I'm going up that way anyhow. If I see him, I'll talk with him. And if I think I can use him, I'll send you the ten dollars."

Mayfield again opened the door, once more admitting the cold, gusting wind. This time, however, Franklin shielded the counter from the force of the wind with his body.

"Oh, Mr. Mayfield, sir! Mr. Mayfield, sir!" Moses called as Mayfield went to step outside.

Mayfield turned part-way around, letting the door stand open and the wind continue to blow in. "You talking to me, uncle?"

"Sir, I don't think you paid Mr. Vasil for them cigarettes you took."

Mayfield felt his face burn. His hand reached for the upper left side of his coat. He dropped it when he noticed Franklin looking at him. "What are you talking about? Are you accusing me of stealing or something?"

Franklin laughed, his face drained of what little color it had. "Oh, don't you pay him no mind, Mr. Mayfield," Franklin said, speaking fast and twirling his right index finger around and around at his temple. "He's all time 'maginin' things." Franklin dropped his hand to his side. "I just let him hang 'round in here 'cause—you know— somebody to talk to—he—"

Mayfield, not waiting for Franklin to finish, charged out the door, slamming it behind him. He got into his car and drove away. A few miles up the road, the rain stopped as did the wind. The cold, however, remained.

As he drove toward Harpers' Joy, Mayfield tried to figure out how the blind man could have determined he had swiped the cigarettes. But before he could reach any conclusion, he spotted in the distance a green and yellow drink truck coming toward him. A billow of grayish, white smoke followed close behind it, obscuring the way up ahead.

Mayfield hesitated a moment, but then pulled off onto the shoulder of the road. As he watched the slow approach of the drink truck, he turned on the Packard's headlights and flashed the brights on and off. The drink truck slowed and took to the other highway shoulder, its cab and drink rack plunging up and down as its wheels encountered bumps and hollows. It rumbled to a stop opposite the Packard and near some red-and-white Burma Shave signs. The cloud created by the exhaust of the drink truck soon caught up with it and settled around both vehicles.

After a moment, a small, slender, younger man with brown eyes and a fixed smile stepped from out of the smoke, up to the side of the Packard, and into Mayfield's life.

***

"Mr. Solicitor, Judge Pryde, he says he wants you," the deputy sheriff called from down the hallway as District Solicitor J. Hopson Fleming opened the door to his ground-floor office.

Fleming waved, acknowledging the message, and walked to the elevator where Inez Roney, a heavily rouged, middle-aged woman sat on a stool stacked high with pillows, her hand on the elevator control.

Inez's face beamed as bright as a London searchlight during the Blitz. "Goin' up?" she asked, giggling as she spoke. The courthouse had only two floors.

Fleming removed his hat and got onto the elevator. The small, ornate car gave a little when he stepped aboard. He inhaled, making a breathing sound. "My dear Miss Inez, that *eau de toilette* you're wearing? Do I detect the scent of Midday in Montgomery?"

Inez laughed. "No, honey, it's Midnight in Paris. I can't afford none of that real expensive stuff," she said, closing the elevator door.

As Inez dispatched the elevator upward, Fleming leaned into the reflective brass of the elevator door to examine his face. Putting fingers to the small triangle that lay between his bulbous nose and his thin upper lip, he smoothed down the sides of his white mustache. He spent the rest of the trip picking lint off his trademark black suit, a suit he told everyone he had purchased from Jordan and Son Funeral Home after they agreed to sew up the back.

When the elevator reached the second floor, Inez opened the door. "Second floor. Writs and subpoenas," she droned.

"Then I'm on the right floor," Fleming responded. He stepped out into the empty hallway. "Thank you, Miss Inez. Whenever I'm down, no one can lift me up like you can."

"Oh, honey. You say that every time."

The elevator door closed once more and a moment later Fleming heard the motor kick in as the elevator started its short descent to the floor below.

Fleming headed for a door at the far end of the corridor. Big black and gold letters on the frosted glass of the door read "The Honorable L. Malcolm Pryde, District Judge."

Marcellus Pondexter, the judge's court crier, jumped up as Fleming entered the office. "Where you been, Mr. Solicitor?" Pondexter asked from behind the secretary's desk.

Fleming guessed the judge's secretary, a do-nothing, must have called in sick, as was her habit.

"The judge, he been callin' all over the place for you. Mmm-huh. He had to go to lunch all by heself today and he don't like doin' that, but you don't need me to tell you that. No, sir. He done cussed out three lawyers already today. Fined one four dollar. Mmm-huh. Four dollar." Pondexter held up four fingers.

Fleming blinked at that unusual bit of news and laughed. "Why four dollars?"

Pondexter shook his head. "I dunno. I just dunno. He ain't told me, and I ain't asked him. Ain't gonna ask him neither. All I know is the judge, he told him—it was a Mr. Turner from over there in Lee County—to pay the clerk of court four dollar. And the judge, he told him he could only pay it with two-dollar bills.

"The man, he didn't have him no two-dollar bills right then and the banks, they'd all done closed up, you know, at two 'clock. So, the sheriff, he was gettin' ready to take him to the jailhouse when somebody just happen to mention somethin' 'bout Miss Inez maybe havin' some. She collects two-dollar bills and Indian-head pennies, you know, for good luck."

Fleming nodded, finding it difficult to believe what he was hearing.

"So, one of the lawyers what was with Mr. Turner, he went and he bought two from Miss Inez and then he give them to Mr. Turner. Mr. Turner, he paid he fine. Miss Inez, she made herself three dollar outta the deal—that be almost as much as the court did. Yes, sir. Almost as much as the court did. Mmm-huh." Pondexter put a hand to his mouth and whispered. "I think the judge, though, he be mighty, mighty put out with Miss Inez for lettin' Mr. Turner have them two-dollar bills of hern. He said somethin' other 'bout gettin' the county supervisor to fire her you-know-what for helpin' them outta-town lawyers like she done, even if she did make herself a little money outta the deal."

"Surely the judge didn't mean it, Marcellus," he said, concerned that perhaps the judge just might have.

"Lord's my witness, he said it. Mmm-huh." Pondexter, his left hand on his heart, extended his right hand toward the ceiling.

Just then the door to Judge Pryde's chambers opened. A round, porcine face protruded from behind the door. "Hop," the Judge said, "I thought I heard you out there."

Fleming bowed an exaggerated bow. "Your Grace."

The judge motioned Fleming inside. "Marcellus, if the county supervisor calls me while I'm with the solicitor here, you tell him to call back in about thirty minutes. I need to talk to him about something," the judge grumped, adjusting with a middle finger black, horn-rim glasses that shielded beady eyes.

"Yes, sir, judge. Tell him call back in thirty minutes. Mmm-huh. Thirty minutes."

Fleming squeezed past Judge Pryde's huge gut and through the open door. As Fleming always did when he came into the judge's chambers, he marveled at how plaques, certificates, and photographs—each one of the judge himself—covered almost every inch of wall space. Fleming maneuvered around stacks of law books and briefs that lay scattered on the floor. He surmised they had never been touched by judicial hands.

Rather than go behind his desk to sit down, the judge chose a wingback chair on the opposite side and pointed Fleming to a similar chair next to it. Serious, intimate, personal conversation with the judge always took place on that side of the desk. The judge lit a cigarette, after offering one to Fleming, who declined it. He inhaled and let the smoke seep up from his lungs and out through his short, pudgy nose and his wide, down-turned mouth. He crossed his legs and pointed the lighted cigarette at Fleming. "Lester Mayfield called me this morning."

"How's Lester?"

The judge took another drag of his cigarette. "What kind of case you got against that cashier that took him for a few thousand down there at the bank? What's his name?"

"Sykes. Hugh Sykes. Enough to get to a jury."

"What's his defense? Got any idea?"

"Claims he didn't do it."

The judge's chair squeaked as he uncrossed his short, thick legs and reached for an ashtray on his desk. "Then who did, if he didn't?"

"Lester doesn't know this yet—I've put off telling him, but I've got to do it. When the bank examiners reinterviewed Sykes the other day, he told them he thinks Lester Junior took the money."

Judge Pryde's face registered incredulity at the mere suggestion that Lester Junior would steal from his own bank. "Did he? Lester Junior, I mean. Did he take it?"

"I dunno," Fleming said. "Grand Jury indicted Sykes."

"The Grand Jury indicted Sykes," Judge Pryde scoffed. "You mean **you** indicted Sykes."

"I had probable cause."

Judge Pryde stared at Fleming, his head turned to the side. "Let me ask you, then, another way. Did Sykes really steal it?"

"That's not for me to say. That's how come we have jurors. I thought you knew that. Aren't you a judge?"

Judge Pryde waved off Fleming's reply, shaking his head. "Well, it doesn't matter."

"It matters to Sykes. And I should think to the bank—and to Sykes' surety down there." He winked. "Then there's my conviction rate to consider, you know."

A break in the conversation ensued as Judge Pryde underwent a coughing spell.

"Are you all right?" Fleming asked, somewhat concerned.

Judge Pryde nodded. "I ought to quit smoking these durn things," he grumbled, pounding himself in the chest several times. "Your conviction rate?" He resumed coughing while crushing his cigarette out and laying the ashtray down. "Didn't know . . . didn't know you kept up . . . kept up with it."

Fleming laughed to himself. He didn't keep up with it and never had. He was just being facetious. He figured Pryde would take him seriously, knowing Pryde had no sense of humor—at least, not a normal one.

"Lester's heard Sykes hired him some fancy lawyer from way over there in Charlotte, North Carolina," Judge Pryde said.

"Charlotte, North Carolina?" Fleming asked, chuckling. "Lot of good that'll do him in Semmes County."

Judge Pryde patted the arms of his chair with his small, plump hands. "Well, don't you worry about him. I'll take care of him for you."

"Who says I'm worried about him?" Fleming said, standing to leave. "I'm sorry, Mal. I've got to go. I've work to do. They don't pay me to sit around, like they do some people."

The judge's clean-shaven head turned pink. "I'll have you know I've got lots of work to do."

Fleming reached for the door and gestured toward the stack of briefs and law books on the floor. "Yes, you certainly do. But the question is, Your Grace, just when are you going to get down to doing it?"

He was out the door before Judge Pryde could respond. As Fleming entered Judge Pryde's front office, the telephone rang.

Marcellus Pondexter picked up the receiver. "Judge Pryde's office—yes, sir. He been lookin' for you to call him. Hold on a jiffy while I go gets him for you."

Fleming shook his head and walked out the door. He headed for the elevator for what would be, he felt sure, his last ride with Inez Roney at the controls.

When the elevator door opened, and he stepped aboard, Inez laughed and said, "Honey, do me a favor. Tell me again what it takes to make a good prosecutor. I tried to tell somebody a while ago what you said one time and I couldn't remember exactly what it was."

Fleming did not feel much like joking around with Inez since he had a good idea what lay in store for her before the close of business hours. "Oh, Miss Inez, I don't think I can remember that either."

"Yes, you can. You know you can. It's somethin' 'bout baby

chickens."

He relented. "To be a good prosecutor, the first thing you do is you go buy you a hundred baby chicks. The next thing you do is you dig you a hundred tiny, little holes and put a baby chick in each one, making sure you bury them up to their little necks."

"And then what?" she said, laughing.

"Then you stomp on them."

"Is that what you done, honey?"

"Who me? Oh, no. I'm too tender hearted. I used itty-bitty defense lawyers."

Inez howled.

***

Dewey Coltraine turned his truck around and, with the gas pedal pressed all the way to the floorboard, followed the speeding Packard up the slick highway. As the truck roared smoking and bouncing in a losing pursuit of the automobile, the wobbling of its front wheels caused the truck to vibrate and the bottles in their crates to wiggle and dance. It seemed to Dewey that each time the front wheels hit an expansion joint in the cement road surface, the harder it became for him to control the truck.

Just when Dewey determined to give up the chase, he saw the Packard turn left onto a narrow dirt road and almost immediately pull into a drive opposite an abandoned cement block building. The Packard stopped at a wooden gate that blocked the way.

Dewey reached the spot where Lester Mayfield, Jr. waited and pulled in behind the car as close as he dared. He wanted to leave room on the dirt road for other traffic. As he checked his side mirror, he heard a door slam and Mayfield shout, "Hey, don't worry about anybody coming down the road. They can wait if they can't get by."

Dewey switched the engine off and watched Mayfield walk to the gate. When he motioned for Dewey to join him, Dewey got out of his truck and hurried over to where Mayfield stood bent over, unlocking the padlock that held the gate to a fence post.

"Come on, Coltraine," Mayfield said, shoving the gate to one side, "I want to show you something. It's right over here."

The two men walked thirty yards or so down the drive. Mayfield stopped and pointed to a structure several yards ahead. The structure, a Stout folding house trailer, sat among several scrub oaks and loblolly pines. "You think you and your wife might like to live in that? It's almost brand new."

Dewey sprung back. "In that over yonder?" he said in disbelief. "Why, Mr. Mayfield, it's plumb beautiful." He ran ahead to get a closer look at the folding house.

"Would you believe it's got a living room, a bedroom, and a kitchen and a bathroom?" Mayfield said, his chest expanded. "And look there," he said, indicating. "A power line. One of the first out this way. You got electricity where you're living now?"

Dewey did not answer, not having heard Mayfield. He stood on tiptoes, his hand cupped against the right front window as he peeked inside. "Mr. Mayfield, it's already got furniture and everythin' in it," he said. "It's real, real nice. Golly gee."

"Tell you something else that's amazing. It's three times the size folded out than when it's a trailer. Isn't that something?"

"Yes, sir. It sure is. I can't wait for Nellie to come look at it."

"Nellie? That your wife?"

"Yes, sir." Dewey smiled. "My wife."

Dewey stepped up onto the lower of the two doorsteps and pulled at the locked door. "Can we go in, Mr. Mayfield, and look around some?"

Mayfield handed him the door key. "You go on in. I've seen it. I'll wait out here."

Dewey disappeared inside the folding house. He reappeared several minutes later. "Mr. Mayfield, is that a heater in the wall there at the bathroom?"

Mayfield laughed. "Yeah. Burns propane. It and the stove. The tank's out back."

Dewey stepped down onto the upper step, turned around, and locked the door.

"Well, Coltraine," Mayfield asked, "what do you think? Think you could live in something like that?"

"And you wouldn't charge me nothin'? Is that right?" Dewey asked.

Mayfield did not answer right away but appeared to study Dewey a few seconds. "Listen, Coltraine, it's not exactly free. You and your wife—you've got to earn your keep." He pointed to his left. "Down that road a piece is a pond and a log cabin. That's where my hideaway is. I'll take you down there in a few minutes and show it to you. Now, whenever I'm not here, you're welcome to fish the pond. Catch as many as you want. It's full of bream and bass. You like to fish?"

Dewey nodded. "Yes, sir. When I get a chance, I do."

Mayfield turned his back to Dewey and continued. "When I'm here—when you see my car down there or see me come through the gate—y'all stay completely away from there. What I do down there and who I bring to stay down there with me, it's none of your business. You understand?"

"Yes, sir."

Mayfield faced Dewey again. "If anybody else comes up, you turn them away unless I'm with them. If you see another car or another person down there, you get in touch with me or the sheriff if you can't reach me. And I don't care who it is either—man, woman, or child. You hear?"

"Yes, sir."

"In other words, Coltraine, you and your wife are going to be this place's caretakers. You take care of it, and it'll take care of you. You help me. I'll help you. It's that simple."

Dewey shook his head up and down. "Yes, sir. And we'll do a real good job for you too. When I ain't here, Nellie, she'll watch out for everythin'. Don't you worry none, Mr. Mayfield."

"That's why I'm letting you move in. This way I get two for the price of one." Mayfield reached into his left vest pocket. "It's settled then?"

"Yes, sir. It is."

Mayfield handed Dewey a set of keys. "There's three keys there. One's to the gate. One's to the folding house and the other one's to the log cabin."

Dewey put the keys with the others he carried on a key ring that included a rabbit foot.

"I just thought of something," Mayfield said. "How are you going to get out here from town? You got a car?"

"No, sir." Dewey nodded toward the truck. "But Mr.

Hammond—he's the man owns the bottlin' plant—he lets me bring the truck home after I get it loaded and all."

"That kind of means when you're not home your wife's stuck out here all by herself, doesn't it?"

"Yes, sir. I reckon so."

Harpers' Joy

Sunday, November 10, 1946

"Southside Dairy time is 10:30 a.m.," the radio announcer for the local Mutual affiliate advised as Candle opened the chifferobe and lifted a bottle of hair tonic from its top shelf. He stepped back, shut the door, and moved in close to the mirror that overlay the door's peeling, wood-veneer exterior.

He shook large drops of the yellow, fragrant fluid into what remained of his dark blonde hair. After working the oil into his scalp with the fingertips of his good hand, he parted his hair with a comb whose teeth held residues of hair and grease.

His hair in place, Candle stepped back and inspected himself in the mirror, turning his head right and left. He frowned. He did not like what he saw. But then, he never did.

Bernard Blumberg's death four days before, though expected, had stunned Candle. Less than two hours after receiving the call from the hospital, Candle had moored his consciousness at Johnny Gray's dark harbor.

Irrespective of whether Blumberg had lived or died, however, Candle would have sought oblivion anyway. In the void, there were no pressures, no worries, no conflicts. The "Great Up-Against-Us," a term Candle believed epitomized these torments, existed only in the conscious world and he saw no need to battle it twenty-four hours a day. Candle liked being unconscious.

Wearing a double-breasted, navy blue suit—the same one he wore in the picture on the mantelpiece in his bedroom—and a snap-brim felt hat, he left his apartment to go downtown. The weather was much warmer and seemed to breed churchgoers, for the street appeared heavy with them. As he sauntered down the sidewalk, several motorists headed in the opposite direction toward, Candle assumed, either the Grace Methodist Church or the First Baptist Church, honked their car horns or waved at him. He interpreted their actions not to be a Sunday-morning greeting but a rebuke for his not attending church. Indeed, two or three had made circling motions with a hand and index finger and pointed in the direction of the two churches.

Candle waved back, declining their invitations to turn around and follow them. He had other gods to appease and other fish to fry.

Besides, he was not, and had never been, a religious person. If he felt anything about God, it was outrage because of the "V-For-Victory" hand that he blamed God for giving him at birth. He never questioned that God was responsible for his disability because all his life he had been told often enough that "it was God's will" that he have it.

The hand, which earned him the nickname "Claw" in grammar school, had kept him from doing many things that he would have liked to have done. Although football had been out of the question because of his being far too skinny, it was his bad hand that hampered his ability to play baseball and basketball, sports he loved almost as much as he now loved his friend Johnny.

His greatest regret, however, was his not being able to join the military during World War II. His Four-F status humiliated and embarrassed him.

While many of his schoolmates from high school, college, or law school served in the armed forces defending America, Candle spent the war years pleading criminals guilty and processing claims for Tekoa's banks against farmers and other borrowers. His low opinion of himself sank even lower when friends and acquaintances began returning home from Europe or the Pacific in sealed caskets as casualties of war.

Apart from his physical deformity, Candle also held himself in low esteem because he never seemed to do anything right. His marriage resulted not from careful deliberation and planning but from an unintended consequence of a frenzied backseat tryst behind the Phi Kappa Sigma house with a girl he had dated only a few times.

When Paula, her eyes red from crying, informed Candle several weeks later that he would be a father, the news had not surprised him. He had expected it, his luck being what it was and had always been. Candle determined to do his duty by the young woman, notwithstanding she was all but a stranger to him. He knew he had no choice, really. It was, after all, the decent thing to do. Whatever he was, he was not a scoundrel.

Right away Candle and Paula went to the home of a justice of the peace near the outskirts of town and got married. At the insistence of her parents, they repeated the ceremony a month later before a Catholic priest. Over the years, he had gotten used to being married to Paula—just like he had gotten used to having only a middle finger and an index finger on his left hand.

Did he love his wife? Did she love him? The answer to both questions was: yes, but not in the romantic sense. Their love was of a type that sprung from close familiarity and mutual dependency, from communal living and common children, from joint activities and shared experiences. In sum, it was a love forged by circumstance.

For his part, Candle entertained no doubt that Fate had willed his marriage to Paula—just like it had willed his deformed hand, the loss of his house and children, the death of his law partner, and all the other lamentable things that had happened to him throughout his life. What else did Fate have in store for him? Candle wondered. Whatever it was, he concluded, it could not be anything good. Not with his luck.

***

The preacher quit preaching and gave the altar call. The choir sang the last stanza of "Just As I Am" three times before the preacher, his head bowed low, ended the service with a benediction and a sigh. No one had come forward.

As Dewey Coltraine made his way up the aisle, he concentrated on the delicate, willowy blonde to his front. Watching his wife as they made their way through the flock and out of the church, Dewey found himself, as he often did, lost in admiration of her. If he lived to be a hundred, he knew that his marrying Nellie Grace Prevatt would be his greatest achievement.

Dewey and Nellie reached her daddy's car, a tan-colored 1939 Plymouth, before her father and younger brother did. They waited for them beside the automobile, a car that had survived World War II but only as one of the rolling wounded.

"I can't wait for you to see it, Nellie," Dewey said, grinning and referring to the folding house.

Nellie smiled and planted a quick kiss on Dewey's cheek. "Dewey, I bet you've told me that a hundred times already. If it'll make you feel any better, I can't wait either."

Nellie edged closer to Dewey as her daddy walked up. Linwood Prevatt, a big-shouldered, bull of a man, opened the driver-side door and pointed at Nellie. "You git yourself up front," he said. "And you git yourself back there in the back," Prevatt said, glaring at Dewey before plopping in behind the steering wheel.

Nellie and Dewey climbed into the car and sat where directed, Nellie hugging the front passenger-side door and Dewey sitting on the edge of the back seat, his forearms on top of the front seat. "Ain't Charlie comin', Mr. Prevatt?" Dewey asked, referring to Nellie's little brother.

"Naw, he ain't," the older man said, his tone none too happy, his face meaner than usual. "He's gonna stay for somethin' other his Sunday School class is doin'. Least, he said they was doin'. I better not catch him goin' to no picture show, I'll tell you that. He might be fourteen, but I can still wear his little fanny out iffen I catch him lyin' to me."

Nellie pressed closer against the door. "Daddy," she said in a soft, guarded voice, "they're all going over to Mrs. Foy's house and work on their Thanksgiving program. She's gonna bring them all home when they're done."

"I hate lyin'," Prevatt said.

Dewey suspected his father-in-law meant to direct his remark about lying to him and Nellie. They had been untruthful to Mr. and Mrs. Prevatt about their intentions that Saturday morning in September when they had told Nellie's parents that they would be going to a student function at Tekoa High School. Instead, they had gone to the courthouse and gotten married despite Nellie's being underage.

Prevatt reacted to the news that evening by slapping his daughter across her face with the back of his hand and cursing her and Dewey in language Dewey thought only drill sergeants used on fresh recruits. After vowing he would get the marriage annulled on the ground neither he nor his wife had consented to it, Prevatt threatened to beat Dewey to death with a pair of brass knuckles that he pulled from his pants pocket. But Nellie stationed herself between her father and her new husband while her brother, in response to Nellie's pleas for help and in disregard of their father's threats against him, telephoned the sheriff's office.

A deputy sheriff arrived at the Prevatt home within minutes of the call. After learning the cause of the furor, the deputy suggested Dewey leave and return later once Prevatt calmed down. Although he agreed to go, Nellie insisted Dewey remain with her. So, he stayed.

Prevatt responded by forcing the newlyweds outside onto the front porch and telling Nellie, "Don't you even look like you wanna leave this house and go off somewheres with that little punk."

Dewey and Nellie, their safety warranted by a deputy sheriff, whiled away their wedding night in a swing, holding hands and affirming over and over again their love for each other, come what may. They spent Sunday evening the same way.

The following Monday, Tekoa High School reacted to the news of Nellie and Dewey's marriage by expelling her. Her expulsion from high school fired her father up once again and necessitated yet another call to the sheriff's office. For a third night in a row, Dewey and Nellie, protected by a sheriff's deputy, awaited the dawn in a porch swing.

Nellie's father relented only after he visited a lawyer's office the day following her expulsion. Upon his return from downtown, he went into the bedroom where Nellie's mother, a stick of a woman and an older, worn-out version of Nellie, spent most of her days in bed. Nellie and Dewey overheard him tell her that it would cost fifty dollars in advance to have the marriage annulled and that the marriage could not be annulled at all if Nellie and Dewey had done what the lawyer called "cohabitated."

When Nellie's mother had asked what the lawyer had meant by the word "cohabitated," Prevatt had answered, "I dunno and he didn't say. But I reckon he meant iffen they'd done done it yet. They probably have, knowin' him."

But in truth, they had not.

Once Prevatt reached his house, he drove his Plymouth into the driveway, parking it behind Dewey's drink truck. He cut the motor and withdrew the key. After he removed it from his key ring, he handed the key over his shoulder to Dewey in the back seat. " 'Fore you ask me again 'bout lettin' y'all borrow my car to move all y'all's stuff, here's my key. I reckon now I'll let you use it. I don't think your boss'd want you usin' his truck and burnin' up his gas doin' it, as little money as you make him."

Dewey accepted the key.

"But you sho' better be careful with it. I'm tellin' you that."

"I'm much obliged, Mr. Prevatt."

Prevatt did not respond.

When they stepped onto the porch, Dewey opened the door and held it for Nellie. As Nellie started in, Prevatt caught Nellie by her arm and pulled her back. "Nellie, I wanna tell you somethin'," he said, squeezing her arm. "I done told you I don't like you goin' someplace where you gonna be all by yourself all day long."

"Daddy, we've already been into that a dozen times," Nellie said, looking down. "Our minds are made up."

"Well, I still don't like it none," he muttered. "It ain't too late for you to change your mind, you know. What with your mama's nerves, I got me enough to worry 'bout as it is, without havin' to worry 'bout that."

"I'll be all right, Daddy," Nellie said. "Dewey says it's got a fence around it. And Mr. Mayfield'll be coming up there some, too. Won't anybody bother us. It's not gonna be like it was during the war when we had all those soldiers from everywhere. They're all gone now. Things are getting back like you said they were before the war."

Nellie stepped back from her father, causing him to let go of her arm. "Would it make you feel any better if we took the shotgun with us?"

Prevatt nodded. "I done thought of that. I know you know how to shoot one 'cause I learnt you how to." He glanced at Dewey. "How 'bout him? He know how to?"

"Of course, I do, Mr. Prevatt. I was in the Army for near 'bout two years," Dewey said, his eyes to the floor.

Prevatt mocked Dewey with a laugh. "I thought you told me you wasn't nothin' but a truck driver."

"We still had to know how to shoot," Dewey said. "I learned to shoot an M-1 and a carbine too. I even shot a machine gun one time when I was in basic trainin'. And I've shot a—"

Prevatt grabbed Dewey by the shirt collar. For a moment, Dewey could not breathe. "Boy, I'm fixin' to tell you somethin', so you better listen up and listen up real, real good," Prevatt said, letting go of him.

Dewey prepared to listen. He was afraid not to. He always felt extremely small and weak when around his father-in-law, a huge man of great physical strength and as mean and threatening as he was big and strong.

"Nothin'—and I mean nothin'—better not happen to Nellie, you got that? Iffen it does, I'll personally come out there and beat the livin' daylights outta you. Then I'll take her off someplace or other you won't never, ever find. She's my daughter and don't you never forget it neither."

Dewey compressed his lips. "Yes, sir."

"Another thing. I seen Nellie git just like her maw sometime. Stayin' in bed all the time, not never eatin' nothin'. Not never sayin' nothin'. Claimin' she's got a headache. You gotta look after her, iffen she ever gits like that while y'all are up yonder."

"Yes, sir," Dewey said, nodding, his face turned away from Prevatt. "I will."

***

Candle Reid left the R&K Cafeteria and went to his law office two blocks away to try and catch up on some things—not everything, just some things. Candle's partner may have died, but their law practice continued. Correspondence needed to be answered, pleadings needed to be drafted, fees needed to be collected, bills needed to be paid, and goodness knows what else needed to be done. He grew weary just thinking about it.

Candle surveyed his desk, groaned, and dropped into his chair. The bitter smell of his unemptied ashtray added to the displeasure of the moment.

He picked up the topmost item, a letter from a lawyer in Charlotte, North Carolina, addressed to his deceased law partner. The lawyer sought Blumberg & Reid's help the following week in selecting a jury in *State versus Hugh Sykes*, a criminal case in which the grand jury had returned an indictment against Sykes for bank embezzlement.

Candle cringed even thinking about going up against J. Hopson Fleming all alone. He had done it once, and what a disaster that had been! Lawyers still talked about the case.

His ordeal came about because Judge Malcolm Pryde called a wreck case for trial while Blumberg was out of town, trying another case in federal court. Fleming, who represented the plaintiff in the case, opposed Candle's motion for a continuance. Judge Pryde forced Candle to trial, notwithstanding the fact that Candle knew next to nothing about the case. In a great show of magnanimity, Judge Pryde gave Candle exactly one hour to review the case file.

Candle's defense in the case crumbled just after he finished direct-examination of the defendant's first witness and offered him to Fleming for cross-examination. All during direct-examination, the man, a one-eyed loom-fixer at a local textile mill, said the traffic light facing Fleming's client had been red. After Fleming began his cross-examination, however, the witness changed his mind and testified the light had really been green after all.

To persuade the witness to change his testimony Fleming had simply to ask the witness if he could identify a folded piece of paper.

Candle learned firsthand that day what it meant to try a case against the lanky, witty, learned-speaking lawyer and part-time prosecutor. The paper Fleming had asked the witness to identify was a bill of indictment that charged the witness with wife beating. It had been returned three years before by the Semmes County grand jury and consigned by Fleming without being dismissed to his so-called "Dependent Docket"; however, the indictment remained subject to retransfer to the active docket and the defendant to prosecution. Fleming justified the practice as "probation on the cheap"—a defendant's avoidance of prosecution would be "dependent" on his staying out of trouble with the law. The practice also allowed Fleming, should he choose to do so, to make virtual slaves of a defendant—for his avoidance of prosecution could be "dependent" on the defendant's doing pretty much what Fleming wanted or expected the defendant to do, irrespective of whether he obeyed the law or not.

Candle's experience that day also taught him to appreciate better an anecdote his law partner Bernard Blumberg said he once heard about Fleming. The story, an unverified tale that now formed part of a growing apocrypha about the solicitor, told how Fleming had once gotten all the witnesses to a highway accident, including the investigating officer, to change the location of a wreck from Semmes County to another county within the judicial district where jurors favored big verdicts for plaintiffs.

Although Candle knew Blumberg had been an honest and just man who had never condoned Fleming's practices—whether real or fancied, he also knew Blumberg had accepted Fleming for what he was and had chosen not to battle him head-on. "Candle," Blumberg had explained, "if Fleming wants to win a case, whether it's civil or criminal, he will win it; and if he wants to lose it, he will lose it. He's that good a lawyer, notwithstanding his other—shall I say?—skills. The trick is to know which cases he's willing to lose. Usually, they're civil cases in which there's no insurance or no other deep pocket to pay a judgment or the occasional criminal case where it's clear beyond all reasoning that the party you represent is not guilty. Unlike our dear district judge, Solicitor Fleming is not totally evil."

"But what if you have a case where you can show it's pretty clear your client's not guilty but it'd go against the interests of those in power for him to be acquitted, what you suppose would happen then?" Candle had asked Blumberg at the time.

"I don't know. I guess it would depend on the type of case it was and what was at stake—you know, exactly whose interests were involved, what all happened, the amount of pressure brought, that sort of thing," Blumberg had answered after a pause. "I just don't know. Probably, your client would lose. But I'm not sure. In many ways, Fleming is his own man."

Based on Blumberg's answer to his question that day, the news reports that Candle read in the local press, and the scuttlebutt that he heard around the courthouse, Candle figured Sykes was a goner—irrespective of whether he aided in his defense or not. The interests of the bank—and hence of the powerful Mayfields—were directly involved and there was, moreover, a strong suggestion of Sykes' guilt.

He switched on the Dictaphone. "Judy," he began, "this is a letter to Matthew M. Futeral, Esquire. His address is on his letter. Re: *State versus Hugh Sykes*. Dear Mr. Futeral. I regret to tell you that my law partner Bernard Blumberg died Wednesday, November 6, 1946, from complications following a stroke. Thus, this office is not available to assist you with jury selection in the above-entitled case. Paragraph. This firm could not have helped you in any event. The bank which employed Mr. Sykes and which he allegedly embezzled, the State Bank and Trust Company of Tekoa, is a major client of ours. We handle most of its loan closings and foreclosures; therefore, I fear we would have a serious conflict of interest to participate in any way in the representation of Mr. Sykes. Paragraph. Thank you for thinking of us and let us know if we can assist you otherwise. I hope you understand our reluctance to become involved in this matter. Sincerely yours."

He picked up the next paper, a letter from Lester Mayfield, president of the State Bank and Trust Company of Tekoa. Candle's heart sank. The Brazeale-Parker deal had not gone through after all and Mayfield wanted Candle to start foreclosure proceedings against the Brazeale property at once, notwithstanding Blumberg's death.

He opened a lower drawer of his desk, peered downward, and spied a quarter-filled bottle of whisky. A year-old set of Supreme Court advance sheets covered the lower half of the bottle. Candle yearned for a drink; however, he wiped his mouth and slammed the drawer shut with his foot. Ol' Johnny would have to wait.

Muttering to himself, he rose from his chair to get the file that contained all the forms needed for bringing a foreclosure action. Lifting the file from the cabinet, he cursed Lester Mayfield for insisting on immediate action against Luther Brazeale at this particular time. Mayfield knew that his law partner had just died.

***

Solicitor J. Hopson Fleming sat opposite Lester Mayfield in the living room of Cottondale Mansion, his hands folded, his elbows resting on the arms of a reproduction Martha Washington chair. Cottondale's white exterior, with its crescent-shaped portico and its balustrade around the edge of the roof, always made Fleming think of the White House, albeit a smaller version of it. Both mansions sheltered powerful men, each a president.

"I hope your wife didn't mind going to the country club alone, Lester. But I needed to talk to you and this might have been our only chance, busy as we both are."

"Aw, Mildred, she doesn't care," Mayfield grumbled as he turned the pages of Fleming's investigative file in *State versus Hugh Sykes*. "Lester Junior and his wife'll probably meet her there. They usually do. That's all she cares about."

While Mayfield pored over the file, Fleming passed the time admiring the mahogany secretary-bookcase by the doorway to the entrance hall and the Persian rug on the gleaming hardwood floor.

Mayfield tapped the open folder with a hand that held a lighted cigar. Ashes, some alive, fell onto the top page, causing small burns. "Let me get this straight, Hop. Sykes now blames my son for taking it?"

"That's my information," Fleming answered, waving away the smoke that he found nauseous.

"Well, my son didn't take it."

Fleming nodded. "Uh-huh. Let me ask you this. And I don't want you flying off the handle when I ask it. We can't afford any surprises at trial. How do you know Lester Junior didn't take it?"

Mayfield, his face now aflame, tossed the file on the floor, scattering papers all about. "Because he's my son! That's how I know. Besides, there wouldn't be any reason for him to take it. He's got money. And if he hasn't got it, I do, and I'll give him any amount of money he wants. All he's got to do is ask." He turned his head to one side. "That's stupid. Just plain stupid, saying Junior stole the money."

"I'm asking about evidence, Lester. What evidence do you have? Anything?"

Mayfield slumped back in his chair and pointed at the file folder down on the floor. "I've looked at your file. There's not a thing in there that shows my son took it."

"Still," Fleming said, "it is possible for him to have taken it. He had access to the money. It's all there in the file. You read that part, didn't you?"

"I'm telling you, Lester Junior didn't steal it," Mayfield said, biting his words.

"Okay. Calm down, won't you? We've got to talk about this, and we've got to do it without anybody getting all emotional and excited. Again, what have you got? What evidence shows me he didn't take the money?"

Mayfield offered no immediate response, but sat in his chair, taking long, deep breaths. His breathing became less labored only after he inhaled a puff of his cigar.

"Well?" Fleming pressed.

"What evidence have I got? My son's word he didn't take it," he said. "That's evidence, isn't it?"

"Yes, it is. And I'm glad you recognize it is. But have you asked him if he took it?"

"I don't need to. I know what he'd say. I know my son."

"I hope you're right. Since the case against Sykes is largely, if not entirely, circumstantial, we'll have to call Lester Junior as a witness. Sykes'll have to testify to establish any kind of defense at all. Then the case'll pretty much turn into a swearing contest: Sykes' word against Lester Junior's."

Mayfield laid the cigar on an ashtray. "I don't want to talk about that anymore." He sat in silence for a moment. "What about that lawyer Sykes got from North Carolina, you find out anything about him?"

"Nothing other than he's somebody named Futeral. Robert, maybe? No, Matthew."

Mayfield shook his head. He appeared perplexed. "Wonder why Sykes'd go all the way to North Carolina to get himself a lawyer? Why didn't he get somebody from around here?"

"I think a secretary in Futeral's firm is kin to Sykes' wife or something. Seems like I heard that somewhere. I don't know. Besides, what lawyer in town would represent him? Who could he have gotten that'd be worth the money he'd have to pay him? Best lawyer he could've gotten just died."

Fleming debated whether to ask Mayfield about one other matter. "There is one thing more I guess we might ought to discuss, Lester."

Mayfield retrieved his cigar and stared hard at Fleming, a frown on his face. "What?" he snapped.

"Would you be opposed to my trying to work out some kind of

plea agreement with Sykes? You know, probation and restitution?"

Mayfield shook his fist. "Why, you better believe I'd be opposed to that! You gone soft or something? The man stole my money."

"Just thought I'd ask. It's a question I usually ask victims, especially of property crimes."

"What kind of message would that send?" Mayfield fumed. "I can't have my employees stealing me blind. When they get caught, they got to pay the price." He shook his finger to emphasize his point.

Mayfield stood. Fleming took this as a signal that their meeting was at its end.

With the messed-up file in his hand, he walked from the living room into the entrance hall. There he reclaimed his hat from off a Chippendale settee by the staircase. He turned and faced Mayfield, who had remained by his chair in the living room.

"All right, then, Lester. Simmer down. We won't offer him any kind of a deal. All I wanted to do in coming out here this afternoon was to make sure you knew exactly what we were up against and to make sure you realized that Lester Junior'd probably have to testify. That's all." He put on his hat and opened the door. "See you next week."

On his way into town, Fleming passed a tan 1939 Plymouth traveling in the opposite direction. Its back seat appeared crammed full of clothes.

***

Dewey turned into the drive and braked for the gate. A few minutes later when he had stopped again, he nodded to the right. "And look back in there, Nellie! See it?" he asked, his voice filled with excitement. "Whatcha think?"

Nellie didn't answer. Instead, she hopped from the car and raced across the patch of ground between the drive and the folding house. Reaching it, she spun around and stood on her tiptoes, looking toward the car. "Dewey, hurry!" she yelled. "I wanna go inside. I can't wait."

Dewey laughed and got out of the car. He walked toward the folding house, patting himself all over. "Now, where did I go and put my keys?" He stopped and turned around. "Now, where could they be at? Heck, I believe we might have to go back into town—"

"Come on, Dewey. Don't do me that way," Nellie demanded.

Dewey came up with a set of keys and jingled them at Nellie as she waited at the door steps. "I found them."

He stepped up onto the bottom of the two steps and unlocked the door, pulling it toward him and exposing the interior of the folding house. Nellie craned her neck to see inside, but Dewey, stepping back down into the yard, blocked her view.

"Come here a second," Dewey said, reaching for Nellie and drawing her delicate body close. He kissed her hair and rested his chin on the top of her head. "Nellie," he said, "your hair always smells so good. Like fresh apples."

Nellie, her head against his chest and her forearms against his shoulders, stood very still. "Dewey, won't you carry me inside now?"

"I will in just a second, Nellie. Just let me hold you a little while out here, then I'll carry you in. I wanna do it just like I've seen them do it in the picture shows. I wanna remember this moment all the rest of my life."

Dewey felt her warm body sag against his.

He lifted his chin from her head and pushed back from her. He stood there admiring all that made her so very beautiful, especially her soft, hazel eyes, and her long, graceful neck. To Dewey, she reminded him of a swan—the prettiest swan in the whole wide world.

"Dewey, please," she said. "Now will you take me inside?"

Dewey nodded and smiled. "Close your eyes and don't you open them up again 'til I say you can."

Sweeping his wife up into his arms, her eyes shut, he turned and climbed the steps. Once inside, he set her to the floor and kissed her. "Now," he said when their lips parted, "you can look."

Nellie opened her eyes. Her mouth agape, she put a hand to her breast. "Why, Dewey! Look, Dewey! A kitchen! It's got a gas stove! And a refrigerator, Dewey! A refrigerator! Not an ol' ice box. And a double sink!" She began to sob. "It's just about the prettiest kitchen I've ever seen. Oh, Dewey. Oh, Dewey. Just look at it! Just look!"

Dewey took hold of Nellie and pulled her close, her sharp chin nestled against his shoulder. "Ain't it pretty, Nellie? Ain't it pretty?" He held her for only a few seconds before releasing her. She took Dewey by the hand and led him into one of the two adjoining wings of the folding house, wiping her face as they went.

"My goodness, Dewey. A dining-room table and a couch. And that door on the side there, I guess it goes to the outside?"

Dewey nodded, smiling.

Nellie turned to her left. "Wonder what's behind this door?" She turned the doorknob and pulled the door toward her. "Look here. It's the bathroom." She peeped in. "It's got a toilet and a sink and shower stall. Can you believe it? A shower stall! Just think, Dewey, now we can take showers."

Dewey reached under her hair with his free hand, lifted it, and pecked Nellie on her neck. She ducked her head to the side, twisting her neck. "Oh, Dewey. This is so wonderful. So wonderful."

"You ain't seen the bedroom yet. Let's go see it," he said, withdrawing and dropping her hand. He stepped aside and let her pass.

They walked across the trailer core to the other wing. Nellie went over to the bed and tested the mattress with her fingertips and, hands on hips, examined the room. "I'll tell you one thing, though." She pointed toward the window. "I can't stand those curtains. You don't suppose Mr. Mayfield would mind if we changed them, do you?"

"I don't reckon," Dewey said, laughing. As Nellie turned to inspect the room further, Dewey took her by the shoulders. "Well, I guess I done okay then?"

Nellie smiled and pecked him on the cheek. "Better than okay. You did wonderful. Next to when we got married, this is the happiest moment of my life. Oh, Dewey, I love you so much. So much," she said, putting her arms around him and laying her head against his chest.

Dewey edged her toward the bed.

"Dewey," Nellie said, "we got to get the car unloaded."

***

"You know, you are a sorry, sorry thing," Lester Mayfield, Jr. heard his wife yell as he stomped out the door, slamming it behind him.

Mayfield went straight to the garage. He propped open its doors, got into his car, and put the gear in reverse. As he backed up the driveway, his eyes on the rearview mirror, the fulsome body of his wife, in a flowing, sheer, baby-blue gown and her platinum-blond hair piled high in pin curls, suddenly appeared between the two concrete lanes of the driveway. For a moment, he had the urge to keep going and run her over; but he stopped, inches away from her naked, fish-belly white legs.

She rushed around the car to the driver-side door and tapped on the glass. "You know what you are? You're a—"

Mayfield did not wait for his wife to finish. He gunned the accelerator to the floor, shooting the car backward.

Once on the street, he paused long enough to turn on the radio and, while it warmed up, to light a cigarette. Both acts brought him almost instant relief. Jan Garber's rendition of "Maria Elena" bridled his fury, while the Camel's blend of Turkish and domestic tobacco relieved his so-called "T-Zone."

He knew his parents would be upset with him, first for not going to church and second for not joining them, as he and his wife usually did, at the country club for Sunday dinner. But he could not abide the dreadnaught's company, not for one more second.

When he had married Georgia Ann Hascall four years before, and even when he had shipped out for Pearl Harbor, she had been a statuesque blonde with a figure and face any movie star would envy. But when he had returned from the war and saw her for the first time in three years, he had initially thought someone was playing a cruel joke on him. What remained of the woman he had left behind lay buried somewhere beneath pounds of flesh.

And not only had her physical appearance changed. Her personality had changed as well. She simply was not the woman he had married or thought he had married. It was as though another woman had taken his wife's place. Alcohol and food had metamorphosed his beautiful wife almost overnight, it seemed, into the creature she had now become, a creature he detested and could not bear even to look upon.

Mayfield cruised downtown Tekoa, studying the marquees of the movie theaters, all of which had opened at one o'clock. None interested him. As he wondered how to spend the afternoon, he suddenly thought of the new caretaker for his hideaway, Dewey Coltraine.

He decided to ride out to see if Coltraine and his wife had yet moved into the folding house. With the car radio blaring Artie Shaw's swing masterpiece "Begin the Beguine," he headed toward Harpers' Joy.

On the way, he tried to visualize what Coltraine's wife looked like. He pictured her as a mirror image of her husband: small, lean, dark-skin, nineteen or twenty years old, country looking. Why, he bet she probably even had buckteeth, thick, protruding lips, a flat nose, and hairy legs and armpits. He laughed at the picture.

Pleased to find the gate open, Mayfield drove into the drive that went past the folding house to his pond and log cabin below.

Mayfield stopped in front of the folding house, just to the left of a tan, late-model automobile. He blew the horn and got out of his car.

The kitchen door opened, and Dewey stuck his head out. "Mr. Mayfield, sir," he called, his voice cheerful, a smile spread across his face. Dewey stepped down into the yard. "Come on in, why don't you? I want you to meet Nellie."

Mayfield nodded and walked past the outstretched arm of his new caretaker, prepared to meet Bucktooth Woman. With Dewey close behind him, he peeled back the door to the folding house and stepped into the kitchen. Just then, Nellie came into the room, fresh lipstick on her lips and her hand pushing back the hair that lay on the right side of her face.

The instant Mayfield saw Nellie he gasped, and his mouth dropped open. He could not believe his eyes. How wrong his mental picture of her had been! Instead of the buckteeth and thick, protruding lips that he had imagined, she had straight, white teeth and thin red lips. And the nose was not the way that he thought it would be either. It was straight and narrow. Her legs, what he could see of them, appeared clean-shaven and well-formed. It was not possible, he thought, for one so lovely to have found shelter in a folding house with a soft-drink salesman for a second-rate bottling plant. But there she stood, her blond hair in rippling folds atop her shoulders, sustenance for the lustful eye.

"Nellie," Dewey said from behind him. "This is Mr. Mayfield."

Suddenly, Mayfield remembered. He had seen her before. She had stood outside the men's room in the county courthouse in late summer, holding a bouquet of bridal flowers. He had wanted her then, just as he wanted her now. He wondered if she remembered seeing him that day. When she extended a soft, slim hand in greeting and smiled at him in a way that made him melt inside, he had his answer.

Harpers' Joy

Monday, November 18, 1946

Candle sat down at the table across from his estranged wife, wondering why she had called and asked him to meet her at the City Café after she dropped the girls off at school. She had arrived first. Judging from the look on her face, Candle concluded she had been waiting for some time.

"Mmm, that bacon sure does smell good, doesn't it?" he said, smiling in a determined effort to steer their initial conversation in a pleasant direction. "Would you like—"

"You'll be late for your own funeral," Paula interrupted, her tone spiked with disgust.

"At least I go to funerals."

Paula dropped her head. "I suppose I deserve that."

"You certainly do," he said, enjoying the high ground for a change.

"The reason I didn't go to Bernie's funeral is I thought it'd—I know how close you were, and I—since the hearing—"

Candle waved away her response. "Oh, come off it, Paula. It doesn't matter."

"I did make it by to see Serena later on though. I don't want you to think I . . ." Her voice trailed off.

Candle frowned. "What did you want to see me for, Paula? If it's more money you want, I just don't have it."

Before she could respond, a waitress approached their booth and handed each a menu and a glass of water. "We just want coffee, thanks," Candle said.

Paula waited for the waitress to return with their coffee before she answered Candle's question. "Candle, I know our marriage has left a lot to be desired. And probably had that—if that accident hadn't happened—I call it an accident—we wouldn't be married now."

"That 'accident' explains the first one, Paula. It doesn't explain the second. And it doesn't explain the last ten years."

Paula again dropped her head and nodded. "I've tried to make a go of our marriage. I really, really have. I know you haven't ever loved me. And I don't know if I've ever really loved you either. But I've honestly tried to be a good wife to you, tried to do my duty. I know you don't believe that." She started to cry.

Candle glanced all around to see if anyone was looking at them. No one appeared to be. He leaned toward her. "For Pete's sake, Paula, get control of yourself! You're in a public place!" He wiggled back in his seat. "You haven't answered my question. Is it more money you want?"

"It's not money I've come to talk to you about, although I could use some more."

Candle turned his head away from her and laughed. "Oh, come off it."

"That's not what I want to talk about. Really," she said, removing a handkerchief from her purse and blotting her eyes.

"What is it, then?" He surveyed the café again.

She lifted her head. "I know we've gone over it a thousand times."

Candle rolled his head about and slumped down in the booth. "You want to talk to me about my drinking. Is that it?"

Paula nodded, her green eyes welling again with tears. She reached again into her purse and withdrew a card. She pushed it toward Candle. "Will you call this man? I've heard he's helped a lot of people who might have a—who might have a . . ."

Candle completed the sentence for her. ". . . a drinking problem. Well, I don't have a drinking problem," he said, pushing the card back to Paula. "I drink, but I don't have a drinking problem. I go to work every day. I take care of myself." He held his good hand, palm downward, over the table and made a determined effort to keep it from shaking as it sometimes did. "Look at this. Steady as she goes. See?"

Paula groaned. "Candle, you **do** have a problem. Everybody knows you do. Why can't you see that and try and get some help? Don't you see what you're doing to yourself? To the girls and me? And now you don't have Mr. Blumberg to depend on, to handle your . . ." She could not finish her sentence.

Candle resigned himself to her crying and to the spectacle she'd created. He lifted his coffee cup and took a sip. "Paula, listen to me," he said, again looking all around and leaning forward. "Listen to me, I said!"

Paula glanced up, her moist eyes meeting his dry ones.

"I know you think I'm an alcoholic, but I'm not one," Candle said. "You drink, too, sometimes. Are you an alcoholic? No, you're not. I know I drink too much every now and then. Everyone does. But does that make me an alcoholic? No, it doesn't. Besides, I got a lot of things on me right now. If I thought I was an alcoholic, I'd do something about it. I'm not stupid, you know."

Paula sat silent for a moment, staring at the table top. She wiped her eyes and withdrew a compact from her handbag. After examining her face and returning the compact to her handbag, Paula slid toward the end of the seat.

"Where you going? You haven't even touched your coffee."

Her sudden decision to leave had caught him off guard.

"Candle," she said, speaking low, almost in a whisper, "I'm putting you on notice. Unless I see some change in you and your drinking habit, when school's out next spring, the girls and I are moving to New York. I'd rather the girls not see you at all than for them to have to watch you slowly but surely destroy yourself. All of this is so confusing for them—and embarrassing. They just don't understand why they can't have a daddy like their friends have."

Paula sat for a moment, appearing to gauge Candle's reaction.

But he did not show any reaction. "Paula, my daddy used to say people'll do what they want to do. If you want to take the girls and go back to New York, then I don't suppose I can do a blessed thing about it, now can I?"

Paula stood, her purse in hand. "Yes, you can. You can quit drinking."

Candle took a sip of his coffee. He saw right through all her talk about his being an alcoholic. She wasn't really interested in him. She was using his alleged alcoholism just as an excuse for her to take the children and go back up north, something he suspected she had wanted to do for years.

He glanced up when he felt her hand on his shoulder.

"I came here this morning," she said softly, "because I thought maybe—just maybe—there might be a chance of our saving our marriage. I didn't do it for me, and I didn't do it for you. I did it for the sake of our two daughters, little girls who love you very, very much. Why can't you quit drinking for their sakes? If you can't, then you are an alcoholic . . . no matter what you say."

Before Candle could respond, Paula spun around and stomped out.

***

Marcellus Pondexter, the court crier, rapped the floor with a long pole and told everyone to stand as Judge L. Malcolm Pryde returned to the courtroom, ending the morning recess.

Judge Pryde wasted no time in addressing Solicitor J. Hopson Fleming. "Any more guilty pleas this morning?"

"No, Your Honor," he replied. "The *Wilkerson* case was the last one for today, unless some of them over at the jail happen to change their minds."

Fleming came forward and handed a bill of indictment to the clerk of court to give to the judge. "However, if the Court pleases, the State is ready for trial in Case No. 13,883, *The State versus Hugh Sykes* indictment for embezzlement of a state-chartered bank."

Pryde made a big show of studying the indictment, turning it this way and that. "All right, Mr. Solicitor," he said, holding up the indictment and waving it about. "Is the defendant Hugh Sykes in the courtroom?"

A middle-age man with a drawn mouth and sad eyes raised himself up and stood in place. "Yes, sir, Your Honor," he said, bowing his head. "I'm Hugh Sykes."

A woman seated next to him reached for his hand and began to whimper.

"Well, don't just stand there," the judge ordered. "Come around here and take a seat at that table there next to the solicitor's. You got you a lawyer?"

Sykes dropped the woman's hand and hurried forward, stopping at the bar. "Yes, sir. Mr. Matthew Futeral of Charlotte, North Carolina." He turned around and pointed toward the back of the courtroom.

A muscular, curly-haired, young man with wire-rimmed glasses scrambled forward and joined Sykes at the bar.

Fleming turned to watch as Futeral held open the gate to the bar for this client with one hand and gripped a thin, gleaming briefcase with the other. Futeral followed Sykes to the other counsel table, greeting Fleming with a smile and a slight nod.

Fleming nodded back and chuckled to himself. Futeral appeared to fit the bill of the type lawyer that Judge Pryde loved to humiliate in a public setting: a polite, polished, erudite, young, out-of-town lawyer with a brand-new briefcase, fancy shoes, and a fresh haircut.

Judge Pryde said something to the court reporter, a woman with gray hair and slender, vein-lined hands and long, liver-spotted arms. She placed a stenographic pad on a table by the witness stand and picked up a fountain pen, ready to write once she heard the first official utterance about the case.

"Mr. Fruity—how do you say it?" the judge said, leaning forward and still holding the indictment.

"Futeral, Your Honor. Futeral."

"Funeral?"

"No, sir. Futeral."

"I've never heard that name before. You spell it like it sounds, F-u-t-e-r-a-l?"

Futeral, his eyes twinkling, smiled. "Yes, sir. Very good."

"Well, I think I'll give myself an A-plus for getting that one right. Whatcha say, Solicitor?"

Fleming shrugged, but the courtroom erupted in laughter. The laughter lasted only so long as it took Pondexter to tap the floor with his pole.

"Mr. Futeral, I gather you are a member of the bar of this state. Is that correct?"

Futeral smiled once again, but the twinkle had fled his eyes. "No, Your Honor, I'm not. I am, however, a member of the North Carolina Bar and of the Virginia Bar."

"I see," Judge Pryde responded. He laid the indictment onto his desk and sat far back in his chair. "Mr. Sykes, have you engaged local counsel?"

"I haven't been able—" Sykes began.

Judge Pryde shot forward in his chair, his face purple. "I asked you, sir, if you have local counsel. Do you or do you not?"

"No . . . no, sir. I . . . I don't."

"That's better. Generally speaking, when—"

"Your Honor," Futeral said, interrupting, "could I be heard, please, sir? May it please the court?"

Judge Pryde, crossed his arms. "Mr. Futeral, sir, are you a co-defendant in this case?"

Futeral glanced at Fleming and then at the judge. "Why no, Your Honor. I'm Mr. Sykes'—"

"How shall I say this?" Judge Pryde took his eyes off Futeral, but only for a moment. "One of the benefits of being a trial judge is I only have to listen to certain people. I listen to witnesses after they've been sworn. I listen to the clerk of court and to the court reporter. And sometimes I even listen to my court crier." Some laughter rippled through the courtroom, especially from Pondexter. "I also listen to officers of this court, you know, licensed lawyers admitted to practice in this jurisdiction. And I listen to the defendants who appear before me—people appearing *pro se,* those representing themselves. That's pretty much it. I don't think, sir, you fall into any of those categories. So, no, you may not be heard. Take a seat."

Futeral sat down, filling his lungs with air in gulps. He glanced again at Fleming, who turned away and directed his eyes toward the floor.

Futeral scribbled something on a yellow legal pad that lay on the table and handed it to Sykes, gesturing.

Sykes began to read from it, his voice unsteady. "Your Honor, I would move that Mr. Futeral be admitted to practice before this court . . ." Sykes hesitated while Futeral whispered something in his ear. "*Pro hac vice,*" he continued, "for the purpose of this case."

"Mr. Sykes, a motion of that kind is one that is addressed to the sound discretion of the court," Judge Pryde said. "Tell me, how long have you known about this case? When were you arrested?"

"Last July."

"Last July. Let's see. July, August, September, October," he said, counting his fingers. "It's now November. Over four months. And the closest lawyer you could find anywhere was one way over yonder in North Carolina and one who's not even a member of the bar of this state?"

Judge Pryde reached inside his robe, withdrew a fountain pen, and stretched his arm. "Let me ask Mr. Futeral some questions here. You can sit down, Mr. Sykes, while I do this. There's no need for you to stand unless you want to say something to me or I say something to you. All right?" He stared down on Futeral. "Counselor?"

"Yes, sir," Futeral responded, springing to his feet.

"When were you retained to represent the defendant, Mr. Futeral?"

Futeral unlatched his briefcase and removed a file folder. He opened it and flipped through some pages. "Let's see. I know it was early September, because I was—Your Honor, I was retained on September the sixth, this year," he said, reading off a paper.

Judge Pryde wrote something on the pad in front of him. "Have you been paid a fee to represent Mr. Sykes or are you doing this out the goodness of your heart?"

"A little bit of both," Futeral said, laughing. No one else laughed and the judge's face became a scowl. "What I mean is—yes, sir. I've been retained."

"Paid you mean? Right?"

"Yes, sir."

The judge wrote again on his pad. "How long have you known the solicitor would be calling this case this morning?"

Futeral consulted his file again. "Uh, since October 7, 1946. That's when I got the solicitor's letter. His letter is dated October 4, 1946."

"October 7, 1946," the judge repeated as he wrote. "All right, now. You filed no affidavit with the court that sets forth information about your competency or your moral character, did you?"

"No, sir."

"And how much of your practice there in North Carolina is devoted to the criminal law?"

Futeral lowered his head. "Very little, if any. I really haven't had much criminal law experience. I handle mostly civil cases."

Judge Pryde threw his pen onto his pad and sat back in his chair. "I suspected as much. You can sit down, Mr. Futeral."

Judge Pryde motioned for Sykes to stand. He shook his head. "I'm afraid, Mr. Sykes, I must deny your motion, as much as it pains me to do so. But you should have spent your money on a local lawyer or, at the very least, one from this jurisdiction, this state. And most certainly one who has experience trying criminal cases." He paused a few seconds. "And one other thing, to try and save some time here. Just in case you're thinking, Mr. Sykes, of moving for a continuance, the motion is denied."

Judge Pryde shifted his eyes to Futeral. "Mr. Futeral, please go take a seat out there, if you don't mind, sir," he said, nodding toward the spectator section of the courtroom. "Okay, then, Mr. Clerk. Give us a jury."

Futeral reinserted the file into his briefcase. He placed a hand on Sykes' shoulder for a moment, turned around, and walked back out into the courtroom where he sat down next to a weeping woman, the same woman by whom Sykes sat earlier.

Back again at his counsel table and with his head down and a hand to his eyes, Fleming sneaked a quick peek at Judge Pryde. Fleming had to credit him. Judge Pryde had made good on his promise to take care of the Charlotte lawyer for him. Fleming suspected the young man also knew he'd been taken care of. Dropped-kicked would be the better way to describe what had happened to him.

***

After filing a foreclosure action on behalf of the State Bank and Trust Company, Candle Reid left the clerk of court's office and stopped by the courtroom to watch some of Hugh Sykes' trial for bank embezzlement. He stole into the courtroom through a hallway door next to the grand jury box, making sure the door made no sound when it closed behind him. No one seemed to have noticed him as he tip-toed past Marcellus Pondexter who sat by the doorway, his pole held to the side.

Candle took an empty seat on the back row of the half-filled grand jury box and stared at the petit jury across the courtroom. Everyone's attention appeared riveted on Solicitor J. Hopson Fleming as he cross-examined Hugh Sykes.

The solicitor stood about three feet from the witness stand, facing the jurors, his left side to Sykes. His voice was even and polite. "Now, sir, you admit, don't you, that you received the $3,500 in question?"

Sykes, sitting on the edge of his seat, a shaky hand to his mouth, offered an all but inaudible "Yes, sir" to the question.

"And you also admit, don't you, sir, that the $3,500 disappeared sometime the same day you got it? Is that right?"

"Yes, sir," he mumbled.

"Yes, sir," the solicitor said, nodding and repeating Sykes' answer. He let it sink in before asking his next question. "All right, sir. Can you account for what happened to it?"

Sykes removed his hand from his mouth and gazed at the jurors. "I just know I didn't steal it," he said, his lips quivering.

The solicitor shook his finger at Sykes, his eyes still fixed on the jurors. "I didn't ask you, did I, Mr. Sykes, whether you stole the $3,500? I asked you, sir, if you can **account** for what happened to it. Now, can you do so or not? Tell this jury, if you can." The courtroom fell silent as all the jurors, most with drawn faces and their eyes on Sykes, waited for his explanation.

Fleming, a hand cupped to his ear, also waited for Sykes' answer.

Candle felt for the poor man. He knew—and he suspected Sykes knew—this was a critical inquiry. Candle hoped Sykes would have a good explanation. He liked the man and saw him as someone who went out of his way to assist bank customers. He always had a smile on his face and something pleasant to say to all who came to his window, rich or poor.

Sykes lowered his head and gripped the arms of the chair. "No, sir. I can't. But since you brought it up, you might ought to be—"

"Wait a minute, now, Mr. Sykes," the solicitor ordered, dropping his hand from his ear and running it through his thick, white hair. "Your Honor, I object, sir. I asked the defendant a question and he answered it. Then he started off talking about something else. It's quite unresponsive to my question."

"Your Honor, can I finish what I was about to say, please, sir?" Sykes said, his tone pleading and strained.

Judge L. Malcolm Pryde pulled at the sleeve of his robe and

frowned. "Let me explain something to you, Mr. Sykes. When you sit down in that chair," he said, indicating, "you become what we call a 'witness.' That means you do not speak unless you are spoken to and, on cross-examination, you answer only the question asked of you. Are we clear about that? So, no, you can't say what you were about to say. It was not responsive to the question the solicitor asked you. You must play by the rules, sir. Objection sustained."

The solicitor moved to the front of the bench and dipped his head toward the judge. "If the court please, I think, in retrospect, I'll withdraw my objection to the defendant's additional remarks." He turned and faced the audience. "I wouldn't want anyone to think either you or I didn't allow him every opportunity to say what he wants to say."

Candle noticed the surprised look on Judge Pryde's face. The look did not strike Candle as genuine.

"All right, Mr. Solicitor," Judge Pryde said, using a disgusted tone. "But I do wish you'd make up your mind." He turned to Sykes. "Go on and say what you wanted to say, Mr. Sykes, and be quick about it. We're wasting time. Lots of time. These gentlemen here," he said, waving his hand toward the jury, "have got businesses to run, cows to milk, hogs to slop, things to do. So what is it? Hurry up and say it."

Candle had seen the solicitor and the judge work this routine several times since his late law partner Bernard Blumberg had first pointed it out to him years before. The solicitor, at a decisive moment in the trial, would object to something and then withdraw the objection. The judge, after pretending to chastise the solicitor, would make the defendant appear to be wasting the jury's time by offering evidence critical to his defense. The purpose of the routine was to induce the jury to either ignore or belittle the evidence.

Sykes seemed flustered. Before he could speak, Judge Pryde again instructed him to hurry and say what he wanted to say.

"You should ask Lester Mayfield, Jr. about the money. He could have taken it," Sykes said.

The solicitor, who had gone to his counsel table and had his back to the witness stand, wheeled about. "How dare you, sir! Shame on you, sir! Shame on you!" The solicitor's voice sounded full of sorrow and his face manifested immeasurable hurt. Most of the jurors dropped their heads, and those that did not, turned their eyes away from the witness.

Solicitor Fleming adjusted his bow tie and picked up a file folder. He walked back to within inches of the witness stand and handed the folder to Sykes. "Here, sir, is the entire investigative file. Do you care to study it?"

Sykes, his hands shaking, took the file but held it in his lap without opening it.

The solicitor turned and faced the jury again. "Sir, you have seen fit to question our investigative efforts, our good faith, our integrity, our competence—"

"I did no such thing. I merely said you should ask Mr. Mayfield."

Solicitor Fleming turned away from the jury and drew closer to Sykes. "Sir, do you think we are amateurs? Don't you think we questioned him? Look in the file there to see all that we did to try and prove your innocence. Look, sir, in the file there. Look and see all that we've done."

Sykes would not open the file. Instead, he sat staring at the floor, his mouth closed, his eyes blinking, his body quivering.

Candle felt for the man and wished he could do something, but he realized he couldn't.

The solicitor reached and removed the file from Sykes' lap. He turned and faced the jury, his lanky frame towering above them. "I didn't think you really wanted to see this," he said, fanning the pages of the file. He walked behind his counsel table and threw the file down next to the water pitcher. "But to show how fair we are, sir, when you are through with your defense we will call Lester Mayfield, Jr.—and any other person you dare accuse—to the witness stand in reply just so you can cross-examine them. We have nothing to hide."

Solicitor Fleming stood for a moment, his hands on his hips, staring at Sykes. When Sykes offered no further comment, the solicitor looked up at Judge Pryde. "Your Honor," he said, "that concludes our cross-examination." He then sat down, folded his hands as if in prayer, and rested his chin on his fingertips.

Sykes stood up and prepared to step down from the witness stand.

"Just a minute," Judge Pryde said, "you have anything else you want to tell these gentlemen?"

Sykes shook his head.

The gesture drew a rebuke from Judge Pryde. "Mr. Sykes, you must answer either 'yes' or 'no.' The court reporter records words. He does not take moving pictures."

"No, sir. I don't have anything else," he responded, his face ashen.

Judge Pryde pointed toward Sykes' counsel table. "All right, sir. You may return to your seat and call your next witness. And don't take all day doing it, either. It's about lunch time and everybody's hungry."

At this point, Candle made his way out of the grand jury box and out of the courtroom. But he had no plans to eat. His stomach felt queasy.

***

Lester Mayfield, Jr. completed his testimony right after the lunch recess. The experience had unnerved him; however, he need not have worried. Solicitor Fleming's continuous objections to Sykes' questions and Judge Pryde's consistent sustaining of those objections stymied Sykes' attempt to cross-examine him about his access to the funds in question and the opportunities he had had to pilfer them. By the time Mayfield concluded his testimony, there was little doubt what verdict the jurors would find. Every one of the jurymen sat gazing at the floor, their heads held low like mourners at a funeral. After asking his last question and having it ruled improper by the judge, Sykes turned and slipped back to his counsel table. He collapsed in a chair, the look of hopelessness etched in his face.

As Sykes sat in the hushed courtroom with his shoulders drawn, his arms between his legs, and his chin to his chest, his wife could be heard crying. Her sobs continued until the court crier, at Judge Pryde's direction, left his post by the hallway door and went over and shushed her, pointing to the judge with his pole as he did so.

After Judge Pryde told Mayfield he could step down, he bounced from the witness stand and flew to his place out in the courtroom.

With sweat pouring from his bald head, he sat next to his father on the front row behind Solicitor Fleming. The older Mayfield acknowledged his son with a smile and a pat on the knee.

Mayfield put a hand to his father's ear after he wiped his head dry with the handkerchief from the breast pocket to his suit. "Dad, if it's okay with you, I think I'm going to take the afternoon off and probably ride up to Harpers' Joy or maybe even over to Neely Springs. I don't feel so good." He rubbed his stomach. "Feel like I'm going to throw up. That's no fun being up there on a witness stand and have everybody looking at you. I hope he gets a hundred years for what he's put us through."

"All right," the older Mayfield whispered out of the corner of his mouth, his blue, icy eyes directed forward.

Mayfield felt relieved that his testimony seemed to have satisfied his father. Before court began that morning, his father had come into his office quite unexpected and had cross-examined him in detail about the Sykes matter. The experience had proven worse than the trial itself.

He thought, however, his answers to his father's questions had satisfied him. What seemed to convince his father of his innocence was his father's own theory that, considering their financial situation, there was no necessity for him to steal the money.

As he walked toward the bank, Mayfield stroked his chin and laughed to himself. But there are other reasons to steal. Like revenge, for instance. Sykes should not have demeaned him in front of the bank examiners the last time they visited the bank. Sykes might not even have known he had done it, but he had done it nonetheless; and Mayfield wasn't about to forget the humiliation he felt at the time.

When he reached the bank, Mayfield ignored the stares and inquiring faces from the tellers and other bank personnel. He hurried to his office where he closed the door behind him and laid his hat on his desk. He picked up the telephone and placed a call. His heart pounded as the phone rang. A female's voice answered.

"Hi. It's me. Can you talk?" he whispered, relieved that the other voice had not been a man's.

"Oh, hello, 'Thelma.' I meant to call you," the woman said. "What time is it?"

Mayfield cursed to himself. "Is he home?"

"Yes, I suppose I am. How about you?"

"Right now I'm at work. I just left the courtroom. I was hoping I could meet you and we could ride up to Harpers' Joy this afternoon."

"Gee, Thelma, I don't think I can go today. George is at home and doesn't feel well. He's got temperature and everything, the poor dear," she said.

Mayfield grimaced. "Okay. I'll call you next week. Maybe we can go then."

"Yes, call me. Don't spend all of Henry's money. Have fun. Bye-bye."

Mayfield tried two other numbers but received no answer to either of them. His mood, already dark, became darker still. He opened his desk drawer and searched for a piece of paper that had a number written upon it. Not finding it, he slammed the drawer shut and got up from his desk. "Just is not my day," he murmured, reaching for his hat.

Miss Thacker gave him a baleful look as he walked out of his office but said nothing.

"My father's still at the courthouse, Miss Thacker. I'm taking the afternoon off. I might get in a round or two of golf."

Miss Thacker smiled a fake smile, causing Mayfield to imagine ways to strangle her, including stuffing a large-mouth bass past her ill-fitting false teeth and down her throat. "Must be nice," she said as she puckered her lips.

Mayfield ignored the cutting remark and headed out of the bank. Across the street he saw a green and yellow drink truck parked in a loading zone. He did not see the driver and figured he must be nearby, probably inside the converted trolley car that housed Shu Ming's Take-Out Chinese Restaurant.

Mayfield peeked through the white's only service window and saw Shu Ming, her back to the window, motioning to Dewey Coltraine to take a loaded hand truck to a far corner in the trolley. He stepped back from the window and went and waited by the truck for Dewey to finish his call.

Dewey came out of the restaurant, pushing his hand truck and its cargo of two flats of empty bottles. "What are you doing downtown, Coltraine?" Mayfield asked as Dewey approached his truck.

Dewey, on seeing Mayfield, broke into a grin. "Mr. Mayfield, sir. How you doin'?" He parked his hand truck and offered his hand, but Mayfield ignored it. He did not shake hands with tenants. Dewey withdrew his hand and adjusted his hat.

"I said what are you doing here in town? I thought you had a country route."

Dewey grabbed the hand truck with both hands and tipped it backwards on its wheels. "Oh, I got three routes. This one here in town, which I run on Mondays and Thursdays, the Harpers' Joy one, which I run on Tuesdays and Fridays, and the Hall's Ferry one. I run it on Wednesdays and Saturdays."

"You're here in town all day Mondays and when?"

"Thursdays."

"And you're out towards Hall's Ferry Wednesdays and Saturdays?"

"Yes, sir. I pretty much got the western part of the county. Mr. Hammond, he's the owner. He does the eastern part his own self on Tuesdays, Wednesdays, Thursdays, and Saturdays. He bottles on Mondays and—"

"I'll see you later," Mayfield said, cutting Dewey off in mid-sentence. "I got some place to go." He left Dewey standing on the sidewalk, still holding onto his hand truck.

Less than thirty minutes later, Mayfield pulled his Packard into the yard of the folding house and blew the horn. Nellie Grace Coltraine came to the door, pushing the screen door to one side and waving. She yelled something, but Mayfield could not make it out.

He leaned to his right and rolled down the front, passenger-side window. "What'd you say?" he yelled back, smiling.

Nellie laughed and came out of the folding house, down the steps, and toward the automobile. She stopped a few feet from the car, tilting her head as she peeped through the opened window. "I said, 'Oh, it's you, Mr. Mayfield, sir.'"

Mayfield turned off the engine and got out of the car. "Who'd you think it was?"

"I didn't know. That's why I got my daddy's shotgun." She turned sideways and pointed toward the door. "It's right there by the kitchen door."

"I saw your husband a little while ago."

Nellie smiled but kept her head lowered. "You did?"

"He was at Shu Ming's, delivering some drinks."

"He was?"

"Yeah. I was on my way to get my car and happened to run into him. I've been in court all morning."

"Court? Ooooh," she said, wrapping her bare arms about herself and drawing in her thin shoulders. "Court would scare me to death if I had to go there."

"I had to testify. An employee at the bank stole a whole lot of money. He'd worked for my daddy—he'd worked at the bank for six years or better. It's gotten where you just can't trust anybody these days."

"Yes, sir. Isn't that the truth?" She turned her head toward the folding house and then back to Mayfield. "Excuse me, Mr. Mayfield, but I better run back inside. It's kinda cold standing out here without my coat on."

Mayfield frowned. "Yeah. It is a little chilly, sure enough. Catch up with you later. Let me know if y'all need anything."

She nodded, waved goodbye without looking at him, and darted back inside, closing the door behind her.

Mayfield climbed back into the car and drove down to the log cabin. Once inside, he turned on the gas heater in the hallway and walked into the living room to where a liquor cabinet and bar stood next to the fireplace. He grabbed up an ice bucket and carried it to the kitchen where he filled it with ice from the refrigerator.

Mayfield waited for the radio to warm up, gulping down his drink as he stood by the radio. In a few seconds, he heard the last several bars of "I Can't Begin to Tell You" sung by Nancy Norman of the Sammy Kaye Orchestra. The station followed with Guy Lombardo's "Seems Like Old Times." The songs made him realized that his thoughts had not strayed far from where they had been when he had last seen Nellie Grace Coltraine.

He returned to the bar and fixed himself another bourbon and water. He consumed it in two, quick gulps. Since he had not eaten since breakfast and had a low threshold for alcohol anyway, Mayfield soon felt the whiskey's effect. The more the alcohol mixed with his bloodstream, the more he thought of Nellie and the more fancied his thoughts of her became.

***

Solicitor J. Hopson Fleming sat alone in the empty courtroom behind a counsel table. One hand held a glass of sour-tasting water and the other a roster that listed the names of defendants and their offenses, lawyers, if any, and expected pleas. Fleming's schedule had been thrown into disarray because Hugh Sykes' embezzlement trial, which Fleming had anticipated would last at least two days, had not consumed even a full day. Sykes' lack of counsel sped things up considerably. Fleming laid the roster aside and began writing on a legal pad the names of the defendants whose cases he would call the following day for disposition.

The door at the back of the courtroom banged open. "Now that's what I call good lawyering. Yes, sir, that's was good lawyering," Lester Mayfield said, laughing and clapping his hands as he walked through the doorway and down the middle aisle toward Fleming. "I don't think ol' Sykes knows what hit him."

Fleming glanced over his shoulder as the shorter, older man came inside the bar. "Well, if he doesn't, he soon will," Fleming said.

Mayfield patted Fleming on the back and sat down on the counsel table, one foot to the floor, the other swinging to and fro. "That'll learn 'em." He smiled. "Yes, sir. That'll learn 'em."

Fleming stood and stuffed the legal pad, file folders, and an assortment of papers into his briefcase. "You sat there, Lester, and heard Sykes and your son testify. You saw the whole trial. Tell me, what you think now? You think Sykes really took your money?"

Mayfield dropped the smile. "Jury said he did."

Fleming recoiled as though someone had slapped him in the face. "Lester, I can't believe this. You mean you put stock in what **that** jury found? You know as well as I they'd have convicted Dwight D. Eisenhower if I had wanted them to." Fleming snapped shut his briefcase. "I heard a lot of people out there in the courtroom grumbling when that verdict came in."

"Let them grumble. Folks who hang around courthouses, they don't know pee-turkey. If they did, they'd be somewhere else. Working, maybe. Doing something productive."

"They were saying they thought your son stole the money."

"I don't care what they think," Mayfield said, his voice raised and angry. "We've had this discussion before, remember? Like I told you then, Lester Junior had no reason to take it. I questioned him myself—just this morning before court and to satisfy my own mind. He convinced me he didn't do it." Mayfield's chest swelled. "And I know my son. He's a good man."

"I'm merely telling you what people said."

"They don't know my boy. He's done more good for this community since he came home from the war than any five people I know about. You know that too. He's pitched right in—feet first. Why, the March of Dimes folks, they told me the other day he was the best—"

Fleming cut Mayfield off with a raised hand. "Lester," he said, "I wouldn't put too much stock in all these so-called good works your son's been doing, if I were you. It gives him power over people and organizations and their funds. He loves power, your boy."

Mayfield stood, his face on fire. "I'm leaving. I'm not going to stand here and listen to you run my son down. I'm surprised at you. How dare you question his good motives!"

Fleming motioned him to sit back down and in a pleading voice said, "Lester, listen to me a moment. I'm trying to be helpful. Now that Mr. Sykes has been convicted, let me tell you a little bit more about this case, so you'll better understand some advice I've got for you and where I'm coming from. Okay?"

"I've heard enough about the case," Mayfield said, sitting down again.

Fleming lifted his briefcase from the counsel table and dropped it to his side. "No, I don't think you have. To satisfy our burden of proof, Lester, we relied on what the law calls a statutory presumption. The presumption we used here is that, when money lawfully comes into someone's hands in trust and the person fails to account for it, the law presumes the person fraudulently appropriated the money."

"What's your point?" Mayfield demanded, his heavy eyebrows knitted together.

"What did Sykes spend the money on, if indeed he took it?"

"How do I know?"

"We found no evidence of unusual spending on his part. We couldn't see where Sykes'd spent any money beyond what you might expect him to spend. We subpoenaed bank accounts, both here in Tekoa and elsewhere. Found nothing."

"Okay, so what? He could've deposited it in another name. Why, he might even have put it in a jar and buried it somewhere out in his backyard, for all I know."

Fleming shook his head and stood staring at Mayfield for a few seconds. "You wanted to know what the point is, Lester? Well, it's this. There's reasonable doubt here. Reasonable doubt. That's my opinion, anyway."

"And so what if there is—in your opinion?"

"What I'm telling you is that your son seems out of control and if you don't keep close tabs on him, he's going to get himself and maybe even you and the bank in a whole heap of trouble—trouble we might not be able to fix, if you know what I mean—like the State Board of Bank Control, the Attorney General. That's what I'm trying to get across to you."

The door by the petit jury box flew open. Marcellus Pondexter stuck his head into the courtroom. "Oh, there you is, Mr. Solicitor," he said, stepping through the doorway. "Went lookin' for you downstairs. Didn't know you still be up here. Y'all ain't heard all the commotion down the hall? Mr. Sykes, he just tried to hang heself in the holdin' pen with he shoe laces. Mmm huh."

"Sykes!?" Fleming asked, stunned.

"Mmm huh. Mr. Sykes," Pondexter said. "That show he must've been guilty, huh?"

Mayfield smirked. "Now, there you are, Solicitor. You be careful what you say about my boy from now on."

***

It was almost eight o'clock when Dewey Coltraine turned into the drive that led past the folding house and down to the pond and the log cabin. He stopped and searched the lighted way ahead. The open gate surprised him. Shifting into first gear, Dewey pulled ahead at a slow speed, pondering whether he should stop and close the gate. He decided not to, thinking Mr. Mayfield might be down at the log cabin.

Dewey drove the truck into the yard of the folding house, parking it next to the front steps. He studied the dwelling for a moment, a hand to his mouth. Something seemed amiss. There were no lights on and the front door stood wide open. He jumped from the truck and hurried inside.

"Nellie!" Dewey called as he searched the darkness for the light switch. Finding it, he turned on the overhead light and surveyed the kitchen. No pots simmered on the stove. No smell of supper being kept warm in the oven permeated the room. Neither dishes nor flatware lay on the kitchen table. Something was wrong all right.

For a moment, Dewey thought she might be down at the log cabin. Perhaps, she and Mr. Mayfield were waiting on him to come down there and join them. But he could not understand why she would do that. If she had gone off, why wouldn't she have left a light on or left him a note? Also, why would she have left the kitchen door standing open?

Dewey peeked into the combination living and dining room. Not finding Nellie there, he walked across to the bedroom. When he turned on a light, what he saw stunned him. The room was in total disarray. The bed was torn up, blood stains speckling the sheets and spread. Nellie's dress and underwear lay strewn on the floor. The dress appeared torn. "Nellie? Nellie?" he called in a quiet voice, his heart pumping fast. "Nellie, sweetheart. It's me, Dewey. You here?"

Thinking he heard something behind him, Dewey spun around and spotted the closed bathroom door. He stepped to the door and tapped. "Nellie, honey, you in there? It's me, Dewey," he whispered, finding it hard to speak. He opened the door and, as light from the kitchen spilled into the bathroom, looked inside.

Nellie sat naked, wet, and shivering in the shower stall, her back against the wall, her arms wrapped around her knees.

"Nellie! Nellie!" he exclaimed, rushing toward her. "What's happened!? What's happened to you!? There's bruises all over your face. And your lip—" He bent down and brought her close. "Oh, Nellie!"

She did not respond. She only stared back through slits in swollen eyes above her high cheeks.

"Nellie, who did this to you? Tell me," he pleaded, dreading the answer.

She still did not answer.

Dewey lifted Nellie from the shower stall and carried her into the living room, grabbing a towel on the way. He laid her on the couch and dried her off. When he turned on a floor lamp and saw more clearly the purple bruises that overlay the right side of her face and her neck, and the scratches and cuts that scored her hands and arms, he began to cry.

"Nellie, we gotta get you seen to and get the sheriff," he said, first wiping away his tears with his hand and then bending down to cover Nellie's trembling body with an afghan that he removed from the back of the sofa. "You think maybe you could let me carry you on out to the truck after I get you some clothes to put on? It's right outside."

"No, Dewey, no," she ordered. "Leave me be."

He stood up straight, looking at her and crying. Then he remembered about the gate being opened. "Nellie, the gate, it wasn't locked when I pulled in a minute ago. Do you know if Mr. Mayfield is down yonder at his place? If he is, maybe he could—"

Nellie suddenly began to wail and shake her head. Her wailing unnerved Dewey. Like that of a banshee, it seemed to carry a warning of something bad about to happen. But before he could ask her anything about what she was attempting to convey, her eyes drew shut and her hand fell limp toward the floor.

Dewey heard the sound of a fast-approaching automobile as it came up the drive from the direction of the log cabin. He wheeled around and raced to the kitchen door, but he was not fast enough. Just as he opened the door to run outside, the Packard blew by, kicking up gravel and dirt in its wake. By the time Dewey reached the drive, the car had turned onto the dirt road and vanished into the night.

***

Lester Mayfield, Jr., his head hurting and his stomach uneasy, closed the garage door behind him and struggled with the lock. His swollen knuckles and the effects of too much alcohol made the task difficult, but after several tries he succeeded in locking the door. He glanced up toward the second floor of his house and was relieved not to spot any hint of light in his wife's bedroom.

Entering his home through the back door, he stopped in the kitchen to search for some aspirin. He found some in a kitchen drawer and took two, chasing them down with a mouthful of water that he drank straight from the faucet. As he rose up, he glimpsed his reflection in the window above the sink and saw the scratches on his head and neck. "The tramp!"

Cupping his hands beneath the faucet, he filled them with hot water and, with his eyes closed, splashed the water in his face to cleanse the wounds and wash off the blood.

Mayfield did not hear his wife come up behind him. He jumped when she spoke.

"My, my," she said, slurring her words, "I've never known you to bathe in the kitchen sink before. Here, let me help you."

She reached for a towel hanging on a rack at the end of the counter; however, he grabbed it before she could and began wiping his face with it.

As he dried his face, she moved to his side, dragging her housecoat on the floor. She leaned around and squinted at her husband. "Oh, my goodness," she gasped, placing a hand over her mouth. "Look at you! You'd better put something on that before you get blood poisoning. What happened?"

"I was in a fight."

"A fight?" She examined his hands as he wiped them with the towel. "Who with?

"None of your business." He threw the towel onto the kitchen counter. "You wouldn't know him anyway."

She scoffed. "Him?" No man would scratch you like that."

Mayfield whirled around, his balance uncertain. "What'd you say, fatso?"

"A woman did that to you. Not some man." She shook her head. "Just look at you. Mr. Pillar of the Community. Witness for the Prosecution. Mr. Big Shot. Who was she? Tell me. I want to know. Was it—"

She did not get to finish her sentence because Mayfield backhanded her across her jaw, knocking her head up and backward. She collapsed against the wall and slid to the floor, unconscious. He then kicked her hard against her right thigh, but she did not appear to feel it.

Mayfield stood at his wife's feet for a few seconds, looking at her and weaving back and forth. He walked out of the kitchen, leaving her on the floor, her head hung to one side and her mouth open.

Bert Goolsby

Tuesday, November 19, 1946

Dewey had tended Nellie all night, holding her head in his lap and anguishing over what to do when morning came. Other than what he saw of her injuries, which were many, and of the bedroom, which he had left untouched, he did not know anything. Who had done this to her? He wondered if Mr. Mayfield had heard anything.

He glanced at the clock on the wall and noted the time. Nellie moaned as her swollen eyelids parted a bit and exposed bloodshot eyes. Dewey kissed her on her forehead. "Nellie, it's 'bout six-thirty in the mornin'. You feel like lettin' me take you to town to see Dr. Kline? While he's lookin' at you, I can go see Sheriff Madison. Also, I need to call Mr. Hammond down at the plant and let him know I can't work the route today." He caressed her swollen cheek with his fingertips.

"Dewey," she whispered, shaking her head, "we're not gonna tell anyone about this."

He shrunk back. "Huh!? How come?"

"We can't tell, that's all."

"Sure we can, Nellie," he said as he eased out from beneath her head and stood. He bent down and lifted her from the couch. "Come on. Let's see if you can make it out to the truck and then—"

Nellie pushed against Dewey's chest with her forearms and stretched her neck backwards. "No, Dewey."

He laid her back upon the couch and resumed his watch in a chair opposite the couch.

A pounding on the kitchen door brought Dewey to his feet.

"I'm comin'!" he shouted, wondering who it could be and, at the same time, feeling grateful that there was at last someone to help him with Nellie and maybe talk her into letting him contact the sheriff. He pushed open the kitchen door. A short, stout figure stepped to the side as the door widened.

Dewey smiled, holding open the door. "Why, Mr. Mayfield, sir! Am I glad to see you! Somethin' awful's happened to Nellie! I tried to catch you last night when you was leavin' but I—"

"Where's your wife, Coltraine?" Mayfield said, stepping into the kitchen.

The smile left Dewey's face. "She's in the living room. Why?" He noticed the Mercurochrome-covered scratches on Mayfield as the man whisked past him.

Dewey followed Mayfield into the room and found him standing over Nellie. She did not move but lay shaking and looking up at Mayfield through battered, half-closed eyes.

"Sit up," Mayfield ordered as he reached down, seized Nellie by an arm, and began pulling her toward him.

Dewey grabbed hold of Mayfield's shoulder. "Mr. Mayfield, you ain't got no right talkin' to her like that and doin' her thataway," he said, pulling Mayfield away from Nellie. "Please, sir, get your hands off of her."

Mayfield dropped Nellie's arm and spun around to confront Dewey. With his free hand, he pushed Dewey backward with his fingertips. "Listen to me, you little hick," he said. "And listen real good. I've already warned your wife. Now I'm warning you. Don't you so much as breathe a word about this to anybody. You hear me?"

Dewey again noted the scratches on Mayfield. "You mean, you did this to Nellie?"

Mayfield drew his shoulders up. "Yeah, that's right. After she attacked me and tried to make what we'd been doing look like rape. I simply defended myself."

Dewey's mouth fell open. "You mean, you—you and Nellie, y'all—"

Mayfield laughed. "Yeah. That's right. We spent all yesterday afternoon in the sack. And about six-thirty or seven, she thought she heard your truck turning into the drive and all of a sudden, she started screaming and carrying on. Hitting me. Scratching me. Look at what she did to me. The little hussy!" He turned and stretched his neck, pointing. "Look at this, Coltraine. She'd have probably clawed my eyes out if I hadn't defended myself. I could get her thrown in the penitentiary for what she did to me. Do you know that?"

Nellie turned her head toward the wall and began to sob. "Oh, Dewey, it's not true what he's saying."

"I know it ain't. Mr. Mayfield, you can't get away with this. I ain't gonna let you."

Mayfield sneered. "Is that right? Well, let Hugh Sykes tell you what happens when you mess with the Mayfields. But I'm not out here to cause you any trouble, understand. The reason I came is to tell you I'm perfectly willing to settle this thing."

Dewey glanced down at Nellie and back at Mayfield. "Settle it? I don't under—"

"I suggest we settle it this way," Mayfield said, interrupting. "I won't say anything; you won't say anything. And just to show you that there's no hard feelings, I'll let you stay here till the end of the week. Then I want ya'll off my place, Coltraine. Got that?"

Dewey looked again at Nellie. Her lost expression sickened him.

"Another thing I want to make clear to both of you is this," Mayfield said, his tone angry again. He kicked the couch. "Listen to me, you little tramp!"

Nellie turned her head toward Mayfield.

"If either of you ever do say anything, anything at all to anybody about this, the very least that'll happen is your wife's reputation'll be ruined. The worst that'll happen is I'll kill both of you, as sure as I'm standing here."

He faced Dewey. "And just to prove I'd do it—" He slammed his fist hard into Dewey's stomach, doubling him over.

As Dewey collapsed writhing to the floor, his arms around his waist, Mayfield left through the side door of the living room, knocking it open with his foot and slamming it shut as soon as he reached the outside.

Once Mayfield drove off, Dewey, breathing hard, pulled himself toward his wife. "Nellie," he gasped, "what we gonna do?" His thoughts were not confined to Mayfield and his threats. They also focused on what Nellie's father had told Dewey he would do if anything ever happened to Nellie.

***

The bell of the clock atop the State Bank and Trust Company of Tekoa chimed the quarter hour and fell silent. Candle Reid studied the obese figure who sat across the desk from him, wiping her eyes with a lace handkerchief. Georgia Ann Mayfield had been there a full half-hour and had talked and cried without letup.

"What am I to do, Mr. Reid?" she asked in her reedy voice. "Tell me."

Candle, thinking of more pressing matters, checked his watch. "I'm sorry. What? What'd you say?" he asked.

"What do you think I should do?"

"Well, have you consi— "

"Like I say, this is not the first time he's hit me either," she declared. "I'm just afraid of him. There's no telling what he'll do to me next time, especially if he ever found out I came and talked to you."

Candle ruffled some papers on his desk. "Tell you what, Mrs. Mayfield. Tell you what."

She dabbed away the tears and looked at Candle, her eyes kindled with hope.

"Have you spoken to your father-in-law about this?" Candle asked.

She lowered her head and rubbed her bruised jaw. "Not this time, but before I have—both him and Mrs. Mayfield. But neither one of them would listen. Those Mayfields stick together." She sniffled and drew herself straight up in the chair. "I guess what I want, Mr. Reid, is o-u-t, out. "Won't you please help me?"

Candle swallowed hard. He thought of all the work the bank sent him, work that, as a rule, was not complicated or adversarial and was always paid for and on time. He bent forward and placed his hands on the pile of papers and things that hid his desktop. "Mrs. Mayfield, you are welcome to come talk to me anytime. You really are. But it'd be a conflict of interest for me to try and help you, ma'am, if that meant going against the legal interest of your husband or his family."

Georgia Ann jarred the floor as she jumped to her feet. "Do the Mayfields own you and everybody else in this town?"

"Yes, ma'am, I think they do," Candle found himself answering. "Including you."

"This has been a complete waste of my time," she said, batting her large purse against her massive thigh and grimacing when she did it. She straightened her hat and her skirt. "Thanks for nothing, you pitiful, deformed coward!" She turned to walk out, retrieving her coat from the chair over which she had tossed it when she entered.

"Mrs. Mayfield, ma'am," Candle said.

"What?" she said, turning back around, her eyes now dry.

"That'll be five dollars. Just give it to Judy on your way out."

"Five dollars!? What in the world for?" she said in a huff. "You didn't do anything."

"Yes, ma'am, I did. I listened to you. For over a half-hour or better," he said. "You know, consultation?"

"Why, I've never," she said and stomped from his office into the hallway, slamming the door behind her.

Candle concluded that this would be the last time he'd ever have to listen to Georgia Ann Mayfield. Just as he had learned from Bernard Blumberg a long time ago to ask for the last paper received whenever any uneducated person came into the office carrying a bundle of documents in a torn, faded, yellow envelope, he had learned from his own experience that if you charged the kind of individual that he suspected Georgia Ann Mayfield was—the kind that liked to talk about divorce but didn't really want one—a small fee for listening, he or she never, ever came back. It worked every time.

He glanced at his legal pad and the few notes that he had recorded during his interview with the talkative woman: *Monday night 11/18/46 husband comes home, scratches on his face, neck, head, hands; drinking, when she asks about, he smacked her lower right jaw Knocked Out!!! Don't know how long - says she's got real big bruise on thigh (didn't see it); there's a bruise on right jaw; says leg hurts; jaw sore; face looks swollen.*

Candle sighed and wished he had a drink right then.

***

As Lester Mayfield, Jr. came into town and drove past the courthouse, he saw his wife close the door to the stairs that led up to the law offices of Blumberg & Reid and hurry toward her car parked in front of the *Tekoa New Dealer*. He blew the horn at her to let her know he'd seen her leave the law offices. He hoped it worried her.

His late arrival at the bank that morning caused no small amount of curiosity, especially after people noticed the scratches about his face and head. Mayfield noted the looks and nods and the whispered conversations. Only one person ventured to ask him anything about the scratches as he walked toward his office: Miss Flossie Thacker.

"Well," she said, adjusting her rimless glasses, her tone cutting as always, "that must've been some game of golf. You must've spent the entire afternoon—how shall I say it?—in the rough."

Mayfield ignored the remark and passed by without greeting her.

He had only managed to hang up his hat and to open the Venetian blind behind his desk before his father popped into his office, carrying a cup of coffee, steam wafting upward from its creamy surface.

"Coffee smells good. Is that my cup, Dad?"

The elder Mayfield shook his head and shut the door behind him with his free hand. "Well, I guess you've notice the bad mood everybody's—" His mouth dropped open. "What's this, son? Georgia Ann do this to you?" He came closer. "Let me look at this."

Mayfield avoided his father's steely eyes. "We had some trouble when I got home last night. She'd been drinking. I doubt if she even remembers much about it. You know how she can get."

The elder Mayfield nodded and continued to inspect his son's wounds. "They look bad. You might better see a doctor."

"It's just the Mercurochrome I put on them. It makes them look worse than they really are. They don't hurt. Not much, they don't," he lied. "What were you going to say about the mood everybody is in?"

Before his father could continue, the voice of Miss Thacker screeched over the intercom. "Mr. Mayfield, Mr. Lucas is here. Mr. Colin Lucas."

Mayfield swore an oath to himself as he flipped a switch on the intercom. "Tell him to have a seat. I'll be with him in a moment. I'm talking to my father right now."

The older Mayfield shook his head and held up a hand. "That's okay."

Mayfield collapsed into a chair behind his desk. "No, Dad. Stay. Maybe he'll leave if we make him wait long enough."

"I expect that depends on why he's here. What's he want from us?"

"More time, I expect. He's way behind on his loan payments and I've already given him one extension. If you ask me, he's just stalling. He just wants to take advantage of us. I'm sick of putting up with him and all his crap."

The elder Mayfield walked to the door, holding his coffee cup. "Well, son, do what you think is best. But I usually try to accommodate folks on things like this if they're not too far behind and there's a good reason why they are."

"That's where you and I differ. The way I look at it, when they don't pay like they're supposed to, that's money out of our pockets."

"I know it is. I just thought—"

"You told me when I took this job I could run it as I see fit. Have you changed your mind?"

The older man smiled. "Oh, no, no. Do what you think's best. I'll catch you later."

Mayfield heard his father greet Lucas as he closed the door behind him. He didn't like it that his father used a familiar tone with the man.

A few seconds passed and the door to his office again opened, revealing the shapeless figure of a woman with the grim look of a prison guard. "Come right on in, sir," he heard Miss Thacker say.

As the door broke wider, Mayfield spotted the sullen, overall-clad figure of Colin Lucas, hat in hand. Clinging to his side was a drooling child with long, knotted hair.

"He'll be happy to talk to you, I'm sure," Miss Thacker announced.

Mayfield found her manner far too cheerful for the occasion. For perhaps the millionth time he wished the woman dead.

Followed by Lucas and the girl, Miss Thacker marched up to Mayfield's desk and laid a file folder down. "You'll need this, I believe," she said, smirking as she said it. She turned around and pointed to the chairs in front of Mayfield's desk. "Y'all come have a seat, Mr. Lucas. It'll take him a moment to review the file." With that, Miss Thacker pressed her hands against her short, wavy hair and left the room.

Lucas and the girl remained standing as Mayfield, taking his time, opened the file, picked up a paper, and pretended to read it over. "What are you doing here, Lucas?" We've already sent this thing to a lawyer, just like I told you we would if you didn't make your payment on time. Didn't you get a copy of this letter?"

"Yes, sir. I got it," Lucas said. "That's how come I'm here. I wanna talk to you 'bout it."

"We've already had our talk. Now, get out." Mayfield gestured toward the child with the bent, stiff wrists. "And take that with you."

Lucas pulled a small pistol from inside his overalls and aimed it at Mayfield's chest. "No, sir. Me and you, we're gonna have us a talk. And my daughter, she ain't no 'that.' Her name's Elsie."

"Now, look here, Lucas!" Mayfield felt the blood leave his face. He started to stand, but Lucas motioned him to stay seated.

"No, sir. You the one looka here!" He tapped the girl with the brim of his hat and nodded toward one of the chairs. The girl stumbled around the chair and sat down, all the while grinning at Mayfield. "I come in here peaceful like, but you done made me do it thisaway," Lucas said, waving the pistol.

Mayfield glanced at the gun but strove not to show any fear. "What is it then? Say what you want to say. I guess you know you're in a lot of trouble right now."

"Trouble? Me and trouble, we're twin brothers, Mr. Mayfield." Lucas, keeping his pistol trained on Mayfield, sat down. He lapped a long, skinny leg over his other and hung his hat on his kneecap. "I want you to git in touch with the lawyer y'all wrote that letter to and tell him not to try and take my land away from me. Least not yet."

"And why should I do that?" Mayfield asked, anger replacing his fear. When his eyes engaged those of Lucas, the latter dropped his head.

"Fer one thing, I'll git y'all all y'all's money paid back 'fore too long. I ain't never borrowed nothin' from nobody what I ain't give it back and then some."

"You seem to forget, Lucas, you signed a contract not only to pay the money back that we lent to you but to pay it back on time and with interest. You didn't do that. You breached the contract. You broke your word."

Lucas nodded. "You're right. I didn't make the payments like I promised I would. My crop, it turned bad on me and I dunno how come."

"We're not responsible for your crop."

"I ain't said you was. But iffen it'd come in like I thought it'd do, we wouldn't be a'sittin' here a'talkin' like we're a'doin'."

"You should've had crop insurance."

"Couldn't 'ford none."

"I'm sorry, Lucas. But a contract's a contract and the law's the law. The whole thing's out of my hands."

Lucas' face tightened. "I'm sorry to hear that, Mr. Mayfield. Both us know the law, it ain't nothin' lessen somebody decides to pick it up and use it. Law's jist like a hammer or a ax. Iffen you ain't careful when you use it, you're liable to hurt somebody with it, includin' your own self."

Lucas stood, his hat in one hand and the gun, still pointed at Mayfield, in the other. He nodded toward the girl who got to her feet at once. "A second reason you might not wanna take my land right now, Mr. Mayfield, is that, iffen you try to do it, I'll come a'lookin' fer you. You can mark my word on that."

Lucas turned to his daughter. "Come on, honey. Let's me and you mosey on home. I think we done done what we come to do." Lucas pocketed the pistol.

Mayfield stood. "You haven't heard the last of this, Lucas. Not by a long shot."

"Oh, I think maybe I have." Lucas took his daughter by the shoulder and directed the stumbling child toward the door.

Lucas turned around only to catch Mayfield reaching for his telephone. "That better be the lawyer you a'gittin' ready to call a'tellin' him not to do nothin." He opened the door and guided his daughter out of Mayfield's office.

It was the lawyer he was calling. He'd teach Lucas to point a gun in his face.

***

Dewey Coltraine pulled the truck onto the shoulder of the road in front of Creel's Roadside Grocery. He checked the time and saw he was three hours behind. He had not wanted to leave Nellie, but she had insisted on his going to work. She promised to keep close at hand the shotgun that her daddy had given her when they moved into the folding house.

Still, he couldn't get his thoughts off her and what had happened to her, not for one second. Notwithstanding Mayfield's threats and Nellie's concerns, he kept debating the question of whether he should report the matter to the sheriff. The strongest argument in favor of his going to the sheriff was that Mayfield shouldn't be allowed to get away with what he had done.

But then there was the risk that no one would believe Nellie's story. And if no one believed her, what would that do to her, to her reputation?

And there was also Nellie's daddy for Dewey to worry about. Suppose he did nothing and his father-in-law somehow found out about the assault? Dewey figured two men would end up dead then—himself and Lester Mayfield, Jr.

Dewey exited the truck and dragged himself into the store building, a wood-frame, unpainted structure plastered with signs that advertised everything from baking powder to cold tablets. He found the owner, Velma Creel, her back to him, standing on a ladder behind the counter.

Dewey learned the third time he came into Velma's store that she, it seemed, could cure physical ailments with Bible verses. One day Dewey had cut his hand on a broken bottle while going through her empties. His wound had bled and bled. The bleeding had stopped once Velma had taken hold of Dewey's hand and recited a verse from *Ezekiel*.

"Mornin', Miss Velma," Dewey said in a weak voice.

Velma, a can of pork and beans in one hand and a dust cloth in the other, brushed back her coal-black, gray-streaked hair and glanced over her shoulder. "Why, Mr. Coltraine," she replied, smiling. "Grace and peace to you."

She wiped off a shelf and set the can down. Throwing the dust cloth to one side, she descended the ladder and turned around. "You kinda late, ain't you, son?"

"Yessum."

He then inventoried the cooler and the stock Velma kept stacked in three neat rows behind it and checked her empty bottles and flats. "Miss Velma," he said, "I think you might could use a case of our orange and maybe even a case of our grape. You got two full crates of empties. You got plenty of Swizzles, I think."

The old woman studied Dewey, her unpainted lips together. "Go get 'em. A case of y'all's root beer too. And a case of Swizzle. Can't never tell. Might have a run on 'em. And then, where'd I be? You know what *Proverbs* 14:4 says, don't you?"

"No, ma'am."

"It says if you ain't got no oxes, then your crib's gonna be empty. Same thing's true 'bout sodas. If you ain't got none, then your drink box, it ain't gonna have none of 'em in it. Then where you gonna be supposin' somebody wants to buy him one?"

After bringing the four cases of soft drinks inside and restocking the drink box with Swizzle-Kola products, Dewey wrote up the purchase order and handed it to Velma. She put it away and paid him after he gathered her empties and placed them on the hand truck.

"Before you leave, Mr. Coltraine, I think maybe you might need to tell me somethin' other. I just might be able to help you." She removed from a shelf behind her a tattered Bible that appeared stuffed with clippings, pictures, and other things.

Dewey, fidgeting, wiped his mouth and looked toward his truck outside. "Miss Velma, beggin' your pardon, but I'm way behind as it is. I ain't got time to—"

"It ain't gonna take you long," she said, interrupting. "Set that empty crate there on end and sit down and tell me what's botherin' you so. I ain't never seen you lookin' thisaway since you been comin' here."

"I can't talk 'bout it. It's kinda private."

Velma turned her head to one side. "Like maybe it's somethin' havin' to do with you and that new wife of yourn?"

"Well, I reckon you could say that. But it ain't what you might think. It's a—"

"I bet y'all done had y'all's first fight, ain't you?"

Dewey started to protest.

"You love her?"

"Yes, ma'am."

"Do you love her so much you'd lay down your life for her?"

"Miss Velma, I really gotta go."

"Wait just a minute while I find what I'm lookin' for. I can't let you leave here without me tellin' you this. Hold on."

Velma began turning pages in her Bible. A faded photograph of a dead baby in a flower-filled coffin fell to the floor. She retrieved the photograph and kissed it. "Mr. Coltraine," she said as she reinserted the picture between the pages of her Bible, "you know what Jesus—bless His holy name!—what He says we're supposed to do when someone does somethin' to us we don't like?"

Dewey sat silent a moment, feeling her stare. "No matter what it is, Miss Velma?"

"No matter what it is, Mr. Coltraine. No matter what it is," she repeated, speaking softly and with great assurance. "Just think what a different world this would be—praise the Lord!—if people done what the good Lord Jesus told us to do. You know, if they'd forgive each other their trespasses."

"Yes ma'am, but—"

"The Lord says right here in *Matthew*," she said, showing him the page and tapping it with the back of her ruddy hand, "we're to forgive 'seventy times seven.' That's what? Four hundred and ninety times, ain't it, or close to it?"

"Does that include every kinda wrong, Miss Velma?"

"Praise Jesus, child! He don't make no exceptions."

"But there's some things, Miss Velma, a man can't hardly forgive."

"Oh no there ain't either! The Lord Jesus expects you to forgive anythin' and everythin'. The onliest way you and your wife'll ever be happy is for y'all to forgive one 'nother."

Dewey got up and walked to where he had parked the hand truck and its load of empty bottles. He pulled the hand truck toward him, thinking of what Jesus expected of him and how difficult it would be for him to do. Lost in thought, he said aloud, "A man's gotta do what he's gotta do, I reckon."

"There now, Mr. Coltraine. Don't you feel better already? Don't you feel just like praisin' the Lord?" Velma said, smiling and lifting her face toward heaven. She picked up her Bible and held it close to her heart.

Dewey did not answer her, for he did not want to lie. If anything, he felt worse. And he did not feel like praising the Lord. Not at the moment, he didn't. He would have to work himself up to that.

As Dewey left the store, he knew now he would not go to the police and report what had happened. He knew, too, he must try to forgive Mayfield.

As to Miss Velma's question of whether he loved Nellie enough to lay down his life for her? Of course, he did. He would do it a hundred times, if he had to.

***

Candle Reid's secretary, Judy Claire handed him a note as he returned to his office from getting a haircut. "Lester the Lesser called you a few minutes ago," she said. "I just hate that man. He said it was urgent."

"I bet it is," Candle grumbled, snatching the note from her hand. He read the note. "Do we have a *Lucas* file?"

"Right here," Judy said, smiling and waving a file folder back and forth. "By the way, nice haircut."

Candle, ignoring the compliment, took the file from her and read the name typed on the file label. "Colin Lucas? Isn't that the fellow with the pitiful little daughter? I think he's got a farm out near Cecelia."

"Yes, I think so."

"Yeah. I remember him," Candle said, turning pages in the file folder. "I think he and some other farmers out in the county had some kind of trouble with their fertilizer or something. Wiped out their crops. Couple of them came in and talked to Mr. Blumberg about it. What did Mayfield want? Did he say?"

"Wanted you to call him just as soon as you came back is all he told me."

As he walked to his office, Candle read the last piece of correspondence clipped to the file, a letter that the bank had sent Lucas a copy of. The letter, dated November 11, 1946, answered his question. Because Lucas had not repaid his loan, the bank wanted the mortgage on his farm foreclosed. But the letter didn't say when the bank wanted him to institute foreclosure proceedings, Candle noted with a broad smile.

As Candle placed the call, he began to think up excuses for not having already done something on the file—just in case the issue arose. A female voice that Candle recognized answered the phone. "Hi, Miss Thacker, this is Candle Reid. I'm returning Lester Junior's call."

"You wanted to talk to me about the Lucas matter?" Candle asked after greeting Mayfield. "Y'all get it settled or something?"

"No, we didn't settle it! He borrowed the money and he didn't pay it back. How you settle a thing like that?"

"Well, I thought maybe you might've given him more time to—"

"I don't know why I'm asking this, but have you done anything on it yet?"

Candle thought of an excuse. "No, I haven't. I started to and then—"

"You want to know something, Candle, I do believe it took the Egyptians less time to build the Pyramid of Khufu than it does to get you to bring a little ol' foreclosure action. I swear, you've got to be about the slowest lawyer there is in America. No, I take that back—in the whole world. I don't know why we bother to fool with you. It's not as though there's a lawyer shortage of some kind. Y'all are like locust—swarming everywhere, destroying anything you can get your greedy little hands on."

Candle suppressed his temper. "Like I was trying to—"

"Oh, just shut up. I'm going to tell you this and I'm only going to tell you one time. And if you don't do what I tell you to, we'll start taking our work to somebody who appreciates our business, to somebody's who's on the ball."

"Well, like I was about to say, your daddy would usually give the borrower—"

Mayfield interrupted. "This ain't Daddy, Candle! This is me! You listen, and you listen good! I want you to get that foreclosure action going against Lucas by no later than five o'clock tomorrow afternoon. You got that? Five o'clock tomorrow afternoon!"

Before Candle could respond, he heard a loud click.

"Yes, sir, boss. Five o'clock tomorrow," Candle said under his breath.

He set the telephone down and walked up front to the secretarial area. "Judy," he said through gritted teeth, "can you stay late?"

"I've already called home," Judy answered. She didn't sound happy.

***

Back at the plant, Dewey finished reloading his truck. Using a forklift, he returned what he had left of the pallet of strawberry drinks to their place in the warehouse among stacks of cased soft drinks. Swizzle-Kola's bookkeeper, a small, humped-back man well into his sixties, opened the door that led from the office to the warehouse as Dewey lowered the half-loaded pallet down onto the concrete floor.

"Coltraine," he called, "Mr. Hammond wants to see you when you get a minute."

"Yes, sir," Dewey answered. "Let me get this lift here out the way and I'll be right there, tell him."

Harling Millican nodded and closed the door.

After parking the forklift next to the bottle washer, Dewey headed for the office. He walked by the glassed-in cubical where Millican, wearing a green eye shade, sat beneath a strong, powerful light, working an adding machine amid piles of bills and receipts. Dewey found Troy Hammond in the lobby, gazing out the front window of the bottling plant. "Mr. Hammond, sir, Mr. Millican said you wanted to see me."

Hammond turned and smiled at Dewey. "You checked up yet, Dewey?"

"No, sir. Not yet, I ain't. I just got through loadin' my truck back up."

"Did you have a good day, I hope?" Hammond asked, nodding toward his office.

Dewey waited for Hammond to enter first and then followed him inside. Hammond sat down and gestured for Dewey to sit also.

"It was 'bout like most days here lately, I reckon. You? How'd yours go, sir?"

"Nothing to brag about," Hammond replied. He frowned and shook his head. "Dewey, I'll come directly to the point." He ran a hand through his graying hair. "I'm sorry, I really am. But I'm gonna have to let you go."

"Let me go?" The news shook Dewey. "But, Mr. Hammond, I was just gettin' where I—"

Hammond interrupted. "I can't help it, Dewey. You can come by tomorrow afternoon. Harling'll have what you've got coming, if you'll let him know how you came out today." Hammond attempted a smile. "I ordinarily wouldn't tell a fired employee this, but I want you to go by the unemployment office tomorrow and tell them I let you go. They'll pay you some unemployment for a while."

"Yes, sir," Dewey responded, not knowing what else to say right then.

Hammond stood and extended his hand. "Like I say, Dewey, I'm sorry. But sometimes I've gotta do things I don't like doing. Business, you know."

Dewey took Hammond's hand. The grip was not tight, and Hammond's hand was cold. "Ain't I been doin' a good job for you, Mr. Hammond?" he asked.

Hammond withdrew his hand and sat down as Dewey continued to stand. "Sure you have. It's not that. It's something else." He drew his lips together and raised his head. "Dewey—and you don't have to tell me this if you don't wanna—but have you had some kinda trouble with Lester Mayfield? The son, I mean, not the old man."

Dewey did not answer Hammond. The question surprised him and reminded him of Mayfield's threats.

"Mayfield called here late this afternoon," Hammond said. "He reminded me that I was little behind on the note I'd signed with the bank, the one I signed to open this plant up with. Then he told me he wanted your—to use his word—'ass' gone from down here and if I didn't let you go he'd call the note. If he did that, Dewey, that'd pretty much put me outta business."

Bert Goolsby

Friday, November 22, 1946

As Georgia Ann Hascall Mayfield drove toward Harpers' Joy, she congratulated herself on her discovery of her husband's hideaway. Her visit to Candle Reid's office had not been all together unproductive. Had the lawyer not charged her a consultation fee, she wouldn't have stopped at Candle's secretary's desk to pay it and she wouldn't have seen an interesting letter from the registrar of deeds.

The letter lay on Judy Claire's desk on the other side of the waist-high partition atop a stack of correspondence in an in-basket. Georgia Ann spotted the letter after she handed Judy the five dollars that Candle had demanded and as Judy bent down to retrieve a receipt book from a bottom desk drawer. The letter referred to "Property of Lester Mayfield, Jr., Narrow Road, Harpers' Joy." The reference jolted her. She knew nothing about any land that her husband owned up in Harpers' Joy.

While Judy prepared the receipt, Georgia Ann read the letter, noting that the property had cost her husband $3,500. Georgia Ann stepped back from the divider and committed the letter's contents to memory as the secretary tore the receipt from the book. She intended to investigate her husband's acquisition.

Moreover, she found it passing strange that the amount he had paid for the property equaled the very sum that a jury determined Hugh Sykes had stolen from the bank. She pulled at her ear. She had some questions for her dear, sweet husband and he had better have some answers.

"Here, you go, Mrs. Mayfield. I hope we've been of some help to you," Judy had said, using a tone not at all sincere.

Georgia Ann had plucked the receipt from Judy's hand and said, "I declare, Miss Claire, you just don't know how much this visit has helped me. You just don't have any idea. No idea at all."

Her husband had blown his car horn at her as she had come from the lawyer's office and headed toward her car. Georgia Ann laughed as she recalled thinking about how her sorry, two-timing, know-it-all husband had no inkling of what she had just learned. His business had become her business. And what fun she was going to have with it. She drove straight to Harpers' Joy and searched out the location of her husband's purchase. After making polite inquiries, she finally found it. She also found a gate blocking the drive that led into the property and a Yale padlock securing the gate.

That evening, while her husband showered, she purloined a set of keys from off the mantel piece in his bedroom. With her heart pounding and her hands shaking, she removed the only Yale key and hoped he would not miss it before she could have it copied the next day.

Luck had been with her. The key had not been missed. With her heart throbbing, and again while her husband showered, she had reattached it the next evening to his key ring.

Two days later during the early afternoon and as the temperature hung in the low seventies, Georgia Ann found herself stopping in front of the locked gate. She jumped from her car and ran stiff-legged toward the gate and the Yale padlock.

She inserted the key and held her breath. The bar sprung free of its housing, prompting Georgia Ann to smile and whisper aloud a thank-you-Jesus.

She opened the gate, returned to her car, and drove through the opening. Once on the opposite side of the gate, Georgia Ann exited her car to close and lock the gate.

As she walked back to her vehicle, she glimpsed the folding house for the first time. She wondered if it represented her husband's hideaway. But because the folding house sat so close to the entrance and because the drive went past it and disappeared as the ground elevation dropped off in the distance, she decided to follow the drive to its end.

Georgia Ann got back into her automobile and eased past the folding house, watching its windows and doors for any sign of movement. She saw none. With the car in first gear, she continued down the drive, glancing every few yards into the rearview mirror until she came within view of a large pond and a log cabin that lay at the end of the drive. Georgia Ann stopped and scanned the area ahead, looking for a car or other signs of an occupant within the log cabin. Taking a deep breath, she stayed in first gear and proceeded on.

When she reached the log cabin, Georgia Ann decided to meet any problem at once and head-on. Looking toward the front of the dwelling, she pressed down hard on the car horn and let it blow for several seconds. When no one came to the door, she got out of the car and walked around to the rear of the log cabin. She climbed the steps to the back porch and knocked on the door. No one answered.

Satisfied no one was in the log cabin, Georgia Ann returned to her car and sat wondering what to do next. She decided she would wait and see what the day would bring. Anyway, she told herself, she had nothing more important to do right then. Besides, she was shopped-out, bridged-out, lunched-out, coffeed-out, and altar guilded-out. And oh, how she would just love to catch her husband with another woman. She'd fix him. She'd fix him good, really good. And the other woman too.

Georgia Ann drove her car behind the log cabin, parking it out of view of the drive. She retrieved some items from the backseat and, with much effort, carried them down to a warm, sunny spot on the bank of the pond. There, she sat down on the grass, propping her back against a tall pine tree. As she waited beneath a cloudless sky for something to happen, she dug into a large bag of chocolate-chip cookies and opened a romance magazine.

**

As his daughter peered out from behind a screen door, Colin Lucas accepted a summons and complaint from Sheriff Bowden "Bo" Madison who stood on the top step of the porch. "I'm sorry, Colin," the sheriff said, his head bowed. "I come myself to serve it 'cause I didn't want you to think I bore you no kinda ill will."

Lucas studied the papers, bringing them close. "I ain't a'blamin' you none, Sheriff. You jist a'doin' what you gotta do. It's Mayfield what's made you do this. I know that."

The sheriff adjusted his hat. "Have you talked to his daddy 'bout the trouble you had with your crop this year, Lucas? I've always found Mr. Mayfield to be reasonable when it comes to helpin' farmers out."

"I went there the other day to talk to him 'bout my problem, but this here old woman made me go talk to that boy of hissen instead."

"Why don't you let me go by the bank and talk to Mr. Mayfield for you? It's worth a try. It can't hurt anything."

Lucas beckoned his daughter to come outside. "No, sir. I can't let you do that. It ain't none of your affair. I'll handle it my own self my own way. But I thank you kindly fer a'offerin'." Lucas folded the papers up and tucked them into a back pocket of his overalls. "Now, Sheriff, since you done done your duty, I'd be obliged iffen you'd be on your way."

The sheriff tipped his hat and backed down the steps. When his feet touched the ground, he glanced up at Lucas who, with his daughter at his side, had moved to the edge of the porch. "Colin, if you change your mind, get in touch with me. I wanna help you."

"I won't be a'changin' it, Sheriff," Lucas said, placing his arm around his daughter's skinny shoulders.

"Colin, I think you're determined to lose this place," the sheriff said, sweeping his hand outward. He nodded toward the girl. "You might oughta think 'bout her some."

"I don't never think of nobody else," Lucas said, squeezing the girl and pulling her closer to his side. "She's all I got since her maw died. Her and my land."

The sheriff shook his head and climbed into his car.

As Lucas watched the sheriff drive off, he took his arm from around his daughter and squatted down so he could talk with her face-to-face. "Honey, wait right here while I go git me somethin' outta the house. Then we're a'goin' someplace."

Less than a half-hour later, Lucas located a parking space for his pickup truck within thirty feet of the Tekoa State Bank and Trust Company. Telling his daughter to remain in the truck, he opened the door to get out. Just as he stepped down into the street, a black, shiny Packard passed him headed in the opposite direction. Lucas recognized the driver. He jumped back into the truck.

**

Dewey had left his wife alone that morning in the folding house and had hitchhiked into Tekoa. He wanted first to try and persuade Troy Hammond to allow him the use later that day of the company canopy van to move his and Nellie's belongings to a garage apartment Dewey had rented the day before in Tekoa. Afterward, he intended to go by the unemployment office and, after that, to look for work.

Nellie's physical wounds had healed somewhat, but her mental condition had deteriorated to the point that she now lay in bed most of each day and had little to say about anything. So great was her fear of Mayfield that she insisted on the double-barrel shotgun her father had given her always being within easy reach and fully loaded. She carried the shotgun everywhere she went within the folding house, whether it was to the kitchen or the bathroom and whether Dewey was about the place or not.

After Hammond promised him the use of the van, Dewey had spent the greater part of the morning and the early afternoon talking with prospective employers suggested by the unemployment office. Two jobs held promise, one as a milkman for Sun Rheay Farms Dairy and the other as a produce clerk for the A&P in downtown Tekoa. Dewey felt good about his chances with the latter since the manager knew Dewey from his employment with the Swizzle-Kola Bottling Company. He had all but told Dewey he could have the job if his former employer recommended him.

As Dewey walked along Main Street on his way to another job interview, he saw a Packard automobile, with Lester Mayfield, Jr. at the wheel, enter the street from the bank parking lot and turn left. The car sped up the street toward the courthouse square. Dewey did not like the looks of it. Beyond the square was the highway to Harpers' Joy.

Glancing at his watch, Dewey decided to forget about the next job interview. He would return to the bottling plant, get the keys to the van, and head straight for the folding house.

The plant lay three blocks away around the corner from the bank. Dewey ran most of the way, after nearly being run over by a pickup truck as it made an illegal U-turn in the middle of Main Street. When he got to the plant, Hammond was not in his office and the bookkeeper had no clue as to his whereabouts. Dewey finally located Hammond in the boiler room behind the plant.

Hammond readily agreed to let Dewey have the van right then and told him to follow him to his office where he kept the keys in a locked drawer.

As they entered his office, the telephone rang. Hammond answered it. He placed his hand over the mouthpiece and motioned for Dewey to leave his office.

Dewey, checking the time on his watch, retreated to the lobby to wait for Hammond to complete his call. Just when he thought the conversation would never end, Hammond appeared in the doorway and beckoned Dewey to come in.

"I'm sorry, Dewey," Hammond said, taking a seat behind his desk, "but that was Mr. Rainsford at the A&P. He was calling about you, wanting to know what I thought about him hiring you as a produce clerk."

"Yes, sir," Dewey replied, anxious to obtain the keys and more worried about Nellie than whether he got the job at the A&P.

"I told him I didn't think you knew an orange from a tangerine." Hammond laughed, his blue eyes sparkling. "But I told him you were a fast learner."

"Yes, sir. Thank you, sir," Dewey said, forcing a grin. He wanted to leave and leave in a hurry. "Mr. Hammond, sir, I don't mean—but I wonder if I could—"

Hammond put both his feet on top of his desk, his work shoes resting upon a bottling magazine. He smiled. "I told him the only reason I let you go was I just didn't think you were cut out to be a salesman. I got the impression he's gonna offer you the job. The A&P's a good company and Mayfield couldn't throw his weight around with them."

"Thank you, Mr. Hammond. I'm much obliged." He again noted the time.

"So, maybe Mayfield, without intending to, did you a favor by pressuring me to get rid of you. To be honest, I don't know how much longer I can afford to stay in business anyway. Things aren't looking too good."

"You reckon I could have them keys now, Mr. Hammond? I'd kinda like to get on home soon as I could and maybe get started loadin' some things in the van."

Hammond unlocked a drawer and got the keys. "Here, Coltraine," he said, tossing them to Dewey. "Keep it until Monday. We won't be needing it over the weekend."

Dewey extended his right hand. Hammond took hold of it. "Thank you, Mr. Hammond," he said. "This is a big help to me and Nellie. You just don't know how much, and I won't never forget it neither."

"I truly wish I could do more for you. I really, really do. I hope you understand why I did what I did."

"Yes, sir. I don't blame you none. And I appreciate you puttin' in a good word for me there at the A&P too."

Dewey hurried from the office and sprinted to the rear of the plant where Hammond kept the van parked. He climbed in behind the wheel and started the engine. He hoped he would not be too late.

***

Nellie awoke to the honking of a car horn. It seemed to come from in front of the folding house. Feeling around for the shotgun with her hand, she found it between the bed covers and an afghan. When she heard the horn again, she sat up, gripping the shotgun barrel with one hand. As she swung her legs around to stand, she pulled the shotgun across the bed.

Once more, the horn blew. "Nellie!" she heard a man's voice call. "Nellie!"

Nellie crept to the bedroom window, sliding the shotgun ahead of her on the floor as she went. She peered out to see Lester Mayfield, Jr., standing by his car.

"Nellie! Come on! I want you to ride down to the log cabin with me. We need to talk about something, you and me. Come on, Nellie! I'm not going to hurt you."

Nellie stepped back from the window, lifted the shotgun, and breached it. She checked both shells and snapped the gun back together as Mayfield continued to call her and blow the horn. Satisfied the shotgun was in firing order, Nellie walked from the bedroom to the kitchen, the stock of the shotgun squeezed under her armpit and the forestock now cradled in her hand.

"Nellie! I've changed my mind about wanting you to move. But we need to talk about it first. Okay? Come on out. I know you're in there."

Harpers' Joy

Nellie opened the kitchen door and peeped out. Mayfield had stationed himself in front of his car and stood with both hands on his hips and his chest extended.

The sight of him brought back the nightmare. The shame, which the nightmare created, now blossomed larger and uglier still as she heard him call her name and bade her outside.

She came out from behind the kitchen door, pressing the stock of the shotgun against her right shoulder and pointing the barrel straight at Mayfield.

"Now, Nellie," Mayfield said, laughing and waving a hand, "let's put that thing away. It's liable to go off and you wouldn't want that to happen, now would you? I just want to talk to you. That's all. You don't have to move. I'm sorry. I'll—I'll even help your husband to—come on now, Nellie, put the gun down." As he spoke, he withdrew to a spot behind the hood of his Packard.

Nellie stepped down into the yard, pressed forward a few feet, lowered the shotgun, and squeezed the trigger. The sound of the shotgun blast flayed her ears and the smell of it assailed her nose and throat. The shot peppered the right side of the Packard's hood, pitted its right-front fender, and punctured the whitewall beneath. The tire wheezed as it deflated.

Mayfield ran around from the driver-side of the car and surveyed the damage caused by the blast. He pointed to the tire. "See what you've done! You're going to pay for this!"

He turned and stepped toward Nellie, but she raised the shotgun and aimed it toward his head. Mayfield stopped in his tracks. "Okay, Nellie. Okay. Everything's all right." He raised his hands above his head. "See? I'm not going to do anything," he said in a calm voice.

Nellie, holding the shotgun parallel to the ground and keeping a close watch on the trembling man with the raised hands, shook her head. She back-pedaled, her foot groping for the bottom-most step of the folding house. Suddenly, she saw Mayfield's eyes grow large and his mouth open wide. Thinking he was about to charge her, Nellie fired again just as Mayfield turned and stepped to his left.

The small, lead pellets burst from the shotgun, spreading apart as they made their flight. The blast seemed to echo off the folding house behind her.

Then, much to Nellie's surprise—and horror—Mayfield collapsed to the ground. She had not meant to hit him.

After seeing what had happened, Nellie felt herself grow faint. Then she lost consciousness.

***

Dewey turned onto The Narrow Road, steering past a late-model pickup. The truck, which appeared occupied, sat in the middle of the road just below the driveway.

As Dewey cleared the gate to the drive, he saw the Packard. And then he saw Nellie, sprawled on the ground, the shotgun at her feet. He drove in behind the Packard, stopped, and switched off the motor to the van. Jumping from the truck, he hurried to where she lay and knelt beside her. "Nellie! It's me, Dewey! Nellie! Nellie!" he yelled as he took her by the arm and pulled her toward him.

He heard her moan and saw her open her eyes for a moment. "What happened, honey?" he asked as he examined her body, looking for signs of injury.

Finding no physical wounds, Dewey laid Nellie back upon the ground. He picked up the shotgun and glanced at the shot-up automobile. That's when he spotted Mayfield, lying in the drive just beyond the front bumper of the Packard.

Dewey stepped to where Mayfield lay. "Mr. Mayfield," Dewey whispered as he bent forward to see him better. "Mr. Mayfield, can you hear me?" Mayfield, his eyes fixed, did not answer.

Dewey stood for a moment, the shotgun draped over his arm, staring down at Mayfield and wondering what had happened and what he should do. After a moment, he decided he would get Nellie inside. Then, he would call the law.

He returned to Nellie. As he knelt and bent toward her, he heard a piercing shriek. Startled, Dewey looked to his right and saw a full-figured woman panting and running toward him. "Murderer!" she screamed. "Murderer!"

With the shotgun still in his hands, Dewey stood and faced the hysterical woman. He watched as she ran forward and flung herself over Mayfield's body, crying and screaming. "You've killed my husband! You've killed him!"

Dewey considered the woman and her accusation for a moment but said nothing. He turned his attention once more to Nellie and laid the shotgun down. "Come on, Nellie," he said, lifting her from the ground, "let me get you inside so I can put you in the bed."

Once inside, he took Nellie into the bedroom. There, he pulled the bedcovers back and set her down. "Nellie, honey," he said, curving over her and pulling the bedcovers up to her shoulders, "can you hear me? Can you?"

Nellie opened her eyes part-way and stared at Dewey. Her eyes held no expression.

"Are you okay?"

She made no reply.

Dewey stood straight and smiled at the expressionless face on the bed. "Sweetheart, I'll be right back. I better go out yonder and see 'bout that woman. It's Mr. Mayfield's wife, I believe. The shotgun's still out there and I better go see 'bout it too, I reckon." He bent down and kissed his wife on the forehead. "Just lay still. I'll be back in a second."

Nellie did not return Dewey's smile or otherwise acknowledge him.

When Dewey left the folding house through the kitchen door, Georgia Ann Hascall Mayfield, trembling and her dress stained with her husband's blood, struggled to stand. "I don't know who you are and why you did this to my husband, but are you planning on . . . on killing me too?"

Dewey reached for the shotgun; but when the woman began begging him not to kill her, he drew himself up straight and left the shotgun on the ground. "I'm ain't gonna hurt you, ma'am. Y'all got a phone down yonder in the log cabin?"

"A telephone?" she said in a whimper, backing away from her husband's body and wiping her eyes with her fingers. "I just don't know if we do or not."

"Tell you what, if you'll go in yonder and look after Nellie—that's my wife," Dewey said pointing to the folding house, "I'll go find a telephone down the road someplace and call the sheriff. I'll be back soon as I can get in touch with him. Okay?"

The woman nodded.

Dewey climbed into the van and started the engine. As he shifted into reverse, he remembered the pickup truck outside the gate and had a sudden thought. Perhaps its driver would be willing to contact the sheriff for him. If so, that would enable him to go back and look after Nellie.

Upon reaching the road, however, he saw the truck was no longer there.

***

When Dewey returned to the folding house, he did not see Mayfield's wife to tell her that the sheriff was on his way. He again viewed Mayfield's body, sighing and shaking his head. The shotgun, he noted, lay where he had left it.

Dewey went inside to await the sheriff. Nellie's condition had not changed. She lay on the bed, her eyes opened and unfocused, her face devoid of expression. Dewey took her by the left hand and folded her fingers into her palm and kissed them. "Nellie, honey," he said, "just wanted to tell you I'm back. I went and called the sheriff. I told them there'd been a shootin' and for them to hurry on out here. I told them where it was and all. They said they were leavin' right then and for me to meet them back here."

Nellie showed no reaction to the news.

Dewey got down on both knees by the side of the bed and, reaching for Nellie's hair, began stroking it with his fingertips. All the while, he kept his eyes, now blurred by tears, fastened on Nellie's beautiful, quiet countenance.

He realized the sheriff would want to know what had happened, and he understood Mrs. Mayfield thought he had killed her husband. Feeling as he did about Nellie and aware of the probable consequences that would result from the manner of Mayfield's death, Dewey decided after much anguish that he had no choice but to take the blame for what had happened. It was, he felt, better for him to die or to go to prison than for Nellie, a circumstance he would not be able to bear.

Besides, all of this was his fault anyway. It had been his idea to move to Mr. Mayfield's folding house in the first place. And he should have reported the rape to the police or maybe even killed

Mayfield himself after he found out it was Mayfield who had assaulted his wife.

The howl of a distant siren prompted Dewey to release Nellie's hand. He got off his knees and went outside to await the sheriff and to confess to having killed Mayfield.

***

Sheriff Bo Madison, the stock of the shotgun tucked under his arm, followed Dewey Coltraine into the interrogation room of the county jail. With a nod, he directed Dewey to sit behind a small, pitted, wooden table. Dewey, his wrists still held together with handcuffs, obliged the sheriff.

The sheriff propped the shotgun up against the table, pulled back a chair opposite Dewey, and took his seat just as a slim, pretty, bright-eyed young woman who carried a green stenographer's pad came through the door and joined them. Dewey tried to stand, but the sheriff motioned for him to remain seated. The woman acknowledged Dewey's gesture with a smile and sat down.

"Coltraine," Sheriff Madison said as he undid his characteristic red tie and unbuttoned the top button of his white dress shirt, "this is Natalie Ward. She's my secretary and she's a notary public."

Dewey acknowledged Natalie with an almost inaudible "ma'am."

Sheriff Madison placed both of his hands upon the table, as Natalie flipped through her notepad. "I've asked Natalie to come in here because I want you to repeat to her what you told me and my deputy when we were up yonder at Mayfield's place. She'll then go type it up; and after she gets done with it, I'll ask you to sign it. You got any problem with that?"

Dewey shook his head.

"Okay, then. You got any questions before we get started?"

"Yes, sir," Dewey responded, "how 'bout Nellie?"

The sheriff tilted his chair backward, resting it on its rear legs. The chair squeaked as he did so. "I think she'll be all right. The ambulance we called got her to the hospital. Also, we got in touch with her mama and daddy. I reckon they've had time enough to get there by now. We'll let you know if we hear anything else."

Dewey hung his head. "Thank you, sir."

"Okay, then, can we get started?"

"Yes, sir."

Natalie raised her pen in readiness.

"All right. Today is Friday, November 22, 1946. The time is 6:15 p.m. Present with me, Bo Madison, here at the jail is Natalie Ward, a notary public, and the accused Dewey Coltraine. He's charged with the murder of Lester Mayfield, Jr. This thing took place this afternoon out there at Harpers' Joy at Mayfield's hideaway, which is just off The Narrow Road.

"Coltraine, have I promised you anything to get you to make a statement?"

Dewey shook his head.

"You're gonna have to answer out loud, son. Understand?"

Dewey nodded and then added, "Yes, sir."

"So, have I promised you anything if you make a statement?"

"No, sir."

"Have I threatened you or done anything to you to get you to make a statement? Have I harmed you in any way, son?"

"No, sir. You ain't. You been nice to me."

"You realize, don't you, this statement you're 'bout to give me can be used against you in court?"

"No, sir. I didn't know that. But I don't reckon it matters none."

The sheriff set his chair upright upon the floor. He scratched an area just above his left eyebrow. "Well, I'm tellin' you it can be. So, now you know that, don't you?"

"Yes, sir."

"All right. Let's get down to brass tacks. Mr. Coltraine, who killed Lester Mayfield, Jr. today up there in Harpers' Joy?"

"I did."

"What did you kill him with?"

"A shotgun. One Nellie's daddy give us when me and her moved out there to Mr. Mayfield's."

The sheriff picked up the shotgun and laid it on the table. "Is this Daly here what you used?"

Dewey could not bring himself to look at the firearm. "Yes, sir."

Sheriff Madison again inclined his chair backwards on its hind legs. This time he placed his feet on the table, exposing his red socks. "Start from the top now. Tell me and Natalie 'bout killin' Mayfield—how come you to do it and all."

Dewey began his account of Mayfield's killing by starting with the day Vasil Franklin told him of Mr. Mayfield's interest in finding someone to look after his place near Harpers' Joy. He ended it by telling how he went and telephoned the sheriff's office and waited for him to come to the folding house.

Sheriff Madison removed his feet from off the table. "Son, that was a smart thing you did—givin' yourself up like that." He looked at Natalie, who had put down her pen. "Tell you what though, old man Mayfield ain't gonna like it a bit you claimin' his boy raped your wife and beat her like he did. How come you didn't report it?"

Dewey squirmed in his chair. "I just didn't. Nellie—"

"Was it because Mayfield didn't really rape her and you're the one who beat her up, maybe after catchin' the two of them together?" the sheriff asked, interrupting.

"No, sir. That ain't it. He forced hisself on Nellie, Mr. Madison."

The sheriff stood. "Uh-huh. Well, let's hope Nellie gets better and can verify your story. That'd help you, but I don't think it'll get you off. I mean, let's suppose you're tellin' me the truth, that he raped her. How many days has it been? Three? Four? You see, son, shootin' him today ain't like it would've been if you'd shot him when you say you first found out 'bout it. You know, Tuesday mornin' when you say he come there."

"It ain't? When he come out there today to do it to her all over again, I figure?"

"Why, son, for all I know, all he meant to do was meet his wife and go fishin' and maybe stop by your place just to make sure y'all was movin' out like he'd told you to."

Bert Goolsby

Friday, November 29, 1946

Three days had passed since the ground in Patriot's Corner, the section of the city cemetery reserved for war veterans, had received the remains of yet another sojourner. An overflow crowd numbering in the hundreds had attended the younger Mayfield's funeral. Solicitor J. Hopson Fleming guessed that every mortgagor in Semmes County, especially those behind on their payments, had not only come to the funeral but had made sure the senior Mayfield knew they had come.

Fleming noticed how the old man had aged since learning of his son's murder. He had little to say to anyone and, when he spoke, the words oozed from his mouth only in whisper form, accompanied by glistening, tear-filled, reddened eyes that appeared not to see. He no longer walked with the swagger of a baron but shuffled forward in slow motion, his body bent as though encumbered with a load much too heavy to carry.

Solicitor Fleming parked his car in the circular driveway in front of Cottondale Mansion. He started up the walkway but stopped midway when he heard the wailing of a siren. He turned and watched an automobile emblazoned with the words "Semmes County Sheriff" and driven by Sheriff Bo Madison leap from the highway into the circular driveway and speed by lion-topped brick columns. Judge L. Malcolm Pryde sat in the front passenger seat, his eyes the size of half-dollars.

The automobile jerked to a stop just inches behind the bumper of Fleming's car. The sheriff and the judge got out at the same time, even slamming their doors in unison. Sheriff Madison paused to adjust his service revolver before heading for the walkway that led to the front door. Judge Pryde, however, cut across the manicured lawn.

"What's the matter with His Grace?" Fleming asked, motioning with his head. "He doesn't look too happy this morning."

"Ask him," the sheriff replied.

"I think you know," the judge grumbled. "I don't like being summoned by Mayfield or anyone else, that's what."

"You'd hate it worse if he didn't summon you," Fleming said, laughing.

"I still don't like it."

Fleming wrapped an arm around the judge's heavy shoulders. "Well, Your Honor, you might as well enjoy it since you're here. Besides, I think he's about to help you. I think he's going to give you instruction on how to try a death penalty case."

"And just suppose I don't do what he says?" the judge asked, rolling his shoulders to shake Fleming's arm loose.

The sheriff and Fleming glanced at each other and laughed. "Uh-huh," Fleming said. "Right."

The three men walked up to the front door and rang the door chimes.

Seconds later, a maid dressed in a black and white uniform opened the door and greeted the three men with a pleasant smile and a curtsy. "Judge, Your Honor, sir. Mr. Solicitor. Mr. Bo. Mr. Mayfield, he be expectin' y'all," she said, holding the door for them as they entered the entrance hall. "Want me to take y'all's hats?"

Each man handed her his hat, which she placed on a nearby table.

"Mr. Mayfield's this way," the maid said, beckoning the men to follow her down the hallway.

They walked by several closed doors and one stairwell before turning down another hallway and being led into a room paneled in a dark-stained wood. In the middle of the room stood a billiard table, a light suspended above it. Save for a stone fireplace, a cue rack, the door and two windows, mahogany bookcases occupied the wall space.

"I'm over here, gentlemen," whispered a voice on the other side of a high-back, brown-leather chair set with three others of like kind and color in front of an empty fireplace that smelled of burnt hickory. "There's coffee right there on a table next to the door, if you want it. And some toast too, I think." A brief pause ensued and then the voice said, "That'll be all, Sill."

The maid smiled at Mayfield and left the room, closing the door behind her.

Judge Pryde and Sheriff Madison passed on the coffee and walked to where Mayfield sat. After shaking Mayfield's hand, they each took a chair across from the old man.

Fleming poured himself a cup of coffee. "Lester, you want me to bring you a cup?" Fleming asked, holding up the coffee pot. When he got no answer, Fleming returned the coffee pot to the hotplate and crossed the room to where the others waited. "This is pretty good coffee, Lester," Fleming said as he settled into the remaining high-back. In truth, Fleming thought the coffee tasted awful. It reminded him of brewed walnut shells.

Mayfield ignored the compliment. "Has that fellow Coltraine got him a lawyer yet?" he asked in a quiet voice.

The inquiry surprised Fleming. "If he has, I don't know it. Any lawyer been to see him, Bo?"

"No, not that I know of," Sheriff Madison said. "Hadn't nobody asked 'bout him, I don't think. No, I take that back. His wife's daddy, he come in. Said if we didn't kill Coltraine, he would."

Mayfield's face darkened. "I'm not interested in that right now. All I want to know is whether Coltraine has a lawyer. Does he have one or not?"

The sheriff offered a weak smile. "I just dunno, Mr. Mayfield. If you want me to, I can let you know later on. Soon as I can get back to town I'll go ask him if he's got one."

"I doubt if he could afford one, from what little I know about him," Judge Pryde said. "Sheriff, you think he could?"

"Well, him and his wife were livin' up there in that foldin' house on Lester Junior's place free of charge and he'd lost his job with the bottlin' plant. So, you're probably right. He wouldn't have any money to hire himself a lawyer with, I don't think."

"That's what I thought would be the case," Mayfield said, nodding several times as he settled all the way back in his chair.

"If he doesn't have any money to hire a lawyer with, I think you better understand, Lester, that the law now requires one to be appointed for him," Judge Pryde said.

"Malcolm, do you think I'm ignorant about the law?" Mayfield asked. "I get awfully tired of the way you and Hop talk down to me about the law. I read the newspapers. I keep up with things. You'd think the law was some kind of big secret or something."

Judge Pryde's round shaven head began to glow. "Well, I—"

Mayfield waved at him. "Just shut up and listen to me. All of you. I don't want y'all to leave anything to chance. I want Coltraine's butt fried, and I want it fried to a fare-you-well. That means I don't want some smart-talking lawyer getting him off with anything less than something that calls for the death penalty."

"That'd mean he'd have to be convicted of murder," Judge Pryde said.

Mayfield glared at Judge Pryde. "I want this thing tried and tried fast. No delays. No continuances. I want quick justice." He pointed at Fleming. "And Solicitor, I want it tried right and tried just one time." He held up one finger. "One time, you got that? I don't want any mistakes. I don't want some goofy, bleeding-heart appeals court giving him a new trial for some stupid error one of you made. "

The three men nodded.

Fleming noticed Judge Pryde open his mouth and sensed he was about to say something stupid. "Don't worry, Lester, we've got things under control," Fleming hasten to say.

Mayfield grunted. "Let's see if you do." The old man struggled to stand and, while the three men watched, dragged himself over to the fireplace. He rested for a moment, one hand on the mantel piece and turned around. "What lawyer do you intend to appoint to represent Coltraine, Malcolm, if he doesn't already have one?"

Judge Pryde glanced at Fleming, his brow creased.

"Well, it'd have to be somebody with some criminal law experience," Fleming said, coming to the judge's aid.

"But not much experience," Mayfield added. "And it'd have to be somebody we can make do what we want him to do."

Fleming studied Mayfield's face for a moment. "You have somebody in mind, I take it?"

"Yes, I do, as a matter of fact. That fellow Reid," Mayfield answered. "Candle Reid. He'd be perfect."

Judge Pryde laughed a contemptuous laugh. "Except for one small detail. He doesn't have much in the way of trial experience, much less criminal law experience, especially felony trial experience."

Fleming shook his head. "Oh, but he does. He just doesn't know that he does. I can think of at least ten cases he tried with Bernie Blumberg, civil and criminal. Felony cases too."

"But Reid didn't do anything, Hop," Judge Pryde said. "He just sat at the table. Bernie did all the work."

"The journals and records all say Reid was co-counsel," Fleming said. "Just because he sat at counsel table and didn't open his mouth during trial doesn't mean he didn't play an important role."

Mayfield nodded in agreement.

"Okay, then," Judge Pryde said, "I'll agree with you about Reid to this extent, he looks good on paper." He eyed Mayfield. "But what about the fact he represents the bank in a lot of foreclosure actions and closings, and so forth?"

"What are you getting at, Malcolm?" Mayfield asked, twisting his head to one side and looking at Judge Pryde out of the corner of his eye.

"Conflict of interest," Judge Pryde said.

Mayfield looked at Fleming. "What about it? Any problem there?"

"Not unless someone makes it a problem," Fleming answered. "And who's going to do that? You, Lester? Coltraine?"

"Reid, maybe?" Mayfield offered.

Fleming smiled. "So, what if he does? You could end that little conflict of interest right quick like, couldn't you? You could simply quit using him and get some other lawyer to represent the bank. That Sturges boy would appreciate some work, I'd expect."

"Would that do it?" Mayfield asked. "Getting someone else?"

"It'd do it enough," Fleming said.

Mayfield's face brightened.

"Anyway, the bank's not a party to the prosecution," Fleming said. "The case is a criminal case, not a civil one. It's something between the State and Dewey Coltraine, not between the State Bank and Trust Company and Dewey Coltraine. That's my view. But just to be on the safe side, we'll keep the record free of any mention of that little fact. Right, Malcolm?"

"All right, if we can. I'll try and take care of it if the question comes up, which it probably will, knowing Reid. He'll think of anything to get out of appearing before me, especially right now," Judge Pryde responded, his tone indifferent.

Sheriff Madison laughed.

"What is it that you find so funny, Sheriff?" Mayfield asked. His expression showed that he found nothing amusing about their discussion.

"What I wanna know is if ol' Candle is appointed to represent Coltraine, who's gonna keep him sober long enough to do it? From what I hear, his drinkin' has gotten a whole lot worse since him and his wife separated."

"Who says I want him kept sober?" Mayfield asked. "That's one candle I want to stay lit."

***

Candle Reid's head hurt like the dickens. He had celebrated Thanksgiving Day the day before by toasting repeatedly the health of Johnny Gray and by giving thanks for his divine, mellow goodness. After swallowing two aspirins, Candle resolved not to take another drink as long as he lived. At the same time, however, he hoped to live long enough to take another one.

Candle had not been in his office more than an hour when he received a telephone call from the clerk of court telling him that Judge Pryde needed him in the courtroom right then. He began to inventory all the things that he was required to do and tried to recall whether he had done them or not. The cobwebs, however, interfered.

So, Candle did the next best thing. He yelled for his secretary, his voice marked by absolute panic.

Judy Claire ran into his office. "What?" she asked, all out of breath, a hand resting over her heart.

"They want me at the courthouse in the courtroom! How come!?" he asked, flipping over papers on his desk in search of some sort of reminder. "Was there something I was supposed to do over there today? Do you know?" His mind shifted to another major concern. "Has my wife done something? Filed some kind of motion? What?"

Judy grimaced. "Tell you what, Mr. Reid. Why don't both of us go on over there and find out what they want. And while you take the heat, I'll run back over here and find the file. It may be something Mr. Blumberg was handling. I just don't know."

"That's a good idea." He grabbed his coat from off a stack of files on the floor and raced from his office, down the stairs, and across the street. Judy followed behind him.

When he got to the courtroom, he was surprised to see no one there except a small, slender young man fitted with handcuffs and leg irons, a deputy sheriff many times the young man's size, and the clerk of court. Candle refused to speculate what all of that was about, certain it had nothing to do with him.

Candle came into the well of the courtroom. "Mr. Honeycutt," he said, addressing the clerk of court, "your office called and said y'all needed me over here for something?"

"Morning, Candle. Judy. Let me go get the judge," Jimmy Honeycutt said, rising from his chair. "Back in a jiffy."

"Can you tell me what—" Candle didn't get to finish his question before Honeycutt hurried out of the courtroom.

Although Candle felt great disappointment in not learning the purpose for his summons to the courthouse, he also felt relief that Honeycutt did not appear angry. Indeed, he struck Candle as downright civil, an unusual posture for Honeycutt whom lawyers regarded as the meanest clerk of court in the whole wide world, living, dead or yet to be born.

Candle and Judy seated themselves next to each other in the petit jury box. As they waited for Honeycutt to return with the judge, Candle found himself staring at the pitiful, manacled young man seated behind a counsel table. Candle recognized from a picture in the newspaper who the prisoner was.

The door banged opened. "Everybody stand," Candle heard Honeycutt say in a voice unnecessarily loud, considering there were no spectators in the courtroom. Candle and Judy jumped to their feet, as did the deputy sheriff and the young man in shackles.

Judge L. Malcolm Pryde, trailed by the district solicitor, marched into the courtroom, his countenance gloomy, his manner regal to the extreme. He sat down in his chair and spread his robe about. Only after he had finished arranging the items on his desk and removed a fountain pen from an inside pocket did he grant those standing in the courtroom permission to sit. He communicated that permission with a hand signal.

"Mr. Solicitor," the judge said at last, "I understand you have a matter you wish to discuss with the court?"

Solicitor Fleming walked from the area next to the door by the petit jury box to a spot in front of the clerk of court's desk. He bowed. "May it please the court, Your Honor, this matter concerns *The State versus Dewey Coltraine*. The accused is in jail awaiting trial on the charge of capital murder. I want the court to inquire of him regarding whether he has a lawyer or the means of securing one."

Candle sprung forward in his chair. He began to sense something wrong. He tried to get Honeycutt to look his way, but Honeycutt would not do so.

"All right, Mr. Solicitor. I understand," the judge said. He opened the black notebook on his desk, turned several pages, and motioned to the officer. "Deputy, bring the prisoner up here."

The deputy sheriff nudged Dewey Coltraine in the side with his elbow. Dewey rose from his chair and, with the deputy leading him by the arm, hobbled over to where Solicitor Fleming stood facing the bench. Dewey, his head bowed low, said something to the judge, but Candle did not quite hear what it was. It sounded like he said "Good morning, Judge, Your Honor, sir." Whatever it was, the judge ignored it.

After a long delay, Judge Pryde spoke to Dewey. "Boy, you got a lawyer?"

"No, sir," Dewey answered, his head still bowed.

"No, sir," the judge said, repeating Dewey's response. "Look at me, boy!" he ordered.

Dewey complied, raising his head.

"Why don't you have one?"

Dewey again hung his head and spoke in a soft tone. "'Cause I don't have any money to hire one with."

"Look at me when you talk to me!" Judge Pryde scolded. "And quit all that mumbling. You got marbles in your mouth or something?"

"No, sir," Dewey said, tilting his head backward.

"Where did you work before all this happened?"

"With Mr. Hammond at Swizzle-Kola, but he let me go."

Judge Pryde sunk back in his chair. "Let you go? Fired you, you mean?"

"Yes, sir. I reckon."

Judge Pryde again consulted his notebook. "You own any property, a car or anything?"

"No, sir."

"Mr. Solicitor?" the judge said.

"Yes, sir, Your Honor," Fleming answered.

"You indicated a moment ago that this is a capital murder case. Is it still your intention to seek the death penalty?"

"Yes, sir."

Judge Pryde crossed his arms. "Coltraine, since you can't afford to hire a lawyer, the Constitution of the United States entitles you to a court-appointed lawyer, so that bunch of yahoos up there in Washington says." He looked at Candle and then looked back at the prisoner. "Any lawyer I appoint must represent you free of charge. In other words, he cannot charge you anything, even if he gets you acquitted."

Candle wanted to protest the impending appointment, but a burst of temper disabled his tongue.

The inevitable command came. "Mr. Reid," he heard Judge Pryde say, "would you please come around? The court has a favor to ask of you." The judge's voice struck Candle as a little bit too sweet, too kind, too nice.

Candle pulled at his collar and, closing his eyes, fought for air.

"Mr. Reid, did you hear me? I said 'come around.' "

Judy shook Candle's arm. "Mr. Reid? Are you okay?"

Candle nodded. Feeling faint and hot, he managed nevertheless to stand and walk from his seat in the jury box to the bench. As he passed by him, Candle could not bring himself to look at his prospective client, a person's whose life would soon be in his hands if he could not get the judge to alter his course. "Your Honor," he heard himself say, "I—uh—"

The judge interrupted. "I know what you're going to say, Mr. Reid. And it's what any lawyer would say. You don't feel up to the task."

Candle felt himself shaking. He did not know if the shaking was due to nervousness, anger, or the effects of alcohol. "No, sir. I really don't. I'm basically just a real estate lawyer. In fact, I represent the—"

The judge finished the sentence for him. "You represent the State Bank and Trust Company, the bank the deceased in this case worked for. Right?"

"Yes, sir, I do in many cases and transactions."

"This case, Mr. Reid, is a contest between this accused and the State. It is not one between him and the State Bank and Trust Company. So, there's no reason for you even to bring the issue up, is there?"

"I suppose not," Candle said, looking around, sweat pouring down his face.

"Even if you did, I'd find no conflict of interest sufficient to disqualify you from representing the defendant in this case. Now, do you wish to raise the issue of disqualification based on a conflict of interest?"

"No, sir."

The judge smiled. He turned a page in his notebook and ran a pointed finger across it. "You were admitted to the bar more than five years ago, were you not, Mr. Reid?"

"Yes, sir. In 1939."

"And you've participated in the trial of felony cases before, have you not?"

"No, sir. I mean, yes, sir. With Mr. Blumberg I have. But I only—"

"Mr. Clerk," the judge said.

Honeycutt vaulted to his feet and faced the bench.

"Let the General Sessions Journal show that I have this day appointed Candle Reid, Esquire, of Blumberg & Reid, as counsel for the defendant Dewey Coltraine, a defendant awaiting trial on a capital murder charge. Let the Journal further reflect that I have found Mr. Reid to have been a member of the State Bar for more than five years and to have felony trial experience. The court will stand in recess."

Honeycutt spun around. "Everybody rise," he called out as Judge Pryde left the courtroom in a great hurry.

Fleming came over to Candle and threw an arm around him. "Don't worry about it, Candle. I'll let you see my file. I'm sure you'll do as good a job as anybody else could do under the circumstances."

With Fleming's arm still around him, Candle said, "Solicitor, you know, the judge knows, and I know I'm not qualified to handle this case for that poor guy."

Fleming removed his arm. "Don't sell yourself short, Candle. You know more than you think you do. Come by my office after lunch. Like I say, I'll let you look my file over. Also, the coroner'll be having the inquest in a couple of weeks and you can learn more about the case then." He tapped Candle on the back and walked out of the courtroom.

Candle stood staring at the floor and feeling sorry for himself until he felt someone touch his shoulder. He turned around and saw it was Judy. Behind her were his newest client and his client's keeper.

"Don't you think you should talk with him a little before they take him back over to jail, Mr. Reid?" she asked, inclining her head toward the prisoner.

Candle nodded his agreement and motioned for all to sit at a nearby counsel table. After borrowing a legal pad from Honeycutt and handing it and his fountain pen to Judy, Candle drew up a chair across from the prisoner and the deputy sheriff. "Mr. Coltraine, I just want to find out a few things about you. We'll talk later about the murder charges and what you've got to say about them. I first want to check out the solicitor's file and maybe talk to Sheriff Madison."

"All right, sir," Dewey murmured.

Candle spent less than five minutes on the interview, asking only general background questions. He ended the interview by asking

Dewey if he had a criminal record. Dewey assured him that he did not.

Candle pushed his chair back and stood. "Like I said, I'll talk to you later on, Mr. Coltraine. I want to educate myself about the charges first."

"Mr. Reid, sir," Dewey said, standing. "I'm real sorry I got you into this thing."

"Well, Coltraine," Candle said, with a slight smile, "there's not a thing in the world either of us can do about it now. Looks like we're yokefellows."

"What's that, sir?"

"In our case, those whom the law has joined together."

***

Dewey Coltraine stood by the window in his cell, gazing through the bars at the world beyond, watching the wine disk of the sun disappear over the tree tops. His thoughts centered on Nellie. Notwithstanding the sheriff's promise to let him know if he heard anything about Nellie, Dewey had not received any word about her since his interrogation when the sheriff had told him she had been hospitalized. His last image of Nellie was of her in the folding house, lying on their bed, her head flat against the pillow and her eyes and mouth half-open. He wondered if her condition had improved. If so, why hadn't she contacted him? If not, why hadn't someone let him know something?

Dewey turned from the window and fell upon his bunk. Resting on his back, he forced himself to think about the day's events. He had been taken that morning to the courthouse and, to his surprise, had been given a lawyer—and it was one free for the asking. This meant he at least would not face by himself what lay ahead.

Still, Dewey was bothered. It was the "free" part that troubled him. The uncle who raised him after both his parents drowned in a boating accident had told him the day that he arrived at his uncle's house, "Boy, if you're expectin' to live with me for free, I'm here to tell you ain't nothin' in life really what you might call 'free.' One way or the other you're gonna have to pay for it." Dewey recalled the uncle had told him this as he handed him an ax and pointed at a wood pile.

A promise of "free" occupancy had enticed Dewey and Nellie to move into the folding house and the experience had proven again the truth of his uncle's observation. Because they had done what they did, Nellie had been raped and had killed a man, and he had been jailed for a crime he had not committed. The price had been high, much too high.

Now that he had a "free" lawyer, he wondered what the real cost would be—for himself, for Nellie, and even for Candle Reid.

Dewey heard the door to the cellblock clang open. Ollie Johns, a jail trusty and man with the face of a thousand pimples and blackheads, came to Dewey's cell door and inserted a key into the lock. "Sheriff, he says come git yo'," Johns said as he opened the cell door. "Somebody here to see yo'."

Dewey followed Johns out of the cellblock. He hoped against hope the person there to see him would be Nellie.

Johns led him down to the first floor. They passed a couple of vending machines, the radio room, and a room Dewey remembered from his first day at the jail, the room where he had given a sworn statement to the sheriff and his secretary. "This'un here, Coltraine."

Johns knocked on the door and a voice answered. Dewey put his head against the door frame. The voice did not belong to Nellie.

Candle Reid held the door open as Dewey walked into the windowless room. "Hello again, Mr. Coltraine. Or do you mind if I call you 'Dewey'?"

Dewey shook his head. "No, sir."

"Take a seat over there, why don't you," he said, pointing to a chair. "I don't have long, and I've got lots to ask you about."

Candle motioned the jail trusty out. "I'll call you when I'm through, okay?"

The trusty nodded, sucking his teeth as he shut the door.

Dewey seated himself and waited for Candle to start the conversation. He noticed a file folder on the table that had his full name on it—Dewey Fletcher Coltraine. Candle removed a pack of cigarettes from his shirt pocket and offered one to Dewey, who declined it with a shake of his head.

Candle opened the file folder and withdrew a legal pad. He fanned through its first several pages before throwing it down on the table. Dewey noticed handwriting covered the topmost page.

"Dewey," Candle began, "after I left the courtroom this morning, I went by the solicitor's office and read everything he's got in his file. I also talked with him and the sheriff. I read the incident report, read the statement you gave Sheriff Madison. I looked at a few other things there in the file—pictures of the shotgun, the scene where this thing happened—the car. You don't—"

Dewey interrupted him. "Mr. Reid, could I ask you to do somethin' for me, please sir? I dunno if it's somethin' you can ask a lawyer to do for you or not."

Candle turned his head to the side. "What?" His tone sounded guarded.

"Would you mind, please sir, findin' out somethin' 'bout my wife? Last I heard, they'd took her to the hospital. The sheriff said he'd let me know somethin' but he hasn't done it yet. I been worried 'bout her. She wasn't doin' too good last I saw her."

"What's her name again? I saw it there in the solicitor's file, but I forget what it was."

"Nellie. Nellie Grace Coltraine."

"Oh, yeah. Okay." Candle wrote Nellie's name on the backside of the file folder.

"I'm obliged, Mr. Reid."

Candle sat back, resting his elbow on the arm of the chair and his chin in the palm of his hand. The hand also held a cigarette. "As I understand it, you shot Mayfield because you say he had raped and assaulted your wife three or four days before, is that right?"

Dewey did not respond.

Candle lifted his head from his hand. "Listen to me, Dewey. You got to tell me everything. Understand?"

Dewey nodded.

"And what you tell me, I want it to be the absolute, God's truth. Understand that too?"

Dewey again did not respond.

Candle took a draw of his cigarette and removed it from his mouth as he let the smoke escape his lungs. "My former law partner,

Bernie Blumberg—he's dead now—whenever he'd interview an accused in a criminal case, he'd always tell them, 'Always, always tell me the truth. I can work with the truth. I can't work with a lie.' "

"Yes, sir."

Candle withdrew a fountain pen from his shirt pocket, unscrewed its top, and turned the pages on the legal pad until he reached a clean sheet. He took one last puff of his cigarette before extinguishing it. "Now, Dewey, tell me what happened out there at Mayfield's place. You can start anywhere you want to."

Before he spoke, Dewey turned his face away from Candle for a few seconds. "I blame myself, Mr. Reid. I was just tryin' to get Nellie off to myself, away from her family and all. Her daddy, he didn't like it none on 'count of me and her runnin' off and gettin' married like we done."

"I'm not following you," Candle said, looking up from the legal pad.

"Mr. Mayfield offered me and Nellie this place of his to live at up there in Harpers' Joy. I took him up on it to get away from her family, mainly her daddy. Then one day while I was at work he—Mr. Mayfield—he done what he done to Nellie. He messed her up pretty bad and she ain't been the same since."

Candle wrote something on his legal pad. "Why didn't you go to the law about that?"

"I wanted to, but Nellie wouldn't let me. Also, Mr. Mayfield come back the next mornin' and threatened to ruin Nellie's reputation and kill us both if either one of us said anything 'bout what'd happened. I think, too, Nellie was afraid of what her daddy might try and do, mainly to me. I'm sure she thought he'd blame me for what happened, for not lookin' after her like I was supposed to, like I'd promised him I would."

"What day of the week was it when you say he attacked Nellie?" Candle asked, without looking up from his legal pad.

"It was on a Monday, a Monday afternoon. It was while I was workin' my route downtown."

"And you shot him on Friday, four days later?"

"Yes, sir."

"What made you shoot him? Tell me about that. What led up to it?"

Dewey hesitated again. "I decided to go along with what Nellie wanted to do. You know, 'bout not reportin' it. Later on, I figured I'd try and forgive him and try and forget the whole thing. I mean, ain't that what we're supposed to do? That's what Miss Velma said the Lord—"

"'Miss Velma,' did you say?" Candle said, writing.

"She runs a store."

Candle glanced up from his legal pad. "Does she know anything about any of this?"

"No, sir."

Candle struck through Velma's name. "Okay then. Go back to telling me what led up to your shooting Mayfield."

"Nellie kept gettin' worser and worser," Dewey said, still directing his eyes toward the floor. "She got to where she wouldn't say nothin', she wouldn't do nothin'. She'd just lay there in the bed pretty near all day. And she started carryin' the shotgun her daddy give her 'round with her all the time. She was afraid Mr. Mayfield—"

Candle sat up straight. "That was **her** shotgun?"

"I reckon it was. Her daddy told her he was givin' it to her. Don't that make it hers?"

"Yeah, I guess it does." Candle lit another cigarette and motioned for Dewey to continue with his story.

"Anyhow, I lost my job there at the bottlin' plant and Mr. Mayfield had done told us to get outta the foldin' house, to go find us someplace else to go live at."

"Mayfield had kicked y'all out?"

"Yes, sir," Dewey said, nodding.

"And you'd lost your job? How'd that happen?"

"Well, whenever I come in off my route and got through loadin' my truck back up, Mr. Hammond called me in his office and told me I was fired, but the Unemployment Office'd help me if I went there and told them he'd let me go."

"Why'd he fire you?"

"He said Mr. Mayfield'd called him up and threatened to close him down if he didn't do it."

Candle puffed on his cigarette. "So, Mayfield assaulted your wife and cost you your job, right?"

"Yes, sir."

"How'd you happen to have the bottling company's van if it had already fired you?"

"Mr. Hammond seemed to cotton to me. He let me borrow it so me and Nellie could get all our stuff moved out."

Candle turned back to the first page of his legal pad and flipped it back and forth several times. "According to my notes here, Dewey, you say in your statement you just happened to see Mayfield in his car riding up toward Harpers' Joy and you followed him up to your place. Is that right?"

"Yes, sir."

"And when you caught up with him, you shot him?" Candle continued.

"Yes, sir." Dewey gulped. "When he saw me come up, he didn't pay me no mind. It was like I wasn't even there or nothin'. That's when I run in the house and got Nellie's shotgun and come back out. It was right after that when I shot him. I—"

"Wait a second."

Dewey stopped talking as Candle went over his notes.

"I thought you told me a minute ago that your wife carried her shotgun around with her all the time. She didn't have it out there with her when you drove up? You had to go into the folding house to get it?"

Dewey swallowed. "Yes, sir," he said, thankful Candle's eyes were again directed toward the legal pad. "I dunno why she didn't have it out there with her right then. He might've caught her outside while she had her hands full with somethin' else. You know, puttin' out the garbage or somethin'."

Candle looked up. "Why'd you shoot him?"

"Mainly, 'cause of what he'd done to Nellie."

"You said something in your statement to the sheriff that you figured he had gone back to attack her again?"

"Well, I believe he would have, if I hadn't followed him up yonder and stopped him."

"Did he have a weapon of any kind that you could see?"

"Mr. Mayfield? No, sir. Not so I could tell."

Candle grimaced as he wrote. "Where was Mayfield standing when you shot him?"

"Standin' in the road in front of his car."

"And you and Nellie, where were y'all?"

"Standin' out in the yard, 'bout ten or fifteen feet from his car, I reckon."

"After you shot him, what happened?"

"That's when I seen his wife. She was yellin' and screamin' at me, callin' me a murderer and wantin' to know if I was gonna kill her too. She seen me holdin' the gun."

"Where was Nellie all this time?"

"On the ground. She was layin' on the ground. She'd done passed out."

"Why had she passed out?"

"I dunno. She just did. I reckon when she seen what'd happen and all, she fainted."

"When did you go try and find the law?"

"Soon as I took Nellie inside and laid her down on the bed. I come back out, and Mrs. Mayfield was still there cryin' and all and still thinkin' I was gonna shoot her. I asked her to please look after Nellie while I went and called the sheriff. Then I left and found a phone down the highway apiece."

Candle put away his pen and stood, his left hand in his pocket. "Dewey, look at me." Dewey, who continued to sit, raised his head but would not look at Candle. "I said, look at me, Dewey!"

"Yes, sir," Dewey responded, directing his eyes into Candle's.

"Let's go back one more time to why you killed Mayfield, okay? You say you shot him because you thought he was there to have another go at Nellie—rape her or hurt her again. Is that right?"

Dewey twisted around in his chair. "Yes, sir."

"Tell me what Nellie was doing when you drove up."

"She was just standin' there. Not doin' nothin'."

"Out in the yard? Without the shotgun?"

"Yes, sir."

"Couldn't Nellie have, if she had wanted to, run into y'all's house and locked the door?"

Dewey took his eyes from Candle. "I reckon she could've, if she'd had a chance. But then he might've come and busted the door down or caught up with her before she made it inside and got the gun. The locks on the doors, they wasn't too strong."

"He didn't chase you, did he?"

"No, sir. I reckon it was 'cause Nellie was still out there in the yard."

"And you left her out there with him?"

Dewey frowned and started to chew on a fingernail. "Yes, sir. But it was just a second or two. No longer'n it took me to get the shotgun."

"What we have here, Dewey, is this: you say a man attacks your wife; yet, you don't report the alleged attack to law enforcement and you don't tell anybody about it; in fact, you don't do anything at all about it at the time; four days later, you follow the man who you say assaulted your wife to your house and when you get there you see him standing outside of his car; he's not armed or anything, at least so far as you could tell right then; you leave your wife alone with him while you run into your house and get a shotgun; you come back outside and shoot both him and his car. Is that your story?"

"Yes, sir," Dewey replied after a pause, his eyes to the floor.

"According to a hospital record that's in the solicitor's file, your wife had been badly beaten recently. And you say Mayfield's the one who did it."

Dewey raised his head. "Yes, sir."

"Tell me this, Dewey. Who's to say you didn't do it? Who's to say you didn't beat her up, huh? And who's to say you didn't do it because you thought Mayfield and your wife had had sexual relations one afternoon while you were at work? Tell me that?"

"Nellie. She'd tell you it wasn't me," Dewey said.

"But Dewey," Candle said, his voice high pitched. "From what Solicitor Fleming tells me, she's not talking. And even if she were and she corroborated everything you say, on the day you killed

Mayfield it'd been four whole days since he had assaulted her. Four whole days!"

"Yes, sir."

"Four days!" Candle repeated, this time louder than before.

"Yes, sir."

"And you went into your house, got a shotgun, came back out, and shot him?"

"Yes, sir."

"And him unarmed?"

"Yes, sir."

"And you shot up his car too?"

"Yes, sir."

"You do that before or after you shot him?"

"After." Dewey caught himself. "Before, I mean."

Candle scratched his head. "Why'd you shoot up his car?"

"Try and scare him off."

"To scare him off? How much time elapsed between your shooting up his car and your shooting him?"

Dewey squirmed. "I dunno. Not long. I seen he wasn't gonna leave her alone but was gonna keep on. So, I shot him."

"Did he come toward you or anything before you shot him? Make any menacing gesture?"

"No, sir. Least, I don't think he did. I don't remember. Everythin' happened so fast."

He stared at Dewey for a moment and sighed, shaking his head as he did so. "What a mess!"

The lawyer sounded so pained and exasperated that Dewey began to feel sorry for him.

Candle leaned back against the wall and folded his arms. "And you've told me the truth now?"

"Tried to."

"What do you mean you 'tried to'?"

"Tried my best. I'm still pretty shook up 'bout everything."

Candle did not say anything for a moment but stood staring at Dewey. He reached for his yellow pad. "All right, I'll tell you another thing Mr. Blumberg used to say. 'Don't ever curse a deaf man.' You know why you shouldn't curse a deaf man, Dewey?"

"No, sir."

"Because it probably wouldn't do any good, that's why. He couldn't hear you do it. So, it'd be a useless thing to do. I think my representing you is going to be just about as effective as cursing a deaf man. It's not going to do you a bit of good. I hate telling you that. But I want to be honest with you too. Plus, I don't want you getting any false hopes."

Candle opened the door and called for the trusty.

"Mr. Reid, sir," Dewey said softly.

"What?" Candle replied, anxious to leave.

"Please don't forget to check on Nellie for me."

***

"What's this you trying to do? I'd quit for the day," Judge L. Malcolm Pryde complained as he held a blue-backed paper close to his face.

"What's it look like?" Solicitor Fleming replied.

"You know I can't read without my glasses," Pryde said, moving about papers and other accumulations on his desktop. He found his reading glasses after sorting through a pile of documents. He flipped out the earpieces and put the glasses on. "State Hospital? You want me to commit Coltraine's wife to the State Hospital for observation and evaluation? How can I do that? She hasn't been charged with anything. You need to go to the Probate Court."

"Oh, but she has been charged. The sheriff served her an hour ago with a warrant naming her as an accessory."

"An accessory? You know they'll have to keep her at least thirty days up there, don't you? Maybe longer, if they decide to get a civil commitment."

"That's what I'm hoping they'll do. Keep her, I mean."

"Then you're not really planning on trying to indict her?"

Fleming shook his head. "Nope."

Pryde looked puzzled. "I thought you were going to use her as a witness."

"Not any more. That's why I'm having her sent off. Only person she could help would be Coltraine."

Pryde reached across his desk and pulled a fountain pen from its holder on the desk set. "What's wrong with her? Why you wanting to send her off all of a sudden?"

Fleming took a chair in front of Pryde's desk and crossed his legs. "The sheriff tells me the doctor told him they've been having trouble getting her to talk or to do anything ever since they admitted her. I understand she'll mostly just lie there in her bed or sit in a chair, staring at the wall, kind of vacant-eyed. Here lately, though, they think she's been hearing voices because sometimes she'll start mumbling to herself and pacing all about with her hands over her ears."

"I guess when she saw what her husband had done it pretty much tore her out of the frame," Pryde said, signing the order. "I think Georgia Ann's been kind of out of it too. My wife heard somebody out at the country club say she hasn't been out of the house since the funeral, and they've had to have the doctor with her once or twice." He held the order out toward Fleming.

Fleming folded the order and put it inside his coat. "Well, anyhow, Bo went out to the hospital this morning to try and talk to Coltraine's wife again—he's been out there several times. When he got to the point where he asked her about her husband shooting Lester Junior, she went absolutely nuts. Bo said she started screaming and crying and carrying on something awful. Throwing things. Running around the room. He said they had to put her in a straight jacket. She kept claiming she was the one who shot Lester Junior, that her husband didn't have anything to do with it."

Pryde grunted and smirked. "So, that's why you had her served with a warrant and why you're wanting me to send her off. You don't want her complicating things for you, do you?"

Fleming sat stony-faced.

"What you think? You think Coltraine did it rather than her?"

Fleming shrugged. "He said he did. And everything certainly points that way. Too, that just might be their idea of trying to cover for each other."

***

After his secretary left to go home for the day, Candle Reid opened a bottom drawer to his desk and withdrew an all but empty bottle of bourbon whiskey. He drank straight from the bottle, quaffing what remained of its contents.

The day had not gone at all like he had planned. But then, it never did. All in the course of one day he had been appointed to represent a shotgun murderer; reviewed the solicitor's file, which contained the sheriff's incident report, a copy of Coltraine's confession, a hospital record concerning Coltraine's wife, and a letter to the solicitor from Dr. Luke Koutrakos in which the physician stated he had examined Lester Mayfield's body and summarized his findings; talked with the sheriff about his investigation; gone by the jail and talked with his new "client"; visited the hospital, inquired about his client's wife, and learned nothing other than she could not have visitors; returned to the jail and told his client what he had learned at the hospital; made it back to his office and reviewed the mail, which consisted of two magazines and seven bills, three of which were past-due; dictated three letters, two of which asked for an extension of time to answer a complaint; signed five checks totaling one hundred and twelve dollars that his secretary prepared for his signature; dodged at least four telephone calls from disgruntled clients and avoided two that paid personal visits to the office; and closed exactly one file for which he billed the client ninety-three dollars.

On top of all that, the clerk of court's office had sent word that the case of *Paula Gachet Reid versus Candle Reid*, the limited divorce action in which Candle, in view of his law partner's death and his lack of funds, now represented himself, had been scheduled for trial before Judge L. Malcolm Pryde on Friday, January 3, 1947, beginning at 9:30 a.m. He had hoped for a different judge. But he should have known better than to hope for that. Candle raised his arm to check the time. His watch had stopped.

With great effort, he lifted himself up from his chair and walked to the outer office where he got the time from a wall clock that advertised a long-defunct funeral home. He saw he had just seven minutes to make it to the liquor store a block and a half away. After setting his watch, he hurried back to his office, grabbed his coat and hat, and ran downstairs. When he reached the bottom step, he realized he had not locked the main door to the office. He ran cursing back up the stairway to do it.

He made it to the liquor store just in time. The liquor store operator was lowering the shade to mark the store closed as he ran up. Candle tapped on the glass. A white-haired, red-eyed man inside raised the shade, looked out, and smiled at Candle. He opened the door, allowing Candle to step inside. "Wondered what'd happened to you," he said. "Somebody said you representin' that fella what murdered young Lester. That right?"

Candle grimaced. "Now where'd you hear that, Pink?"

"Fella come in here. Said he'd heard it. Expect you'll make pretty good representin' him, won't you?"

"Millions," Candle answered, his tone sarcastic but cordial. "Let me have a pint of your Johnny Gray there."

Pink went behind the cash register, got a bottle from off a shelf, and dropped it into a sack. The bottle made a whacking sound when it hit the bottom of the bag. Pink exchanged the package for the money Candle had already laid onto the counter.

Candle's apartment lay two blocks away. Every evening, almost as soon as he entered it, Gloom and Despair walked in with him; however, they never got to stay long. Candle's smooth, liquid buddy would chase them away before they could settle down.

The cold, dark apartment greeted Candle with the smell of country-fried steak drifting in from his landlady's kitchen on her side of their common bathroom. He closed the door and stood for a moment with his eyes closed in the cold and the dark, savoring the greasy, peppery scent. He reached up and pulled the light string. The light did not come on.

"What else can happen today?" he exclaimed aloud.

He walked into the kitchen and turned on its light. Enough of the light in the kitchen fell into the bedroom that he could see to light the gas heater. Once he did that, he went into the bathroom and knocked on the door that led to his landlady's side of the house. "Mrs. Blankenship," he called, "could I talk to you a moment, please ma'am?"

The door opened. A woman, several years older than Candle, but not looking her age, greeted him. "Why, hello, Mr. Reid. Is there something wrong?" Louise Blankenship asked, wiping her hands on a worn apron.

"Could you let me borrow a light bulb? The one in my bedroom is burned out."

The woman smiled. "I think about all I have is a seventy-five-watt bulb. Can you use that?"

"Yes, ma'am."

She opened a closet door, reached in, fetched a light bulb, and handed it to Candle. "I heard on the news a while ago you're representing the man that killed Mr. Mayfield."

"Afraid so," Candle answered, his mind set on returning to his apartment and fixing himself a drink now that he had what he came after.

"What is the world coming to?" she asked, sounding exasperated.

"The worst, probably."

"I believe that. Armageddon's just around the corner, you know."

"I've got to go, Mrs. Blankenship. Thanks," Candle said, holding the bulb up and turning to leave. He felt she was about to take off on Jehovah Witness doctrine and he didn't care to hear it.

"I'll tell you one person who's delighted that man killed him, though."

Candle stopped and turned back around. "Who?"

"My cousin, Colin Lucas. I ran into him at the Colonial Store—out in the parking lot. He said the man saved him the trouble of doing it. He said he'd been thinking about killing Mayfield himself—and also Mayfield's lawyer, whoever that was. He said there was one down and one more to go."

Candle felt his heart skip. He seemed to lose his breath. "I sure hope you reported that to the police, Mrs. Blankenship?"

Mrs. Blankenship batted the air with her hand. "Aw, Colin was just running his mouth. He wouldn't do anything like that. He's not that type. Besides, he's got that daughter to look after. Poor, pitiful little thing."

Harpers' Joy

She studied Candle for a couple of seconds. "Why, Mr. Reid, you look plumb white. Is there something wrong?" She grabbed a chair. "Here, sit down, why don't you?"

Candle dismissed the offer with a shake his head. "It's nothing. I guess it's because I haven't had anything to eat since breakfast, I've been so busy."

"Then why don't you stay and have supper with me? I've got plenty. Country-fried steak. Mashed potatoes. English peas." She turned, stepped to a cupboard, and opened a door.

Candle's thoughts were not on eating. Whatever appetite he might have had, Louise Blankenship had just finished off. His thoughts were focused on Colin Lucas and what Lucas might do to him. After all, the foreclosure action he had brought as counsel for the State Bank and Trust Company against Lucas was still ongoing. Dewey Coltraine's killing of Mayfield had not changed that.

He cursed to himself about the burned-out light bulb. Had it not gone out, then he would not have knocked on Mrs. Blankenship's door and he would not have talked to her and learned of Colin Lucas' threat. No, the day had not gone well at all. "Please, Mrs. Blankenship. Don't bother."

Mrs. Blankenship stood with plate in hand, ready to lay it on the table. "Are you sure, Mr. Reid? It's awfully good. Don't you smell it?"

Candle opened the door to the bathroom. "Thank you, but I better not. Some other time, maybe. It smell's good, though. Goodnight, ma'am."

He closed the door behind him and almost ran to where he had put the sack of whiskey. He unscrewed the cap and, as he had done at the office, drank straight from the bottle.

Very soon, Candle forgot about Dewey Coltraine, the State Bank and Trust Company, Colin Lucas, the work left undone at the office, his upcoming divorce hearing, and all the other problems that faced him right then. That was the way it was when he and ol' Johnny got together. Ol' Johnny made him forget, bless his heart.

***

"Coltraine," Bo Madison said, "I had them bring you downstairs, so I could give you some information. I wanted you to hear it firsthand."

Dewey ducked his head. "Yes, sir?"

"Your wife's been taken to the State Hospital in the upper part of the state. Judge Pryde signed an order on her late this afternoon."

"State Hospital?"

"The insane asylum. She's had what they think is a complete nervous breakdown. I'm sorry, Coltraine. I know you got enough problems right now." He lowered his eyes and shuffled some papers on his desk. "If I hear anything else, I'll let you know."

"You mean they think Nellie might be insane?" Dewey asked, his eyes fixed on Madison.

"They're checkin' her to find out now, son," Madison said. "That's why she's up yonder. You know, to see if she really is or not."

"Did they say how long it'd take them to find out?" He continued to study Madison's demeanor.

Madison shook his head. "There's just no tellin' 'bout things like that. Coupla weeks. Maybe a coupla months. I just dunno."

"Coupla months?" Dewey heard his voice quiver as he spoke. "Do you know if anybody's told her mama and daddy?"

"Yeah. They were there at DeBusk-Inman Hospital when we went to get her."

"I don't reckon you feel like tellin' me what they said or anything."

"Like you, they're upset. Her daddy, though, blames you for everything. He wants you dead, he told me. Said when they got ready to juice you, he'd pull the switch."

"Yes, sir."

Monday, April 7, 1947

Candle Reid did very little to prepare for Dewey Coltraine's trial. He had been too busy earning a living during the day and too occupied recovering from the effort during the night.

Besides, he had felt no real need to prepare. He had convinced himself early in the process that the outcome was a foregone conclusion anyway and that the Supreme Court, like it did in Hugh Sykes' case, would affirm the conviction, if not on the merits, then on some technical grounds. His participation as Dewey's counsel was nothing more than constitutionally mandated window dressing. Everybody knew that.

Indeed, other lawyers in town, when he ran into them in the clerk of court's office or elsewhere, reinforced Candle's notion that Dewey was beyond the help of judicial science and, thus, any effort spent on Dewey's defense would be totally wasted. "Hey, Candle," one had said, "you joined the electricians union yet? Better hurry." Another had joked about the State's method of execution, cracking as he prodded Candle in the rib cage, "You know what day of the week they'll electrocute your boy Coltraine on, don't you? On Fryday. Get it? Fry-day. You know, Fryyyyy?" These and other remarks of similar nature made Candle detest his involvement with Dewey Coltraine's case all the more and question why he had become a lawyer in the first place.

On what had been Candle's last visit to the jail three days before, which was to let Dewey know the solicitor would call his case as the first one for trial at the upcoming Spring Term of the Court of General Sessions, Dewey had shown little interest in what lay ahead. Candle suspected he, too, knew his situation was hopeless. Dewey had only wanted to know whether Candle had heard anything about his wife beyond her being committed by the Probate Court to the State Mental Hospital following her initial court-ordered, thirty-day observation. Candle didn't have any information about Dewey's wife because he had neglected to make any inquiries about her; however, he had promised he would do so before court opened. As to the length of trial, he had told Dewey, "It'll probably go pretty fast, I suspect."

The whole time Candle had sat in the client-interview room with Dewey that Friday morning, Candle had felt like he was looking at a corpse. Dewey resembled one, in fact. His confinement had whitened his skin to the color of fresh sheets. Worse still, his body emitted a gamy odor.

The interview that morning had produced little meaningful conversation between the two. Candle's mind kept returning to the things he must do at the office and to the relief that he would feel once this dreadful experience was behind him—when Dewey was at last out of sight and out of mind, which, in Dewey's case, meant convicted and sent away to prison to await execution.

Candle sat waiting for Dewey to be brought into the courtroom for his arraignment on murder charges. As he waited, Candle contemplated how his friend Johnny Gray now mistreated him. His hands often trembled so he could not write in a clear hand. During the morning hours, his temples pulsated with pain, making concentration difficult, if not impossible; and his stomach, for long periods each day, felt the queasiness of storm-tossed sailors.

Suddenly, the door by the petit jury box opened, jolting Candle out of his melancholy. He looked up to see a deputy sheriff ushering a manacled, head-bowed Dewey Coltraine into the crowded courtroom. A rustling resonated throughout the spectator section as Dewey, a sorrowful expression on his face, shuffled across the floor toward Candle, his bonds jangling, his shoulders bent.

The appearance of the prisoner at the bar and the commotion that it incited in the courtroom jarred Candle. The sight of him and the sound of his coming depicted for Candle an image of reality that he had not before perceived. For the first time, Candle felt more pity for Dewey Coltraine than for himself.

Candle began to shiver, not from the effects of alcohol, but from panic, a panic born of a sudden realization that he was not ready to defend the wretched man who, with his shackled feet dragging across the bare wooden floor, now moved toward him. He was not prepared in any way for the task that lay ahead.

And why was it that he was just now gripping reality? It was because, heretofore, the defense of Dewey Coltraine had neither form nor substance. It could not be seen. It could not be heard. It could not be touched. Now it could be. A full-blown trial in which a man's life was at stake was about to ensue. Candle's representation at trial of the man with the woebegone countenance was no longer a hypothetical endeavor, if indeed it had ever been.

It now dawned on Candle that he needed more time, time that he could not waste—not if he was to provide any meaningful assistance to this unwanted client of his. He needed it to formulate a defense. He also needed it to clear his mind, steady his hands, calm his stomach, and free his head of the throbbing pain. Dewey Coltraine might represent dead meat, but that did not mean Candle had to help cook him. He wondered what he could do to get the additional time that he now felt he needed so very much.

As Dewey, dressed in khaki pants and in a matching long-sleeve shirt that he had buttoned at the collar, drew closer, he raised his chin and smiled at Candle. When their eyes met, Candle felt his stomach knot up. He grew faint and wished himself a thousand miles away with his friend Johnny Gray. But—if he could—he had to stay away from Johnny for a while, at least until after the jury returned its foregone conclusion in the form of a guilty verdict.

"Mornin', Mr. Reid," Dewey said as the deputy removed the shackles and cuffs from his ankles and wrists. "You hear anything more 'bout Nellie?"

Candle, lost in thought, did not hear Dewey's question. "What?" Candle said.

With the cuffs now off, Dewey held a hand out toward Candle in greeting. Candle shook it without getting up and motioned for Dewey to take the chair next to him.

"Have you heard anything 'bout Nellie, Mr. Reid?" Dewey asked as he sat down.

"No, Dewey," Candle said. "Nothing. Maybe the sheriff'll have some information when he gets here in a few minutes, or the solicitor. Okay?"

Dewey nodded and dropped his head.

"They're to arraign you this morning, Dewey. You'll have to stand in that pen-looking thing over there," he said, indicating. "It's called a dock."

Dewey appeared to study the small wooden enclosure that resembled a cage. "Reckon they'd mind puttin' me a chair in it?"

"A chair?"

"I don't think I could stand in it the whole trial. I feel kinda weak."

Candle smiled. "Oh, I'm sorry, Dewey. You won't have to stand in it the whole trial. You just have to stand in there for the arraignment, that's all."

"How long will that take?"

"A minute or two. Not long."

"Why can't I just stand right here? Right here at the table?"

"I don't honestly know. It's just like so much of what happens in court, I guess. No reason, except that's just the way they've always done it."

"Yes, sir," Dewey said, his head bowed again.

Candle heard a door creak open and saw Solicitor Fleming enter the courtroom. He came in by the door next to the grand jury box, a box occupied by the eighteen men who comprised the Semmes County Grand Jury. He carried a stack of indictments and a large black notebook.

Fleming grinned at the grand jurors, pausing to glad hand the foreman and most of the others seated on the first row. He waved to those on the back row as he walked past them and headed for his counsel table on the opposite side of the courtroom, the table closest to the petit jury box.

"Well, looka here, why don't you?" he said, smiling toward Candle. "Aren't you the eager beaver? What are you doing here so early, ol' sport? Trying to get a leg up on me with all these fine folks?" He nodded back toward the men seated beyond the bar on the first several benches behind Candle. The men—all of them white—had been summoned to serve on the petit jury venire.

Candle forced a smile. Anymore, he felt very uncomfortable, if not intimidated, in the presence of Fleming. At the January hearing on his wife's petition for a limited divorce, Fleming's cross-examination of him when he had taken the witness stand to testify in his own defense had been a frightening event. Whenever Candle thought back on the experience, it still unnerved him. Though Candle, as a fellow lawyer, understood Fleming was just doing his job, Candle thought he had done it a little too well.

"You said to be here by ten o'clock," Candle said.

Fleming laid the notebook and the bills of indictment down on the counsel table next to Candle's and extended his right hand. Candle took Fleming's hand and shook it from a seated position.

As Candle withdrew his hand, he glanced at the caption on the topmost indictment. He saw it was the murder indictment that the grand jury had returned against Dewey four months earlier. Although he knew about it, Candle had not read the indictment before. He had seen no need to do so since he had read a murder indictment once before and figured the only differences between the language in it and in Dewey's would be the names of the victim and the accused, the date on which the murder allegedly occurred, and how it had been committed.

The sight of the indictment prompted Candle to remember a maneuver that his late law partner had once employed to get a murder case with which Candle had been involved carried over from one term of court to the next. Candle now knew how he could gain more time within which to prepare for Dewey's defense. Dewey's arraignment upon the indictment would provide Candle the means.

"Solicitor, you're just going to arraign Dewey this morning, right?" Candle asked, tipping his head sideways toward Dewey.

"Arraign and **try** him," Fleming responded.

Candle frowned. "Try him? I thought after the arraignment we were entitled under the statute to a ten-day sight of the indictment."

"Yeah, you are. But we want you to waive that, so we can go on and get started on Coltraine's case first thing this morning. I've got a lot of people in jail and a whole bunch of others out on bond. One or two of them want trials, so I understand. Judge Pryde doesn't want any dead time."

"But I thought I could count on the ten days. You know to get—"

Fleming laughed and finished Candle's sentence. "Get ready? Is that what you were fixing to say? Get ready? Get ready for what?"

He picked up the indictments and began shuffling through them. "Tell me, Candle, if you had ten more whole days to prepare, exactly what would you do? Now tell me honestly."

"Well, I could—"

"This thing could be over and done with by late this afternoon or by the middle of tomorrow morning, at the latest."

"Still, the statute—"

"Listen, Candle, I know the statute gives your client the right to a ten-day delay between his arraignment and his trial, but everybody waives it. You know that." Fleming's chest rose and fell. "Are you telling me Coltraine there, who's been sitting in jail for nearly five months waiting to hear what's going to happen to him, wants to wait even longer? Is that what you're telling me?"

"No. It's—"

"I wish I knew what idiot legislator put that stupid statute on the books. I'd try and indict him for something, just to put him away someplace where he couldn't do any more harm to our legal system. Criminals have enough rights as it is."

"I thought—you know, due process—"

"Due process? Look here, Candle, your man has had more due process than he knows what to do with. I let you see my file. The coroner held an inquest that you went to. The grand jury acted on the indictment which you've known about since December. You could have come to my office at any time and asked for it. I tell you, it's nothing special. It's just a regular ol' murder indictment."

"I know. That's not my, uh, my—"

"And now, I'm ready to arraign his fanny and then pick a jury and go to trial. I thought you were, too."

"Well, I'm—"

Fleming's tone became angry. "Let me tell you something, Candle. You know every case in which there is an indictment pending is scheduled for trial the first day of court. Your case is no different."

"I know that. But I still have a right—"

"And I've got witnesses subpoenaed—I thought of all people you'd be ready, anxious as you must be to get shed of this case. But, if you want me to, I'll go back yonder and tell Judge Pryde you want your ten days. Just say the word and I'll go. But it's you he'll be chewing out for messing up court week. And I'll expect he'll be doing it in front of all them out there." He pointed to the prospective petit jurors. "That'll do your practice a lot of good, now won't it? You really should have said something to me earlier about this."

Before Candle could respond, he heard the voice of Sheriff Madison from behind him. "Mornin', Solicitor. Candle."

Candle stood and turned to greet the sheriff, but he did not stop. He headed for Solicitor Fleming and put his arm around his shoulder. The two, their backs to Candle, engaged in an animated conversation and laughed as they shared what Candle guessed was a private joke. He wondered if it was about him.

Candle walked to where the sheriff and solicitor stood. "Sheriff? Excuse me, you got a minute?" he asked.

Madison removed his arm from the solicitor and turned around. "Sure. What you need?"

Candle, whispering into Madison's ear, asked if there was any new information concerning Dewey's wife. The sheriff whispered back, a hand covering his mouth. Candle shook his head as he received the sheriff's report.

"Thank you, Bo. All right if I tell Coltraine?"

The sheriff scrunched his shoulders. "Go ahead. I meant to tell him myself, but I just plain done forgot all 'bout it," he said.

Candle returned to his counsel table and sat down beside Dewey. "Dewey," he said, facing forward. "The news about your wife isn't good."

Candle felt Dewey look at him. "Sir?"

Candle lowered his head. "The sheriff told me he understands she's had to have shock treatment there at the State Hospital."

"Nellie? Shock . . . shock treatment?" Dewey said, his voice breaking.

Candle patted Dewey on the knee. "I'm sorry, Dewey. I really am."

Dewey's head bobbed, and his shoulders shook as he began to cry. Candle, feeling awkward and looking all around, continued to pat Dewey on his knee. "Come on now, Dewey," he said, "you've got to get hold of yourself. People are looking at you."

Dewey lifted his head and turned his face toward Candle, tears streaming from his eyes and his lips quivering. "I can't help it, Mr. Reid. I can't help it. Did they really have to give her shock treatment?"

Candle felt discomfited. He knew only he, and probably the sheriff, understood why Dewey was crying. He wanted to stand and explain to everyone the reason that underlay his client's emotional state, but he knew he could not do that.

Mercifully, Marcellus Pondexter, wearing a navy-blue blazer and a brass badge that read "Court Crier," rapped the floor with a pole right then. "Be upstandin' for the court," he shouted in a loud, bass voice.

Everyone in the courtroom stood and watched the Honorable L. Malcolm Pryde, his robe unbuttoned and his round, hairless head held high, sweep behind the bench.

When the judge reached his chair and turned to face the lawyers, policemen, jurors, witnesses, defendants, bail bondsmen, and the rest, Pondexter again rapped his pole on the floor. Only this time he cried, "Hear ye! Hear ye! All persons havin' business before the Court of General Sessions for Semmes County, draw near and pay attention, for the court, the Honorable L. Malcolm Pryde, presidin', is now in session. God save this honorable court."

Judge Pryde, gesturing, directed everyone to sit. He appeared to be in a bad mood. Then his mood seemed to worsen as he appeared to read from a note handed him by the clerk of court. Judge Pryde folded the note and had everyone stand again as he called on a local Presbyterian minister to pray.

The minister read a long prayer from a prepared text, botching every fourth or fifth word and having to repeat it.

Once the minister finished, Solicitor Fleming presented bills of indictment to the grand jury to act upon and swore all the witnesses that the grand jury would hear in support of the indictments.

After the grand jury left the courtroom, Judge Pryde directed the clerk of court to call the names of those summoned to serve on the jury venire and to bring before him those who sought to avoid jury service based on hardship. He excused an accountant, a department store manager, a paving contractor, a radio station owner, and a pharmacist, but refused to do the same for an automobile mechanic, a house painter, and an unemployed tire salesman who had a bedridden, cancer-stricken wife to care for at home. Judge Pryde several times reminded those whom he would not excuse of the importance of jury service, telling them that one of the reasons this country fought the Germans and Japanese was to preserve the right of trial by jury.

Dewey's arraignment, as Candle had predicted, took only a couple of minutes. It ended with Dewey being told to say "by God and my country" in answer to the solicitor's question regarding how he would be tried. The solicitor, not Candle, told Dewey to say what he did. Candle had forgotten what a defendant was required to answer when asked the question.

Candle's answer to the solicitor's final question made Judge Pryde bounce upward in his chair. When the solicitor asked, "Are you ready for trial?" Candle replied, "No, sir, we are not. We want a ten-day sight of the indictment."

Judge Pryde removed his glasses and glared at Candle with cold eyes. "Say, what? What's that you say, Mr. Reid? Did you say something about wanting ten more days?"

Perspiration dampened the top of Candle's head. "I'm sorry, Your Honor. But, uh, I need the, uh, time."

"Time? For what?" Judge Pryde asked, leaning back in his chair and looking befuddled. "Haven't you had enough time? You've had four months just about to get ready. Most lawyers in your position waive—"

Candle felt perspiration start to trickle down behind his ears. He reached for his handkerchief. "Your Honor, I'm sorry," he said, wiping away the sweat. "But you know ever since Mr. Blumberg died, I've had to run the office all by myself. I've got other clients. I really didn't count on being—"

"Mr. Reid, Mr. Reid, Mr. Reid," he said, interrupting. "I must say this is a very big disappointment to me personally. I appointed you to represent this defendant because I thought you were the best man for the job. I knew your reputation—or thought I did. And now look what you're doing. Just look!" Judge Pryde glanced at Solicitor Fleming, who had moved to a spot beside the petit jury box, several feet away. "Mr. Solicitor, do you have anything else we could be trying the next ten days?"

Solicitor Fleming shook his head, his face evincing great unhappiness. "Well, Your Honor, I thought we'd be trying this case. You know, starting today. Mr. Reid never—"

Judge Pryde appeared agitated and began to fidget. "You see there, Mr. Reid? You see what you've done?" He pointed to the jury venire. "Tell me this, Mr. Reid. Just what are all these gentlemen out there to do for the next ten days while they're waiting for the trial of your client to get underway? Are they just expected to sit in here, twiddling their thumbs? Is that what you want?"

"No, sir," Candle answered in a meek voice.

Judge Pryde jumped around in his chair. "Mr. Reid, I'm curious. Did you tell the solicitor that you'd insist on a ten-day sight of the indictment?"

Candle started to answer.

"Before today, I mean."

"No, sir."

"Is this some kind of clever move on your part, some kind of defense tactic? Some defense trick? If it is . . ." Judge Pryde did not complete his sentence.

Candle could sense the aggravation and disapproval that everyone in the courtroom felt toward him at that moment. The newspaper reporters who had taken the seats vacated by the grand jurors were giving him looks of disgust and dissatisfaction, especially the ones from out of town. Members of the petit jury venire could be heard grousing. Several lawyers seated with the press in the grand jury box made no effort to hide their snickers. City policemen and sheriff's deputies seated in or standing near the petit jury box, looked at each other and shook their heads or made faces.

"Your Honor, I appreciate the problem," Candle said, his hands and voice shaking, "but could you just give me until next Monday morning? I hate to impose on the court and all these gentlemen," he said, turning around and pointing to the petit jury venire, "but I really need the time."

"Are you saying, Mr. Reid, that you'll waive the ten-day requirement if I'll give you until next Monday morning to be ready for trial? In other words, you want a seven-day sight of the indictment, right?"

"Yes, sir," Candle answered, counting his fingers. "Seven more days. Until next Monday."

Judge Pryde sat looking at Candle, saying nothing. His face registered no expression. "All right," he said, "let me ask the solicitor something." He rolled backward in his chair and braced his hands against the edge of the bench. "Mr. Solicitor, if we were to start the trial of the Coltraine case next Monday morning, would you have enough business to justify keeping the court in session?"

The solicitor walked to the front of the bench. "I can't really say. I know I've got enough for today and tomorrow and maybe Wednesday. I've got about thirty or so guilty pleas that I had kind of hoped to work in when you had time to hear them. Most of them are jail cases. Only seven or eight of them have a lawyer."

"Very well, then," Judge Pryde grumbled. "Monday morning, we will begin the trial of *The State versus Dewey Coltraine*. In the meantime, if we break down and have to take a couple of days off, then we'll just have to break down and take a couple of days off, courtesy of Candle Reid, Esquire, of the Semmes County Bar." He glared at Candle. "And Mr. Reid, you'd better be ready to try the case next Monday morning or come packed to spend some time as a guest of our fine jail. Got that?"

***

When Candle Reid reached the landing at the top of the stairs, he paused to rest until his heart assumed a regular beat. The morning had taken its toll on him both physically and emotionally—and professionally too, he imagined, judging from everyone's reaction to his insistence on a delay in the trial of Dewey Coltraine's case. The task that lay just ahead seemed overwhelming, since he had come to better appreciate the gravity of his client's situation. How he wished Mr. Blumberg still lived. He would know what to do.

Candle opened the door to his office, his eyes catching at once those of Judy Claire. They appeared wide and frightened as she twice pitched her head to her left. Candle turned to see Colin Lucas, sitting in a chair, a young girl on his lap.

Candle's first thought was to slam the door shut and scamper down the stairs, for he remembered all too well the remark Lucas had made to Candle's landlady after Lester Junior's death about there being one down and one more to go; but Candle knew it was too late to run away. Lucas had seen him already.

Lucas and the girl stood as Candle entered the waiting area. "Lawyer Reid, I'm here 'bout that there foreclosure business."

Candle ignored Lucas and decided to try and reach the sanctuary of his office down the hall. "I'm sorry, Mr. Lucas, but I can't talk to you this morning. I'm involved in a death penalty case over at the courthouse." He hurried by Lucas and the girl without looking at them. "How about checking with me next week when I've got more time?"

He made it only to the hallway entrance before Lucas grabbed him from behind by the shoulders. Candle yelled for Judy to call the police while struggling to free himself from Lucas' grip. Undaunted, Lucas pushed Candle down the hallway and into his office, kicking the door closed behind them and leaving his daughter outside the door.

"Go on ahead and call the police. Let 'em come. I ain't 'fraid of 'em," he said, his arms now wrapped around Candle, who continued to twist and buck in an effort to break free.

"You jist be still, Lawyer Reid. I ain't a'gonna hurt you. Least not yet, I ain't," Lucas demanded. "I jist wanna talk to you, that's all. I'll let you go, iffen you promise you'll talk to me peaceful like."

Candle, not a strong man to begin with, went limp, quitting the fight. "All right," he said as he felt Lucas' hold loosen, "what is it you want?"

Lucas removed his arms from around Candle and backed up a couple of steps. "I want you to drop that there lawsuit and give me another chance to pay what I owe the bank."

"That's not my decision to make, Lucas," Candle said, exhausted and feeling faint. "That's the bank's."

"Then you go talk to Mr. Mayfield and tell him," Lucas said.

Candle, gulping for air, collapsed into a nearby chair. "Why don't you do it yourself?"

Lucas towered over Candle. "I'd whole lot rather talk to you. Mr. Mayfield, he done suffered enough, I figger, what with that boy of hissen a'bein' shot down in cold blood by that woman like he was."

The last bit of information startled Candle. "What do you mean 'by that woman'?"

"Jist what I said."

Candle sat up straight. "Nellie?"

"I dunno her name."

Candle felt his strength returning. "How do you know she shot him?"

"I jist know, that's all."

"The only way for you to know that is for you to have been up there and seen it happen."

"I was there, and I seen it."

"You saw Coltraine's wife kill Lester Junior? What you trying to pull here, Lucas?"

"I ain't a'tryin' to pull nothin'."

"What were you doing up there?"

Lucas rocked back and forth on his heels, his arms crossed behind his back. "I'd followed him up there—Lester Junior. I wanted to try and talk some sense into him, see iffen he'd give me one more chance to catch up on what I owe. I figgered iffen I could talk to him 'way from the bank—you know man-to-man like—he'd let me do it."

"Uh-huh. Did you talk to him?"

"Didn't git no chance to. After I parked my truck up there on the road, right there by the driveway, I marched myself a little ways down to where he was a'standin' out there in fronta this here trailer house, a'yellin' fer this woman to come outside." Lucas grinned and dipped his head. "She come outside, all right, and commenced to shootin' at him. Hit his car first time she shot. Second shot's what got him. Then 'bout that time, the Coltraine boy, he drove up and seen what'd happened and all; and that's when I skedaddled outta there. I didn't wanna git mixed up in nothin' like that, you know. Still don't and I ain't gonna be, provided Mr. Mayfield'll do like I want him to. You go tell him what I told you. Every word. And you tell him, too, I won't be no witness fer the Coltraine boy iffen he'll drop ever' thing and let me have a chance to pay what I owe 'em. It won't cost him nothin' to do that, now would it?"

Candle heard the blare of a police siren on the street below, just outside his window. He stood to take a look-see as Lucas rushed to the door and peeled it back, exposing his daughter on the other side, standing in the doorway. Lucas took her by the hand. "Come on, honey. Let's us be a'goin' afore the polices git here." Lucas turned to leave as the sound of the siren died down. "I'll be a'waitin' to hear from you, Lawyer Reid. Iffen you know what's good fer you, you'll do what I say do."

Candle followed Lucas and his daughter up the hallway. Entering the waiting area, he saw Judy hugging the wall by her desk and heard the sound of feet pounding up the stairway outside.

"Are you all right, Mr. Reid? That should be the police," Judy said.

"He's all right," Lucas said, answering for Candle. Lucas, with Candle close behind him, opened the front door just as a police officer reached the top step. He eased his daughter out the door. "Mornin'," he said. "What's all the fuss?"

The officer, his hand on his revolver and his feet planted on the top step, said nothing and looked at Candle, who stood just inside the doorway.

Candle smiled. "It's okay, officer. False alarm. Sorry."

The officer didn't appear convinced, but he didn't question Candle. Taking one step backward, he turned sideways and allowed Lucas and the girl to squeeze past him.

When Lucas and his daughter reached the bottom step, the officer came into Candle's office. "You sure everything's okay, Mr. Reid? Somebody called from here and reported you were being attacked." The officer peeked around Candle, looking toward Judy who now stood behind her desk.

"I called you," Judy said. "That man—"

Candle interrupted, smiled, and shook his head. "Officer, Judy just misunderstood. I'm fine, really. Thank you for coming so quickly."

"But Mr. Reid!" Judy exclaimed.

"That's okay, Judy. Everything's all right now," Candle said, giving her a look and motioning for her to sit down.

"You sure?" the officer asked.

"I'm sure. I tripped, and Mr. Lucas kept me from falling. Judy must've thought he grabbed me. Like I say, it's just a misunderstanding, that's all."

"Okay then," the officer said, turned, and walked out the door, closing it behind him.

In fact, Candle was not sure everything was all right. His defense of Dewey Coltraine had now become a more complicated endeavor. If Lucas were to be believed, Coltraine had voluntarily and knowingly signed a written confession to a murder he had not committed and one that could, and no doubt would, put him in the electric chair. The question was could Lucas be believed? Had Coltraine's wife really killed Lester Mayfield, Jr.?

"Well, that was a fine how-do-you-do," Judy complained from behind the counter. "Why did you tell the officer you were okay? That man attacked you in your own office right in front of me."

"Just forget about it, Judy. I'm all right," Candle replied, embarrassed.

"Forget about it? How do you think that makes me look? What do you think the police'll do if I ever have to call them again?" She spun around, flopped down in her chair, crossed her arms and legs, and turned her head away from Candle.

"When you calm down," Candle said, laughing a nervous laugh, "would you call Mr. Mayfield's office and see if I could see him this afternoon? The earlier the better."

"It'll take me a few minutes. I don't know when I've been so mad. I ought to quit." She all but spit the words out.

Candle retired to his office to await Mayfield's response to his request for a meeting. It took longer than he anticipated. In the meanwhile, he relived all of the morning's events and wondered what he was going to do about the new worries those events had spawned. The worry that he felt for Dewey Coltraine had only been made worse by Lucas' visit. The worry that he had felt for his own safety had been made worse by Lucas' visit as well: if Lucas was capable of assaulting Candle in his own law office in front of his secretary, what else was Lucas capable of doing?

***

Lester Mayfield made Candle Reid wait for nearly thirty minutes past the time for which his secretary had scheduled the appointment. When at last Mayfield received him, Candle wished he had not asked for the meeting. Mayfield remained seated behind a large desk as Candle entered Mayfield's office. He sat with his head bent over a ledger book, its soft-green, lined pages filled, from the look on Mayfield's face, with some hard realities.

Candle, his left hand buried in the pocket of his coat, walked up to the edge of the desk and waited to be recognized. Much to his dismay, his stomach growled, making a loud, gurgling sound. He hit himself in an effort to make it stop. The growl continued for a second or two more.

"What's that you say, Reid?" Mayfield asked, looking up.

Candle felt his face flush. "Just hello."

Mayfield pointed to a chair. "I started not to see you, you know. I heard about the stunt you pulled over there in court this morning."

"Mr. Mayfield, sir," Candle said as he sat down. "After I left—"

"I don't suppose you ever lost a son or daughter before, have you, Reid?"

"No, sir." Candle then realized he had lost his daughters or rather was about to do so once school was out, if his wife carried through on her threat.

"I didn't think you had. If you had, you wouldn't feel too kindly toward somebody that was trying to help the fellow that took him away from you, I'll tell you that."

"Yes, sir. But you know I was appointed to represent him, Mr. Mayfield. I didn't ask to do it. And I'm not getting paid anything. I—"

"What is it you want?" Mayfield snapped. "Is it about my son's case?"

"Well, it is and it isn't."

Mayfield sunk back in his chair. "Now, what does that mean?" he asked, his upper lip curled.

"You remember Colin Lucas? He owns a farm out near Nye's Packing Shed, right before you get to Cecelia. He's the one that's got that spastic daughter."

"What about him?"

"Well, before he died, Lester Junior insisted on my filing a foreclosure action against him. Lucas'd gotten way behind on his payments and had some things happen that interfered with his ability to pay off the loan y'all had made to him."

"I know all about it."

"I filed suit like Lester Junior told me to. Lucas then went into default. He didn't answer the complaint like he was supposed to."

"I know what default is. Get to the point. I hate a mystery."

"Lucas wants you to authorize me to drop the suit and he wants you to give him more time to come up with what he owes the bank."

"The answer is 'no.' You can tell him I said that."

Candle nodded. "All right, sir. But there's one other thing."

"Which is?"

Candle collected himself before speaking again, so certain was he that the rest of Lucas' message would infuriate Mayfield. "Lucas said if you didn't agree to drop the foreclosure suit and give him an opportunity to pay off his debt, he was going to come testify at Coltraine's trial and say Coltraine's wife killed Lester Junior. That Coltraine didn't have a hand in it."

Mayfield appeared shaken. "What!?"

"Yes, sir. He'd say Coltraine didn't kill your son. That Coltraine's wife did and that he saw her do it."

"Is that something you put him up to saying, Reid? Is it?" Mayfield said, his eyes wide and angry. "When Malcolm called me a while ago to tell me what you did in court this morning, he said you just might be up to no good."

"Now, you know better than that, Mr. Mayfield."

Mayfield sat for a moment as if in thought. "No, I don't reckon you did. You wouldn't have sense enough."

Anger welled up inside Candle and he tried to avoid showing it. His effort in that regard made no difference, however, for Mayfield had turned his attention back to the ledger.

"That's about the nuttiest thing I've heard lately," Mayfield said, turning a page. "You don't put any stock in it, do you? I sure don't, and I don't see how anybody else could either." He lifted his eyes from the ledger and glared at Candle.

"I, uh—"

"Well, do you or not?"

"No, sir. I don't. I mean, he admitted doing it, Coltraine did—to me and to the sheriff." Candle instantly regretted including himself as one to whom Dewey had confessed. He had violated a confidence.

"You get in touch with Lucas and you tell him that the bank isn't dropping a thing and that, as far as I'm concerned, he can testify for Coltraine till the Second Coming. He must think me an idiot."

"All right, sir. I'll tell him. But he isn't going to like it. And to tell you the truth, I'm scared of him myself."

"Scared of him?"

"Yes, sir. What I didn't tell you is that he assaulted me in my office late this morning."

"You don't look like he did."

"Well, he did, and he did it because I'm the bank's lawyer. I heard on the grapevine he wanted me dead, too, because I represent the bank."

"Are you saying you don't want to be our lawyer anymore, Reid?"

"No, sir. I'm not saying that. I'm just telling you what happened at my office and what I've heard. I don't think Lucas is anybody to fool with."

"Who's fooling with him? I'm sure not. You call him and tell him what I said. You can also tell him I said to go to Hell."

Candle stood to leave. "I'll let him know the bank intends to go forward with the foreclosure action."

"You gonna use Lucas as a witness?"

"I don't see how I can, do you?"

"You're the defense lawyer."

Walking back to his office, Candle tried to answer the question about the possible use of Lucas as a defense witness. He doubted he would use him. For one thing, there might be a legal problem associated with the admission of evidence of that kind—courts ordinarily disallowed evidence that someone other than the defendant committed the crime alleged in the indictment. Then there was Coltraine's own voluntary admission to his having killed Lester Mayfield, Jr.

Aside from all that, Candle had to agree with the senior Mayfield's assessment of Lucas' testimony: no one would find it credible. Certainly, no fair-minded juror would do so. First, Lucas had conditioned his testimony on the bank's refusal to drop the foreclosure suit and Candle himself, as directed by Lucas, had disclosed that fact to Mayfield who was sure to tell Fleming. Second, Lucas had not said anything earlier to law enforcement authorities about Lester Junior's being killed by Coltraine's wife, notwithstanding the news about the killing was widespread throughout the area. Third, any skilled cross-examiner—and there was none better than Solicitor Fleming—could easily persuade the jury that Lucas' pointing of a finger at another as Lester Junior's killer represented nothing more than a blatant but pathetic attempt to exact revenge on the Mayfields and their bank for foreclosing on his farm.

As Candle climbed the stairs to his law office, he determined he would not make any effort to talk with Colin Lucas about Mayfield's decision to continue the foreclosure action. Instead, he would write Lucas a letter, telling him. And he would write the letter in such a way that it would, he hoped, cause Lucas to focus his fury on Mayfield alone. He would definitely put in the letter that Mayfield had expressly told him to tell Lucas "to go to Hell."

***

After signing the letter to Colin Lucas, Candle picked up his Coltraine file and placed it under his arm. He walked out of his office and handed the Lucas letter to Judy. "I'm headed over to the jail to talk with Dewey. If Colin Lucas comes back, you immediately call the police."

"Don't worry. I will," Judy said, folding the letter and inserting it into an envelope. "Though I doubt if they'll pay any attention to what I tell them."

Candle interpreted her last remark as a cut.

He went straight to the jail next door to the courthouse. Within minutes, the jailer brought Dewey Coltraine to the client-interview room. Candle lit a cigarette as Dewey sat down.

"I've got something to ask you about, Dewey."

Dewey, his eyes toward the floor, nodded without speaking.

"Well, before I do, I want you to know again I'm sorry about your wife. I know how upset you are, especially since you can't see her or be of any help to her."

"Thank you, sir," Dewey mumbled.

"You feel like talking?"

"I reckon."

Candle drew on his cigarette. "Do you know a man named Colin Lucas?"

"No, sir."

"He assaulted me this morning in my law office." Candle studied Dewey for a couple of seconds to see if Dewey manifested any reaction to the news. He did not. "This man Lucas hated Lester Junior because he blames him for the bank's trying to take his farm."

Dewey continued to stare at the floor.

"Anyway, he told me you didn't kill Mayfield, that it was your wife who did it."

Candle thought he saw Dewey flinch.

After a moment, Dewey raised his head but said nothing. His expression changed in a way that made Candle uncomfortable. Dewey appeared uneasy.

Candle continued. "Lucas said he was out there when it happened. That he saw your wife shoot him."

"He wasn't there, Mr. Reid," Dewey said, not looking at Candle. "Wasn't nobody there exceptin' Mr. Mayfield, Nellie, and me. And then, Mrs. Mayfield, she come up."

"You've said Mayfield had earlier assaulted your wife. Wouldn't that be a reason for Nellie to kill him? If she thought he was there to do it again?"

Dewey directed sad, red eyes at Candle. "My wife, Mr. Reid," he said softly, his lips quivering, "she ain't no murderer and yet look at what they done done to her already. They sent her off way up yonder. Then, after they got her there, they started electrocutin' her, givin' her that shock treatment and all, and there ain't nothin' I can do about it." He laid his forearms flat onto the table, laid his head down upon them, and began to cry.

"Look at me, Dewey," Candle said. "Look at me. Did Nellie kill Lester Mayfield? Tell me. What you say will stay right here in this room. I promise. I need to know, if I'm to be of any help to you. "

Dewey raised his head. "I'm the one killed Mr. Mayfield, not Nellie. She wouldn't hurt a fly. If you knew her like I do, then you'd know she couldn't have done it and you wouldn't be askin' me what you're askin'. I dunno why that Lucas fella told you what he did. He wasn't out there. Like I say, wasn't nobody there but the three of us to start with—and after I shot him, Mrs. Mayfield."

Candle extinguished his cigarette. "All right then, what is your defense?"

Dewey wiped his nose on his shirt sleeve. "I don't reckon I got no defense. It's kinda like that time my aunt caught me and my cousin eatin' this lemon meringue pie she'd just got done bakin' and'd put out on the table to cool off some. Both us had it all over our face and fingers when she come in there and caught us. I mean, what could we say? We'd took the pie."

Candle could not help it. He smiled. "You could've said, 'We thought that pie just needed eating.' "

Dewey wiped his nose again. "That's sorta like what my cousin said. He told her we thought she'd fixed it for us to eat and that's why come we ate it. But what he told her, it didn't do no good. She switched the fool out of both of us anyway."

Candle talked with Dewey for only a few more minutes before summoning the jailer to return Dewey to his cell. As he walked back to his office, Candle found himself thinking, of all things, about Dewey and his cousin's defense to their taking of the lemon meringue pie. Why wasn't the defense of "the pie just needed eating" a good defense? Isn't that why lemon meringue pies are made? Aren't they supposed to be eaten? What had made the defense fail? Why hadn't his aunt bought it? The answer was an obvious one, he concluded: Dewey's aunt might not have fixed the pie for him and his cousin. Maybe the wrong persons ate the pie, a pie that just needed eating.

His thoughts shifted to Dewey's killing of Mayfield. Was it true that Dewey had no defense, as Dewey himself had suggested? Perhaps Dewey had no legal justification or excuse for what he had done, but did that mean Dewey did not have some sort of a defense on which the jury might hang an acquittal?

Suppose, Candle asked himself, he could prove that Mayfield had indeed raped Dewey's wife; wouldn't that make Mayfield in the eyes of the jury somebody who just needed killing? But, as in the case of a pie that needed eating, what about the question of who could properly do it? Certainly, the State could have killed Mayfield, provided it could have proved beyond a reasonable doubt that he had raped Nellie. Rape carried the death penalty, even for rich, young white men. Could he prove Dewey was the right person to have killed Mayfield and thereby earn a jury's pardon?

First, he would have to prove that Lester Mayfield, Jr. was indeed somebody who needed killing. And that might prove so difficult he would not get to the second question of whether Dewey was the right person to have done it.

When Candle reached his office, he headed straight for his desk and picked up a yellow legal pad. After clearing clutter from his desktop, he laid the legal pad onto his desk and withdrew a fountain pen from his shirt pocket. Turning to a clean page, he wrote on the top line in all-capital letters, SOME FOLKS JUST NEED KILLING. Several lines down he wrote *Why Lester Junior needed killing*, drew a line, and vertically listed the numbers one through ten.

He pushed back in his chair and studied for a moment what he had written. Pitching forward, he laid the legal pad back upon his desk and wrote beside the number one, *Assaulted and raped Nellie Coltraine—brutally*. By the number two, he wrote, *Beat up Dewey*; by the number three, he wrote, *Told them to move out*; by the number four, he wrote, *Came back to meet wife at cabin*; by the number five, he wrote, *Stopped at Dewey's place to—*.

Candle couldn't finish the last entry. He didn't know why Mayfield had stopped at the folding house. Colin Lucas, if he were to be believed, had said Mayfield had called Dewey's wife outside. To prove that, Candle would have to use Lucas as a witness and, if Lucas were true to his word and in view of Mayfield's refusal to drop the foreclosure action, he would willingly be available as a witness for the defense.

But what if Lucas during his testimony, either on direct or cross-examination, should assert that Nellie, and not Dewey, had shot and killed Mayfield? How would that look to a jury, especially since Dewey admitted to having killed him? The "some-folks-just-need-killing" defense could not work, Candle decided, if Lucas in his testimony should accuse Dewey's wife of the murder—not with Dewey as the defendant. No, Candle concluded, he could not risk using Lucas as a witness, not if Dewey's defense was to be "some folks just need killing."

The "some-folks-just-need-killing" defense was proving harder to establish than expected. Who besides Dewey and his wife could offer evidence of the rape? And judging from the information he had about Dewey's wife, she was not mentally competent to testify, or so he had been led to believe. He would have to check on that.

Candle fiddled with other ideas for about thirty minutes before he glanced at his watch and saw it would soon be five o'clock. Out of habit, he pulled open the bottom desk drawer but banged it shut when he spied his drinking buddy Johnny. The bottle lay there, waiting for him. Candle bounded from his chair, threw on his coat, and hurried to the secretarial area. He wanted to put some distance between him and the bottle.

Candle paused in front of his secretary's desk. "Judy, I'm going to head on out, if you don't mind. I'll see you in the morning."

"I'll lock up," Judy said, without once taking her eyes off the form order she was typing. "This'll be ready for you to have the chancellor sign in the morning. It's the *Andrews* case."

When Candle reached the street below his office, the chimes of the Tekoa State Bank and Trust Company began striking five o'clock. He wiped his mouth and looked down the street toward the liquor store. He resolved to resist the temptation to go there, no matter what.

***

As Candle approached his apartment, he was delighted to see his landlady outside sweeping off the front steps of her house. If he was to avoid alcohol, he needed someone to spend an evening with.

Candle figured she might fit the bill. Besides, he could not be too particular. The urge to have a drink had become almost overpowering for him to handle by himself. Calling his wife was out of the question.

The only thing that gave him any pause about perhaps spending a few hours with his landlady was the prospect of having to fend off her attempts to tell him about the Jehovah Witnesses. That seemed to be all she ever wanted to talk about—that and what a bargain his rent was, considering the prices of things. He snapped his finger. He would just chance it.

"Hey, Mrs. Blankenship," Candle said, standing at the brick walkway that lead to his apartment on the north side—the coldest side—of the house. "You started supper yet?"

The woman quit her sweeping and, gripping the end of the broom with both her hands, glanced down at Candle from the top step, a startled look on her face. "Why no, I haven't. I've been working out here most of the afternoon, the weather's been so nice."

"Good," Candle said. "Why don't we—you and me—go out some place and eat? Hadn't neither one of us got anything else to do tonight, now have we?"

Louise Blankenship did not answer Candle right away. She stood looking at him, a tongue to her cheek. "Well, I was kinda planning on doing some Bible study."

"Aw, come on. You can do that later," he said, his voice cheerful.

"Where are you thinking about going?" A note of uncertainty replaced the note of surprise evident in her voice moments earlier.

"Oh, we could walk down to the cafeteria."

Mrs. Blankenship removed a slender hand from the broom. "I don't believe I feel much like walking anywhere, tired as I am."

Candle sensed the battle was about to be lost. "Well, if you don't mind taking your car, we could ride out to Stagg's Fish Camp. It's a good place to eat."

"I hear their food's mighty greasy."

Candle laughed. "Well it is. That's what makes it good. Besides, you know, everybody needs an oil change every now and then. It'll make the ol' joints work better." He bent his arms and started flapping them.

"You remind me of a chicken," she said, laughing. "Okay, we'll do it. But you'll have to give me about fifteen or twenty minutes. I don't want to go looking like this."

The fifteen or twenty minutes turned out to be thirty or forty minutes, and they were the longest thirty or forty minutes Candle could remember he had ever spent while waiting on somebody. He wanted a drink in the worst sort of way. He resisted the urge by drinking water. Lots of it. He also busied himself washing dirty dishes and otherwise straightening up his apartment.

When Mrs. Blankenship surrendered the bathroom after what seemed forever, he gave himself the fastest shave of his life, cutting himself only twice, and washed his face, hands, and underarms.

He caught the evening news on the radio as he dressed. Dewey Coltraine's arraignment led off the news and Candle heard his name mentioned as Dewey's counsel. Hearing the radio announcer speak his name both embarrassed and pleased him at the same time. He wondered if his wife had also heard the announcer and what her reaction was, if she had.

Candle heard Mrs. Blankenship return to the bathroom. She knocked on the door and told him she'd meet him in the garage. He turned off the radio, checked himself out in the chifferobe mirror, straightened his necktie, and put on his dark-blue sport coat. Backing up, he glanced one more time in the mirror, this time to see how well his tan pants matched his navy-blue coat. He frowned at what he saw.

By the time he got outside, Mrs. Blankenship had opened the doors to the garage, exposing a black, mint-condition, 1937 Nash inside. "Here," she said, dropping the car keys into his hand, "you drive."

The trip to Stagg's Fish Camp took less than thirty minutes. Candle had braced himself for an exposition by Mrs. Blankenship about Jehovah Witness beliefs, but it never came. On the way, they talked about small things, avoiding topics concerning religion and government. The closest they came to discussing her religious faith was when Mrs. Blankenship mentioned her husband had died on V-J

Day after he refused a blood transfusion following an accident at his workplace. Her conversation then veered off into how much her life had changed since her husband's death and the loneliness she often felt.

At the fish camp, both ordered the all-you-could-eat catfish dinner. Candle, however, was not prepared for how much Mrs. Blankenship, a tall, angular woman, could eat. He measured her intake of fish, not in servings, but in schools. As for himself, he could not eat very much. He blamed Johnny Gray for his want of an appetite and ate what he could of all he could eat.

When they returned home, Candle maneuvered the Nash into the garage, parked it, switched off the ignition, and turned off the headlights, Candle and his landlady sitting in pitch-black darkness. As he gave Mrs. Blankenship back her car keys, his hand quite by accident brushed against her left thigh. She appeared not to notice and took the keys without comment. With them still in her hand, she touched Candle's shoulder. "Would you like to come in for a little while, Mr. Reid?" she asked in a sweet voice.

Candle did not answer her at once, so great was his surprise. He groped for a proper response after losing his breath for a moment. He wondered if her invitation had anything to do with his touching her thigh. He concluded that it did. "Why, yes. Yes, I would," he said, swallowing hard. "But here, let me get out and turn on a light so you can see to walk without falling over something."

He hurried to exit the car and turn on the outside light. Once out of the car, he realized his hands trembled and his throat felt dry. It had been a long time since he had been with a woman. He ran around to the passenger side of the car, opened the door for Mrs. Blankenship, and escorted her out of the garage to her backdoor step. "I'll be over in a few minutes. I've got to do something first, if that's okay," he said.

"Don't be long," she cooed.

"I won't," he assured her before racing around to the side of the house and a half block down the street to the Sinclair Oil Station.

He went to the men's toilet, shut the door, and inserted coins into a vending machine above the urinal. The machine, on which someone had scratched "*EXODUS* 20:14," returned Candle a round, half-dollar-size, gold-foil package. Glancing around the empty restroom, he slipped the package into his pocket and hurried back to Mrs. Blankenship's house.

"Here I am," Candle announced as he came through Mrs. Blankenship's back door, after knocking. His heart was racing, and his breathing was heavy.

Mrs. Blankenship ushered him from her kitchen into the living room where she had already drawn the shades and had turned on only two lamps. She pointed to the sofa. "Just have a seat, Mr. Reid—or do you mind if I call you 'Candle'?"

"Nope. Sure don't. And I'll call you 'Louise,' Louise," he said with a grin.

"Good. I'll be right back," she said, drawing out the word "right." She disappeared into her bedroom.

Candle imagined her turning off lights and turning back bedcovers. As he pictured what the next hour or so would be like, he thought of *Exodus* 20:14 and guessed at what the verse probably referred to—adultery. The thought of the verse and its probable meaning served to remind him that he was still a married man. Meng the Merciful had granted his wife only a limited divorce.

He tried to suppress any thought of his marital status. What did his being married matter now anyway? he asked himself. Wasn't Paula going to New York in a few weeks once the children's school-year ended? Then too, what better way was there to overcome the urge to drink than having a brand-new bed partner? And a widow woman at that! He wondered how long it had been for her, whether she had been with a man since her husband died.

Candle heard Mrs. Blankenship walk across the bedroom floor, pause, and head back toward the living room. In a short while, he thought, he would be lying next to her in bed and knowing a woman for the first time in ages. This was going to be better than anything Johnny Gray could offer him—at least right then. He was sure of that.

Mrs. Blankenship stole from the bedroom into the living room, a new scent signaling her approach. Candle, too embarrassed to look up, waited for her to come sit next to him on the couch. "Candle," she said, as she sat down, "could we talk about love?"

"Sure," Candle said, fumbling with the small packet in his pocket and trying to be agreeable. Then he looked at her. Her hands held a Bible and a *Watchtower* magazine.

Harpers' Joy

Monday, April 14, 1947

Before Candle Reid realized it, the week that he had been granted to prepare for trial had been gobbled up. To divert his attention from his craving for alcohol, Candle had thrown himself into his work, preparing for his defense of Dewey Coltraine. He went over the notes that he had made when he had examined the solicitor's file and interviewed the sheriff. He reviewed the memo that he made after attending the coroner's perfunctory inquest at which the sheriff only told of finding Lester Mayfield, Jr.'s body and read Dewey's sworn statement. He studied and restudied the jury list, making discreet inquiries of other lawyers and friends about those listed. He made several visits to the jail and had Dewey rehearse his testimony. Candle also wrote down questions essential for him to ask the prosecution witnesses on cross-examination and, should he take the stand, his own client on direct-examination.

Candle's hard labor had worked. His mind seemed some clearer. His headaches were not as severe, nor did his hands shake as much. Although he did not feel like a new man, he did not feel hung over and he woke up sober every morning.

Not that Candle didn't want a drink. He did. Indeed, he longed for the end of Dewey's trial when he could have one—and a big one at that. He had come close to taking a drink the first night, after he discovered he had misread his landlady's intentions regarding what the remainder of their evening together would be like.

But, in retrospect, her effort to interest him in the Jehovah Witnesses had been for the best. She had talked for almost an hour, explaining about Armageddon, what Jesus' role in the great battle would be, and what the world would be like after Satan's defeat. She had so exhausted him with her presentation that when he returned to his apartment he gave no thought whatever to Johnny Gray but went to sleep almost as soon as he crawled into bed.

Jury selection had taken less time than he had imagined it would. Judge Pryde had excused only one member of the jury venire, the town's only known Republican. The man, a Quaker who hailed from Pennsylvania, did not believe in the death penalty and was disqualified to serve on the jury. To a man, the others on the jury all swore they could set aside their prejudices and dismiss from their minds what they had either read or heard about the case that was about to be tried and they could deliver a fair and impartial verdict based on the law and the evidence. Candle wondered if they each could actually do so, but he had no way of finding out if they could. He would just have to take their sworn word for it, whatever that was worth.

Candle turned and studied his client. He struck Candle as being calm, relieved even. "Dewey," he said, "I don't know what to tell you about the jury. I know most of them. The three or four I don't, I got some information on. I guess we got about as good a draw as we could expect. Whether they'll live up to their oath, I couldn't tell you."

"Yes, sir," Dewey said.

"I mean, everybody in the county knows a little something about the case. And everybody knows the Mayfields. A lot of people are indebted to them."

"All right, Mr. Solicitor," Candle heard Judge Pryde say from the bench, "you may publish the indictment."

Indictment in hand, Solicitor Fleming took a sip of water and stepped toward the petit jury box a few feet to his right. About midway, he stopped. Looking up at the judge, he said in a serious tone, "May it please the Court."

Judge Pryde responded with a nod.

Fleming turned and walked to the end of the jury box, waiting until he had the attention of all twelve of the jurors and the two alternates. "Mr. Foreman and gentlemen of the jury, please listen as I read to you the indictment returned by the Semmes County Grand Jury against the defendant Dewey Fletcher Coltraine." He turned toward Candle and Dewey. "Mr. Reid, would you have your client stand right there at the table, please, sir, while I publish the indictment?"

Candle nudged Dewey with his left elbow and both men stood.

"Thank you, sir." Fleming again faced the jurors. Each one wore a suit and sported a tie. "Mr. Foreman. Gentlemen of the jury, look upon the prisoner at the bar. Prisoner at the bar, look upon the jury."

Glancing at Dewey, he said, "If you answer by the name of Dewey Coltraine, raise your right hand."

Dewey began raising his hand, but before he could get it all the way up Fleming said, "Put it down." Dewey complied.

Fleming unfolded the indictment and, using a very grave tone, began publishing it to the court and the jury. When he finished, Fleming looked at Dewey. "How say you, prisoner at the bar, are you guilty of this felony for which you stand indicted or not guilty?"

Dewey opened his mouth to speak, but Candle spoke first. "He pleads not guilty, Mr. Solicitor."

"Is he ready for trial?"

"He is," Candle answered. He spoke with a loud voice, a voice that did not shake.

Fleming nodded. "Then, may God give him due deliverance," Fleming said. He refolded the indictment, laid it on the clerk of court's desk, and walked to his table where he continued to stand. He turned toward the audience seated beyond the bar. "If it please the Court, the State calls as its first witness Dr. Luke Koutrakos. Would you come around and be sworn, please sir?"

A handsome, olive-skin man, a file folder in his hands, rose from his seat on the first row and, brushing back thinning, dark-black hair, came forward. After the clerk of court administered the oath, he stepped up onto the witness stand and sat down, resting one leg over the other. He smiled at Judge Pryde, who smiled back and whispered something to him.

"Dr. Koutrakos, you practice medicine here in Tekoa, sir?" Solicitor Fleming began.

"That's right. Just since the war."

Fleming had Dr. Koutrakos recite his qualifications to the court.

"You are licensed to practice, I take it, sir?"

Koutrakos smiled. "Oh, yes, indeed."

Fleming moved from behind his table and stood to the rear of the jury box, making Koutrakos turn and face all the jurors as he testified. "While you were in the Army Medical Corps, did you ever treat battle casualties such as gunshot wounds?"

"I couldn't begin to tell you how many."

"Doctor, did you know Lester Mayfield, Jr., a war veteran like yourself?"

"Yes, I knew him. I once played golf with him and with his father."

"Tell us this, sir. Did you see him on November 22, 1946?"

"Max Jordan called my office around six o'clock that evening and asked that I come to his funeral home. He said the coroner wanted me to look at a body. I went and that's when I saw the body of Lester Mayfield, Jr."

"Did you examine Mr. Mayfield's body, sir?"

"I did," Koutrakos replied. "I went to Jordan and Son Funeral Home and examined it there."

Dr. Koutrakos opened a file folder that lay in his lap as Fleming returned to his counsel table and picked up a black notebook filled with several pages. Fleming opened the notebook and ran his finger down the first page. "Dr. Koutrakos, would you please tell the court and the jury what your examination showed?"

Koutrakos lifted a paper from inside the folder, read it over, and returned it to the file. "I found—"

"Excuse me, Doctor, Mr. Solicitor, Your Honor, sir," Candle said, standing and interrupting the solicitor's direct-examination, "but what was that you just read?"

Koutrakos again withdrew a paper from the file and held up it for all to see. "This is a carbon copy of a letter I sent to Solicitor Fleming. It contains a brief summary of the autopsy report I'd prepared for the coroner."

"So, that's not the autopsy report itself?" Candle asked, uncertain of where he was headed with his inquiry and of whether he should object to the doctor's testimony on the ground that the summary was not the best evidence.

"No, sir. I sent that to the coroner." Dr. Koutrakos turned toward the solicitor, a helpless look on his face. "I'm sorry, should I have kept a copy of that too? I'm kind of new at this sort of thing."

Solicitor Fleming looked at Candle, his eyebrows arched. "If the court please, I don't quite understand Mr. Reid's problem," he drawled. "Right after you appointed Mr. Reid to represent the defendant, I gave him complete access to my file. The original of the doctor's letter was in the file then. As for the autopsy report, I believe the coroner filed it with the clerk of court shortly after the inquest. Is that not right, Mr. Honeycutt?"

Jimmy Honeycutt, the clerk of court stood, and faced the bench, nodding all the while. "That's right, Your Honor. Mr. Reid could have asked me for—"

Candle, still standing, shook his head. "Your Honor, we don't have any objection if all the doctor's going to use the summary for is to refresh his memory," he blurted out before Judge Pryde could say anything. "We just don't want it in evidence. It's not the—"

Solicitor Fleming interrupted. "Your Honor," he said, using a condescending tone, "we have absolutely no intention of introducing the summary in evidence."

"There you are, Mr. Reid. Satisfied? Now take a seat and do it quick," Judge Pryde barked. "You're wasting everybody's time."

Solicitor Fleming continued. "You were telling us, Doctor, what you found when you examined Mr. Mayfield's body."

Koutrakos removed another paper from the file and held it out toward Solicitor Fleming. From where Candle sat, the paper appeared to be a sketch of some kind. "I found two wounds on the right side of Mr. Mayfield's head," Koutrakos said, pointing to the paper.

"What part of the head are we talking about, Doctor?"

"The temple area and just above it. Right here and here," Dr. Koutrakos said, indicating with his free hand. "Only one wound—one shot—pierced the skull. The other one glanced off the skull and went beneath the skin. I removed a flattened piece of shot from between the skull and the scalp when I folded the scalp back."

"How about the other one? Did you recover it?"

"No, sir. It had penetrated the brain and was deep inside the cranium. I didn't try to get it because I didn't want to bother with removing the scalp."

"Was that shot, sir—the one you didn't take out—sufficient in and of itself to cause death?"

"Yes, it was."

"Doctor, what in your opinion caused the death of Lester Mayfield, Jr.?"

"The shot that penetrated his skull and lodged in his brain."

"What did you do with the piece you took from his head?"

"Same thing that I did with the autopsy report. Gave it to the coroner."

"You don't have it with you, then?"

"No, sir. The coroner has it. Least he did."

"Thank you, Doctor. Please, sir, answer any questions Mr. Reid may have for you."

Fleming sat down and poured himself a glass of water as Candle heaved himself up from his chair to begin his cross-examination.

"Dr. Koutrakos, what's that you're holding in your hand?" Candle asked as he walked toward the witness.

Koutrakos glanced downward. "Oh, this?" he said, holding the paper up for Candle to see. "It's just a rough, free-hand drawing for me to use here at trial to approximate the placement of the two head wounds. I prepared it from the autopsy report—that's got a more accurate drawing in it, if you want me to get it and show it to you."

From behind him, Candle heard footsteps. It was Solicitor Fleming walking toward him. "If Your Honor please, if Mr. Reid wants us to introduce the autopsy report, we'll be happy to get it for him and put it in evidence. We've nothing to hide."

"What about it, Mr. Reid?" Judge Pryde groused. "You want the autopsy report in or out? Your call. But if it comes in, it goes to the jury. What do you want me to do?"

Candle stood for a moment, a hand grasping the back of his neck. He did not want the autopsy report in evidence, not with all its gory detail and technical language. The medical evidence was bad enough for Dewey as it was, plus he had no reason to question the cause of death: Mayfield had died from a shotgun wound to the head, pure and simple. "Your Honor, I just want to look at the doctor's drawing a second or two. That's all."

Judge Pryde sighed, waving his hand. "Go on ahead and do it. But if you want the autopsy report in evidence, just say so and I'll make the solicitor put it in."

"Yes, sir. I mean, no sir. Like I said—"

Judge Pryde suddenly shot forward, a sneer on his face. "And while we're at it, Counsel, if you want them to get that metal piece they took out of Mr. Mayfield's head, I'll even make them get that for you too. I want to accommodate you in every way I can." He turned toward the jury and smiled.

Candle gulped. He certainly did not want the piece of flattened shot in evidence. He could think of nothing more prejudicial and inflammatory.

Judge Pryde leaned over the bench. "Mr. Honeycutt?"

Honeycutt leaped up. "Yes, sir?"

"Have somebody go get the autopsy report and that other thing. We might need them," Judge Pryde said, looking straight at Candle.

Honeycutt reached into a lower drawer of his desk. "I have them right here, Your Honor, with all the inquest material." Honeycutt held a document with a blue cover at waist-level while holding a small opaque bottle aloft. "I kinda figured we might need the coroner's file before all was said and done."

Candle notice several jurors straining their necks to get, what he assumed to be, a better look at the bottle, which Honeycutt had now begun to shake and rattle.

"Good," Judge Pryde fumed. "If Mr. Reid mentions the autopsy report just one more time, I'm going to have everything introduced as a court's exhibit and I mean everything."

Koutrakos handed Candle the drawing, which Candle studied for a moment before giving it back and walking over to his counsel table. He removed from a file folder a page from a legal pad on which he had made some handwritten notes. "I notice, Doctor," Candle said, looking down at his notes, "your drawing does not show some other wounds which, according to my notes, your letter to Solicitor Fleming said was on Lester Junior's face and on his neck and head and other parts of his body. Why's that?"

Before Koutrakos could respond to Candle's question, Judge Pryde interrupted. "What's this? Are you talking about the autopsy report again, Mr. Reid?"

"No, Your Honor," Candle replied, sensing he might have opened a door that he could not close. "I just want to ask the doctor about some things he mentioned in his letter to Solicitor Fleming. I'm not asking anything about the autopsy report."

"You're this close to getting it in, Mr. Reid," Judge Pryde said, his hand stretched toward Candle, his thumb and index finger almost touching. "Understand?"

"Yes, sir. Thank you, Your Honor," Candle said. He repeated his question to the witness. "Why's that?"

"Why's what?" Koutrakos asked.

"Why doesn't your drawing show those other wounds?"

"I suppose I didn't think them to be significant. They did not appear to be fresh wounds, like the ones on the right side of his head did. I guessed them to be a few days old. They certainly were not fatal wounds."

"How many of them were on him and where were they exactly?"

"Goodness, I don't know—"

"A lot of them?"

"A good many. But, like I say, they weren't significant—"

"Where were they located?"

"I'm speaking mainly from memory now. I don't even think the autopsy report details their exact locations. I only spoke of them in general, both in my summary and in the autopsy report. So, I could be a little off."

Fleming rose from his seat. "Your Honor, I must object to any speculation. He can't—"

Judge Pryde did not wait for the solicitor to finish stating his ground of objection. "Overruled," he said. "Continue, Doctor."

"Like I say, I might be a little off. But as I recall, there were marks—minor cuts, really—on his hands, his arms, his chest, some on top of his head, his face and neck. Some on his back, I think. There were some bruises also."

"Could these 'cuts,' as you call them, have been caused by being shot with a shotgun?"

"Not hardly."

"What could have caused them?"

Fleming sprang to his feet and faced the jury. "If the court please, I don't know where counsel is going with this cross-examination. He's asking the doctor to speculate on where these cuts came from. Also, I don't see how they're even relevant. If I had thought they were, I'd brought them out myself."

Judge Pryde motioned to Candle, twirling his finger in the air. "Mr. Reid, how are they relevant? Is it your position that the defendant acted in self-defense or something?"

"No, sir. That's not our defense." Candle looked around at Dewey.

"Then, sir, what in the world are you attempting to prove by this? I mean, we're talking about some old wounds, not new ones."

Candle found himself unable to speak. Fleming's objection, which he had not anticipated, had unnerved him as did the tone of the judge's voice. Candle's mind had gone blank. "Well, Your Honor. Uh, uh, I think. I mean, it—"

Judge Pryde cut him off. "Oh, go ahead," he said with a frown and a wave of the hand. "Your objection is overruled, Solicitor." He settled back into his chair, mumbling something Candle could not understand.

Candle, relieved at being rescued, resumed his cross-examination. "Excuse me, Doctor. I forgot what I was asking you about."

"You wanted to know what could have caused these cuts," the doctor said, his tone somewhat sarcastic.

Candle glimpsed the jury, his face suddenly warm. "Yes, sir. Right. Do you have an opinion?"

"It appears to me he'd been in a scuffle of some kind. The wounds were consistent with having been made by fingernails—in other words, scratch marks."

"A woman's?"

"I couldn't say. Both sexes have them, you know."

The whole of the courtroom erupted in laughter.

"You asked for that one, Mr. Reid," Judge Pryde observed, chuckling and provoking more laughter, laughter that he made no attempt to stop.

Candle felt mortified. Not only did the witness's response embarrass Candle, it drowned the point he had attempted to make in waves of hilarity.

Bowing his head and rolling his tongue against his cheek, Candle retreated to his counsel table and waited for the laughter to subside.

"Thank you, Dr. Koutrakos," he muttered when all became quiet. "That's all I have."

As Candle seated himself, Judge Pryde asked the solicitor if he had any additional questions. Fleming said he did not and called his next witness, the sheriff, Bowden "Bo" Madison. The sheriff, who had been sitting in the end seat of the grand jury box, hotfooted it to the witness stand. He placed one hand on the Bible, raised his other hand, and swore an oath to tell the truth.

"Sheriff," Solicitor Fleming began, "let me direct your attention to Friday, November 22, 1946."

The sheriff nodded, turned toward the jury, and smiled. Most jurors smiled back.

"Did you, sir, have occasion to be in the Harpers' Joy community of Semmes County on official business?"

"Yes, sir. I did."

"Would you tell us about that, please sir?"

The sheriff recounted the events leading to his arrival at the crime scene.

"And what did you find when you got there, sir?"

"When we got there, we saw a '39 Chevy truck—actually it was one of them canopy vans. Belonged to Swizzle-Kola, come to find out. It and a car—a new Packard—they were parked out in fronta what they call a foldin' house. It's a—you know—a kinda trailer that folds out like and makes—"

"Did you see anyone?"

"Yes, sir. The defendant yonder," the sheriff said, nodding. "And Mr. Mayfield."

"When you say 'Mr. Mayfield,' do you mean Lester Mayfield, Jr.?"

"Yes, sir. Him."

"Where was he, sir?"

"Sorta to the fronta the Packard, left side there, on the ground, little bit in the road or drive or whatever you call it. He was layin' flat on his back, his legs kinda folded underneath him like."

"And the defendant, sir?"

"Standin' at the door of the foldin' house."

"What else, sir, did you see right then?"

"I noticed that the car—the front right side of it, the side closest to the foldin' house—had been shot up pretty good. Its front tire had done gone flat as a pancake."

"Other than the defendant and Mr. Mayfield, you saw no one else there at the time?"

"Not outside, I didn't."

"When you and your deputy arrived at the scene, what was the condition of Lester Mayfield, Jr.? Was he alive or dead?"

"Dead."

"You looked at him, sir?"

"Yes, sir. Me and Ezell, my deputy, both did."

"What, if anything else, sir, did you find outside?"

"A shotgun. A Daly. Twelve-gauge."

Fleming reached beneath his counsel table and picked up a long, narrow article wrapped in brown paper. He handed it to the sheriff who tore away the wrapping, exposing a shotgun. The sheriff broke the shotgun apart, peered into the breech and down both its barrels, and locked it back in place. "It's empty," he said.

"Can you identify this shotgun for us, Sheriff?"

"Yes, sir. That's the one me and Ezell found out in fronta the trailer. Out in the yard there."

Fleming took the shotgun from Madison and turned and walked toward the defense table. "Your Honor," he said, speaking as he walked, "we offer the shotgun in evidence." He stopped and held the shotgun out to Candle, who had stood as Fleming approached his table.

Before the judge could ask Candle for his position regarding the solicitor's proffer, Candle announced the defense had no objection to the shotgun being marked as an exhibit in the case.

Fleming walked to the court reporter's table and held the shotgun as the court reporter placed on its stock a red sticker that identified the shotgun as State's Exhibit Number One. Afterward, Fleming laid the shotgun on top of the dark oak divider that ran along the front of the jury box. Several jurors stretched forward to view the shotgun.

Fleming again reached beneath his counsel table, this time retrieving a smaller package. As he had done with the shotgun, he handed the package to the sheriff, allowing him to open it. "And what's that you're holding, Sheriff?" he asked.

Madison held two small cylinders up where all could see. "Two empty shotgun shells. Winchester. Number Four shot. I personally removed them from the Daly. See? This is my mark right there, on this one and on this one," he said, pointing.

Fleming turned and faced Candle. "Any objection, Mr. Reid?"

"No, sir."

"Your Honor, we offer these into evidence as State's Exhibit Numbers Two and Three."

"Without objection," Judge Pryde said.

Once the court reporter had marked the shell casings, Fleming placed them on the divider, next to the stock of the shotgun. One juror reached and picked them up, examined each one, and handed them to the juror seated to his right. The juror in turn passed the shells to the juror seated next to him.

Fleming waited until each juror had an opportunity to inspect the shell casing before he resumed his examination of the sheriff. "Now, Sheriff, you indicated the defendant was standing there at the door to the trailer. Did he do or say anything when you and the deputy got there, sir?"

Sheriff Madison related that Dewey had peacefully surrendered and that Nellie Coltraine had been taken to the hospital due to some sort of nervous disorder.

The solicitor next inquired of Sheriff Madison about whether Dewey had given him a signed, written statement. The sheriff acknowledged Dewey had done so and, withdrawing the statement from a file folder that he carried, identified it. Without objection from Candle, the court allowed Dewey's written confession in evidence. After the court reporter marked the statement as a State's exhibit, Solicitor Fleming directed the sheriff to publish the statement to the jury.

When Madison finished reading Dewey's confession, Solicitor Fleming announced he had no further questions. Before returning to his counsel table, Fleming took Dewey's written statement from the sheriff and gave it to the foreman of the jury.

Candle, his left hand concealed in the pocket of his coat, rose from his chair to begin his cross-examination of the sheriff; but before he began, he walked over to the jury box and retrieved Dewey's confession from the foreman. The foreman, who had begun to read the statement, did not appear happy to give it up.

Candle stationed himself between the witness stand and the jury box. "Sheriff," he said, hitching his britches with the hand that held Dewey's signed, written confession, "there's something I want you to read one more time to the jury, if you don't mind, please sir." He gave the statement to the sheriff and placed his finger below one line on the page. "Start reading from right there. Read it out loud for me."

The sheriff lifted the paper, holding it toward the light that shone through the windows above and behind the jurors. "It says, 'I come home from work. It was night when I got home. I had to load the truck and all and check up. When I got home, I didn't see a light on in the foldin' house. At first, I thought maybe Nellie had gone off some place. But I knew that wasn't like her. Besides, she wouldn't have no way to go, except to walk. I come in the house and called out for her but didn't get an answer. I went in the bedroom. It was all tore up and there was blood all over the bed there. Then I thought I heard somethin' in the bathroom. I looked in there and that's when I spied Nellie. She was sittin' in the shower stall and didn't have any clothes on. I turned on the lights so I could see better and that's when I saw she had scratches on her and bruises. There was blood on the floor. I asked her what'd happened, and she wouldn't tell me nothin'. I told her we ought to call the sheriff, but she wouldn't let me.' "

Madison paused to clear his throat. Fleming offered him some water, but he declined it.

" 'The next day Mr. Mayfield come and that's when I learned he had forced himself on Nellie. He warned us both not to say nothin' 'bout what he had done to her. He then hit me in the stomach real hard and told me he wanted us to move out of his foldin' house too. Sometime after he left, Nellie made me go on to work. She wouldn't let me go call the sheriff, so I didn't. Later on that week, I went downtown and borrowed a van from Mr. Hammond at the Swizzle-

Kola Bottlin' Company. I happen to see Mr. Mayfield drivin' toward his place up at Harpers' Joy. I followed him out there. He got out there way 'head of me. When I got there, I saw he was out in fronta the foldin' house, standin' by his car. Nellie, she was outside. He was yellin' somethin' other at her. I thought he'd come back to hurt her again, like he did that other time when I wasn't there, when I was out on my route. After I got outta the truck I was in, I run in the house and got the shotgun and come back outside where I shot his car up to try to make him stop botherin' Nellie and leave her alone. That didn't make him quit, though. He kept right on. That's how come I shot him.' "

The sheriff laid the statement onto his lap and waited for Candle's next question.

Candle went back to his counsel table and reviewed his notes. He returned to where he had been standing. "Did you get a good look at Mrs. Coltraine—Nellie Coltraine. Did you get a good look at her?"

Madison shifted around in his seat. "Well, yeah. I reckon. I looked at her."

"Did you see bruises and scratches about her arms?"

Madsion nodded. "On her hands too."

"How about on Mayfield, see any?"

"Any what?"

"Scratches. Bruises. Cuts."

Madison did not answer right back. He crossed one leg over the other, clutching the shin of the top leg. "Tell you the truth, Mr. Reid, I didn't look all that close at him. My main concern was securing the scene and the evidence there." He dropped his right leg to the floor. "And if you'll look there in Dr. Koutrakos' report—and I thought you mentioned this when you were questionin' him a while ago—somethin' is said 'bout the scratches and all bein' on Mayfield's face and other places."

Candle turned to go back to his counsel table. When he looked at Dewey, his expression startled him. Dewey appeared disinterested in the sheriff's testimony. Candle turned around and faced Madison once more. "One other thing, Sheriff. Did you see anybody else up there at Mayfield's place?"

"Not when we first got there, we didn't. After the coroner come, Ezell rode down to the cabin Mr. Mayfield had there by the pond. He found Mrs. Mayfield. She was down there. She told him she had run up the road and had seen Coltraine—"

Candle held up his hand much like a traffic cop ordering a motorist to stop. "Just a minute, Sheriff. You're about to say something I didn't ask you about."

Sheriff Madison smiled and nodded. "I'm sorry."

"Other than Mrs. Mayfield, did y'all see anybody else there?"

"Huh-uh, we didn't."

Candle stood for a moment, thinking if he had any other questions for the sheriff. He decided he didn't. "I guess that's all, Sheriff. Thank you." He came back to the defense table and squatted down beside Dewey. "Anything you want me to ask the sheriff, Dewey?"

"No, sir," Dewey said, shaking his head. "I can't think of nothin'."

The solicitor started up from his chair, but before he could say anything Candle asked the judge if he could put one more question to the sheriff. Solicitor Fleming sat back down, and Candle, without waiting for the judge to respond, asked the sheriff whether he had noticed any bruises, scratches, or cuts on Dewey.

Sheriff Madison shook his head. "No, I didn't. But then I didn't look for any, Mr. Reid."

Candle came from behind his table and walked over toward the jury box. "You didn't look for scratches and cuts and bruises on Dewey here. Is that what you said?"

"Mr. Reid, I was investigatin' a murder and I got a statement from the person who told me he was the one done it." For the first time, Sheriff Madison sounded irritated with Candle. "What did I need to look for scratches on him for?"

"You saw scratches and bruises and so forth on the defendant's wife, right?"

"Yes, sir."

"You saw scratches and so forth on Mr. Mayfield, right?"

"I didn't say that. The doctor did," the sheriff responded. He glanced at the jury, appearing pleased with his response. One of the jurors, a snaggle-tooth, red-haired man on an end seat of the second row, beamed at the sheriff and elbowed the juror to his right.

"These scratches and bruises on the defendant's wife, do you know where they came from?"

"No, sir. I don't."

"Could they have been caused by Mayfield?"

Solicitor Fleming stood, scraping his chair against the floor as he did so. "Objection, Your Honor."

"Sustained," Judge Pryde said with a tired tone.

The judge's ruling did not bother Candle. He felt he had made his point. At least, he hoped he had.

***

After a brief recess, the trial resumed when Solicitor Fleming called to the witness stand Georgia Ann Hascall Mayfield. The large woman, her hair cut short and curled in tight ringlets against her head, lifted herself from a front-row seat and made her way to the clerk's table. After being sworn, she squeezed herself into the chair on the witness stand.

Georgia Ann began to sob and shake as soon as she sat down. The tears seemed real enough to Candle, but he couldn't be sure.

Fleming, his lips together and one hand atop the other, stood behind his counsel table, staring at Georgia Ann with what Candle surmised was feigned sympathy. He let her cry for a while before he asked if she felt like going forward. "I'm sorry, Mr. Fleming," she said, wiping her eyes and twisting her handkerchief. "I tried not to do this. I really did. Please ask me your questions."

"Before directing your attention to that awful day up in Harpers' Joy, Mrs. Mayfield, would you tell the jury something of your background, your marriage to Lester Mayfield, Jr.?"

"Yes, sir. My daddy is Robert William Hascall. He's the city judge here in Tekoa. We're originally from Georgia. Hence my name," she said, sniffling. Mrs. Mayfield went on to tell about her education and how she met and married Lester Mayfield, Jr.

"He served in the Pacific during the last war, I believe?" Solicitor Fleming asked.

"Yes. He was very proud of that."

"Tell me this, Mrs. Mayfield, and I don't mean to pry," Fleming said, turning toward the jury, "but was your husband a good husband?"

"Yes, he was," Georgia Ann said, ducking her head. "However, I wouldn't want to create the impression that all was sweetness and light, Solicitor. No, it was not like that. Like most married couples, we had our little spats. We sometimes would—"

"Spats?" Fleming approached the witness stand. "What do you mean by the term 'spats'?"

Georgia Ann dropped an arm into her lap and directed her eyes downward. "You know, spats. Yelling and carrying on—quarreling. Maybe slapping at each other. Calling each other names. You know. I blame the war. He was different when he came back." She raised her head and searched the faces of the jurors. "I think the war changed a lot of people. Unlike before the war, he was nervous, high strung. He was different," she said. "And he drank more than he should, and that made him—" The tears started again, this time gushing.

Fleming walked to the clerk of court's desk and picked up a water pitcher. He filled a clean glass with the water and handed it to Georgia Ann. Before asking another question, he waited until she had finished, returned the glass, and dried her eyes. "Mrs. Mayfield, there was some mention earlier by Dr. Koutrakos that your husband had some scratches on him. Some were on his arms, some on his head, his face. Maybe elsewhere, I forget at the moment. You know anything about that?" he asked.

"Yes, sir. We had a spat, and I put them there," Georgia Ann said, her head held low.

"You put them there, you say?" Fleming repeated.

Georgia Ann nodded. "Uh-huh."

"When did this happen?"

"Three or four days before he was murdered by that little man over there."

"I see."

"I got extremely upset with him," Georgia Ann said, her voice choking. "I think we both had had too much to drink that night and . . ." She stopped to wipe her eyes and ask for another glass of water, which the solicitor hurried to get for her. She took a sip and handed the glass back to the solicitor. "After he came home that night, we had some words and then—all of this is so embarrassing now. We—I didn't know one day I'd—"

"I think we get the picture, Mrs. Mayfield." Fleming turned to the jury and nodded at them. Several jurors nodded back. They all looked toward the floor. Fleming moved to the end of the jury box. "Where were you on the afternoon of November 22, 1946? That's the day this thing happened."

"I was at our little place there in Harpers' Joy."

"Why were you there?"

"I was waiting on my husband."

"What did you do while you were waiting?"

"Oh, nothing really. It was a pretty day. Warm and sunny out. Felt like spring. I walked out to the pond. Sat down under a tree and read some."

"Did you stay outside the whole time?"

"Yes."

"Did something unusual happen while you were outside?"

"Yes, but I'm not sure about the time. I think it was around three-thirty. I thought I heard something that sounded like a gun shot. Then a little bit later I heard another one. So I decided to go see what was going on. I thought the sound came from up near the highway, near the folding house trailer. I thought at first it could have been some hunters, and I knew my husband wouldn't approve of someone hunting on our property. When I walked up the drive and got close to where the caretaker's house was, that's when I saw that man right there." She pointed to Dewey. "And my husband. The man, he—"

"Where was your husband, Mrs. Mayfield?"

"On the ground. Lying on the ground, near the front of his car."

"And the defendant—the man you just pointed to—where was he?"

"Closer to the folding house, twenty or thirty feet away, if I had to guess. When I first saw him, he had a shotgun in his hand. He then threw it on the ground and bent down over this girl who was lying there. I must have screamed or something because he turned and looked my way. He had this real mean look on his face. I was petrified, I was frightened so."

"How far is the pond and the cabin from the caretaker's house, please ma'am?"

"Half mile maybe? Quarter of a mile? I don't know. Seemed like a hundred to me," Georgia Ann said, fanning herself with her hand.

"You say the defendant had a shotgun in his hands and he had a mean look on his face?"

"Yes, sir. And I thought he was—"

"Did you say anything to him at all, ma'am?" Fleming took a few steps forward and faced the jury.

"I said, 'You've killed my husband' or something like that. I might've said 'You've killed Lester.'"

Fleming leaned into the jury box. "You accused the defendant of killing your husband?"

"Why, yes, I did. I mean, he was holding a shotgun. And there wasn't anybody else around, except this girl who was lying there on the ground—and of course my husband."

Fleming turned and faced Georgia Ann. "When you accused the defendant of killing your husband, did he deny it?"

Candle stood to object to the solicitor's question on the ground of hearsay, but then sat back down as he suddenly remembered the rule of "probative silence." That rule held that a failure to deny an accusation could constitute an implied admission if it could be reasonably expected that a person in the accused's position would protest the statement as untrue. Candle felt the rule certainly applied here.

Georgia Ann twiddled with a button on her blood-red jacket before she answered Fleming. "No, he didn't."

"Did he threaten you in any way?"

"Well, I guess not. He just picked the woman up and took her into the folding house. After a few minutes, he came back out. I was trying to help my husband right then, although I could tell he was already dead. I mean, all you had to do was to look at him and see that. I had blood, my husband's blood on my—"

"What happened after he came back outside, please ma'am?"

"He scared me to death. I thought for a moment he was coming back to kill me too. He said he wasn't going to, but I couldn't be sure. You know, I was a witness. I told him somebody had better go report what had happened to the sheriff. Surprisingly, he said he'd do it, and then he got in his truck and left."

Georgia Ann shifted around in her chair. "I stayed with Lester a little bit longer; and then since there was nothing I could do for him, I thought maybe it'd be safer for me to go back down to where my car was and wait down there." She looked at the jury and began crying again. "I mean, he was dead. And I didn't know right then if the man might change his mind or not about letting me live. I might should've gone on and left from there and tried to find somebody myself, but I was just too nervous and scared to drive right then or to even think straight. I tell you, I was just shaking all over—sort of like I am right now. See my hand?" Georgia Ann held a shaking hand, lighted with diamond rings, out toward the jurors. Several jurors nodded and frowned.

"So, I stayed down there in my car with my doors locked for I don't know how long until—thank the good Jesus—this deputy came. I can't tell you how happy I was to see him. I was just so afraid and so upset about Lester. I couldn't stop crying. And his blood, it was on—"

"Thank you, Mrs. Mayfield." Fleming nodded and bowed to the witness. "I know this has been an awful strain on you, forcing you to relive that terrible, terrible afternoon and testify about intimate details of your marriage. I hope you will forgive me. Please answer any questions Mr. Reid might have for you."

"Yes, sir," she said, her voice catching. "I'll try to."

Georgia Ann dabbed at her eyes with a handkerchief as she waited for Candle to stand and begin his cross-examination.

Candle felt reluctant to cross-examine Georgia Ann even though he did not believe she put the scratches on her husband's face. His notes of their conversation that he had made when she last visited his office indicated as much. The jurors' solemn faces and the downward gaze of their eyes, however, suggested to Candle that they very much sympathized with Georgia Ann. Still, he needed Georgia Ann to paint for the jurors a picture of the brutality of which Lester

Junior was capable, especially when liquored up. The encounters between Georgia Ann and her husband sometimes went way beyond being mere "spats." Candle knew this of his own knowledge for he remembered the bruised, swollen face that his notes spoke about.

Candle stood and pulled from a file folder the yellow sheet that held the notes of his conversation with Georgia Ann five months before. After his appointment to serve as Dewey's counsel, he had placed them in Dewey's file since they concerned Lester Junior and how he looked on November 18, 1946, just days before he was killed. Candle glanced over them. He didn't know if it was proper for him to use the notes or not—since the information reflected on the sheet came during a confidential consultation—but he was going to make use of the information anyway. Why should ethics get into the way of truth?

"Mrs. Mayfield, would you describe the fight you and your husband had that produced these scratches we've heard about?"

"It was just a little one. I wouldn't call it a 'fight.' "

"Did he hit you?"

"He might have. I don't remember."

"Did he knock you unconscious?"

Fleming yelled out an objection. "Your Honor, this is not a domestic relations case. I think counsel should be reminded that the defendant in this case is Dewey Coltraine, not Lester Mayfield, Jr. What Lester Junior did or didn't do in the privacy of his home has nothing whatever to do with this case. Absolutely nothing."

Judge Pryde shook his head and pointed the handle of his gavel at Candle. "I will not, Mr. Reid, allow you to pursue this any further unless you can connect it up somehow with what happened on the twenty-second of November last year. Objection sustained."

The judge's ruling surprised Candle. "Your Honor, I thought the solicitor opened the door for me to ask about their fight when he asked her about the scratches on the deceased's body?" Candle deliberately chose the last two words. His former law partner had once told him that in the trial of a murder case a good defense lawyer should attempt to depersonalize the victim by avoiding the use of the victim's name.

"Well, you thought wrong, Mr. Reid. Now, continue with your examination."

Candle glanced down at the yellow sheet. "We know what injuries your husband had, Mrs. Mayfield. Didn't he bruise your thigh and your jaw that night?"

Again, Fleming objected as Georgia Ann made a face that registered amazement.

"Sustained," the judge responded, shaking his head and frowning. "Mr. Reid, I must not have made things clear to you, sir."

"We talked about Mr. Mayfield's injuries. Can't I ask her about hers?"

"Mr. Reid, no you cannot," Judge Pryde barked. "The solicitor limited his inquiry to the injuries found on Mr. Mayfield and how they might have gotten there. That's a rabbit, sir, that you let loose in here when the doctor testified. I'm not going to permit you to let another rabbit loose. One's enough. So, let's be clear about this, okay? In the exercise of my discretion, I will not allow you to go into any other details about any argument or spat the Mayfields might have had. Are we clear about this now?"

Candle nodded his understanding while glancing again at the notes of his conversation with Georgia Ann, particularly the entry that read, "comes home, scratches on his face, neck, head, hands, drinking." Candle swallowed a breath of air. "Your Honor, couldn't I just ask her—please sir—about what caused this spat during which she says she put the scratches on her husband?"

Judge Pryde folded his arms and leaned forward. "You're pushing things, Mr. Reid."

"All right, Your Honor. Thank you. I'll go to something else. Mrs. Mayfield, you weren't really afraid of Dewey that day, were you?"

"I certainly was. I was scared to death of him."

"Yet, you didn't leave. You stayed there at your place until the sheriff came."

"Is that a question, Mr. Reid?" Judge Pryde asked.

"After Dewey left to go get the sheriff, did you pick up the shotgun and hide it?"

"Of course not."

"Was that because you weren't afraid of Dewey Coltraine, Mrs. Mayfield?"

"I wasn't thinking straight. Yes, I was afraid of him. I still am. Anybody'd do what he did is liable to do just about anything."

Candle did not like her last remark. He saw two jurors nod in apparent agreement. He figured he had best sit down. Already, he sensed his "some-folks-just-needed-killing defense" was going nowhere. "That's all I have, Your Honor."

The judge, staring at Candle and making no attempt to hide his displeasure, shook his head. He turned to Georgia Ann. "Thank you, Mrs. Mayfield. You may stand down."

Georgia Ann whispered a thank-you and wiped her eyes.

Solicitor Fleming helped Georgia Ann from the witness stand and escorted her to the bar, kissing her on the cheek when they reached the gate. After she sat down, Fleming returned to his counsel table and picked up the indictment. "Your Honor," he said, turning the indictment over, "that's the State's case."

Judge Pryde, with both his elbows resting on the bench, looked toward Candle. "I suppose you have a motion to make, don't you Mr. Reid?"

Candle stood. "Yes, sir."

"I thought so," Judge Pryde said, his tone disrespectful. "Mr. Foreman and gentlemen, I'll have to ask you to go to your jury room. It won't be but for a minute or two, so if you light up be ready to put it out pronto."

When the last juror disappeared through the door, Candle rose from his chair. He opened his mouth to speak, but before he could do so Judge Pryde addressed him. "I suppose, Mr. Reid, you want me to direct a verdict of not guilty of murder, is that it?" Judge Pryde's voice sounded tired.

Candle again started to speak.

"That motion is denied. Are you ready to go forward with your defense?"

Candle turned toward his client, who sat staring into his lap and rolling his thumbs. "I guess so. Yes, sir."

"How many witnesses do you have, Mr. Reid? I'd like to know what to expect so I can plan what to do today."

"I think maybe just two, Your Honor."

"All right. Two witnesses." Judge Pryde stood and banged his gavel against the top of his desk. "Let's take five minutes."

***

The recess concluded, Judge Pryde signaled the bailiff. "Bring the jury back."

Candle watched the jurors reclaim their seats. He never understood why each juror insisted on taking the same chair that he took when he was first seated. Candle got up from his chair ready to launch his proof that Lester Mayfield, Jr. was one of those folks who just needed killing. "If it please the court, the defense calls as its first witness, Mr. Troy Hammond."

Candle spun around and surveyed the audience, looking for the bottling company owner. "Mr. Hammond, would you come around, please sir?"

Hammond, his blue eyes directed toward Candle, his face grim, came forward to be sworn. He raised his hand only halfway when he took the oath.

"Mr. Hammond," Candle began, "you're the owner-manager of the Swizzle-Kola Bottling Company?"

"I was, yes, sir."

"What do you mean by 'I was'?"

"The plant's closed."

Candle grimaced. "I'm sorry. I truly am. I didn't know."

"That's okay. It happened long after we talked."

"Did the defendant Dewey Coltraine work for you at one time?"

"Yes, sir. As a route salesman."

"How long did he work for you?"

"Oh, not long. Couple of months, maybe."

"Why did he leave?"

"I let him go."

"Let him go?"

"Yes, sir."

"Why was that?"

From behind him, Candle heard a chair grate against the floor. "Objection, Your Honor. I don't think that's relevant at all," Fleming said.

"Overruled, Mr. Solicitor," the judge said. "Go ahead, Mr. Reid." Candle gestured for the witness to continue.

"Why'd I let him go?" Hammond said. "Because Lester Mayfield told me to fire him, that's why."

"Which Lester Mayfield, Senior or Junior?

"Junior."

"Why did Lester Junior want you to fire him?"

"I don't know. He just told me to fire him."

"What words did he use in telling you to do this?"

"Told me he wanted him gone and if I didn't do it, he'd call the note the bank had on my plant."

"And you fired him, is that right?"

"That very evening, when he came in off the route."

Candle went back to his counsel table. "Thank you, Mr. Hammond. The solicitor may have some questions for you."

Fleming stood and walked back to the bar, resting against it. "Mr. Hammond, what kind of salesman was the defendant?"

"I've seen better."

"You say Lester Junior didn't tell you, sir, why he wanted you to let the defendant go?"

"No, sir."

"Did you ask him?"

"No, sir, I didn't."

"Well, I declare," Fleming said with a laugh and a quick glance at the jury. "Was Lester Junior concerned about your repaying the loan the bank had made to your bottling company?"

"Yes, sir. We'd talked about it. The note was past due."

"Did you get the idea, sir, he wanted you to fail in business?"

"No, sir."

"He wanted to help you, is that right? That's why he didn't call the note, isn't it, sir?"

"Yes, sir. I suppose."

"And y'all, the two of you, y'all discussed the problems you were having down there, didn't you?"

"Some of them, yes, sir."

"Wasn't one of these problems personnel?"

"I don't remember that."

"Well, now, hasn't just about everybody had a problem with help? You're not some kind of exception, are you, Mr. Hammond?"

"Well, I may have had some help problems from time to time. I just don't remember discussing them with Lester Junior."

"You discussed Dewey Coltraine, didn't you?"

"Yes, sir. In a way."

"And he was a problem, wasn't he?"

"Well, he wasn't the best salesman in the world, if that's what you mean."

Fleming turned and faced the jury. "Isn't what happened, Mr. Hammond, sir, Lester Junior simply recommended that you lay Dewey Coltraine off because he wasn't doing you any good as a salesman and if you didn't do something to improve your sales the bank was going to have to call its note?"

"That's not the way I remember it, Mr. Solicitor. No, sir."

"You say you're no longer operating the bottling plant? Why's that?"

"I was forced into bankruptcy."

"Was it the bank that did it? Forced you into bankruptcy?"

"No. It was a bottle manufacturer out of Georgia."

"But the bank tried to help you, didn't it? Tried to keep you afloat, right, sir?"

"Yes, sir."

"And Lester Junior advised you to get rid of Dewey Coltraine not too long before you went under, is that right?"

"I guess you could say that."

Fleming took a moment to search through his file folder. He removed a paper and read it over. "One other thing, Mr. Hammond," he said, looking at the paper. "What boards or committees did you serve on with Lester Junior?"

"Two."

"And they were, please sir?"

"The Semmes County Airport Committee. We're trying to get the War Department to let the city acquire DuBose Field when they're finally done with it. They're in the process of closing it down now."

"The other one?"

"The board out there at the TB sanatorium—Blue Springs Cottage Sanatorium."

Fleming turned and nodded to the witness. "Thank you, Mr. Hammond. No further questions."

"Any re-direct, Mr. Reid?" Judge Pryde asked.

Before answering, Candle went over in his mind about what had just happened. Fleming had neutralized Hammond and there was nothing Candle could do about it. "No, Your Honor," Candle said, trying not to look bothered by the turn of events. "The witness may come down."

Candle nudged Dewey. "Your Honor," he said," I call Dewey Coltraine."

Dewey, his head down, eased himself up from his chair and walked past Candle on his way to the witness stand. He stopped at the clerk of court's desk as the other witnesses had done and took the oath.

His direct testimony consumed very little time. After questioning Dewey about his background, including his past employment and his army service during the war, Candle moved to the events that led up to what had brought everyone together there in the courtroom. He dwelt on Dewey's recollection of the evening when he found Nellie in the shower, battered, raped, and bleeding, and his recollection of the following morning when he learned the identity of her attacker. Dewey also told of Mayfield's threats, his assault on him, his order to vacate the folding house, and his getting him fired at the bottling plant. Candle spent very little time asking Dewey about the killing itself, figuring the less said about it the better. After inquiring about Nellie's whereabouts, Candle offered Dewey to Solicitor Fleming for cross-examination.

Solicitor Fleming took his time before starting his cross-examination. He read over his notes, jotted some things down on his legal pad, and sorted through some papers that lay on his table. Candle thought the delay was a trial tactic designed to make Dewey apprehensive and to focus the jury on what was about to unfold. After what seemed like forever, but which consumed less than a minute, Fleming rose from his chair and took several steps toward the witness stand. "You say your wife's in the State Hospital, sir?" he began.

"Yes, sir."

"Is that why you're not calling her as a witness, sir?"

"I don't think she's able to come."

"How do you know that, sir?"

Dewey did not answer the solicitor's question but looked at Candle with a helpless expression on his face.

Candle could do nothing.

"Did you try to subpoena her, sir, and get her here so His Honor could determine if she were able to testify or not, sir?" Fleming said, facing the jury, his back to Dewey.

"I dunno, sir, if we did or not. I don't reckon we did." Dewey appeared confused.

"You don't reckon you did, sir?" Fleming wheeled around. "And she's the only person who could verify these absolutely awful things you've had to say a minute ago about Mr. Mayfield, the man you shot and killed, sir?"

"I just heard she's real bad off and she won't talk or nothin' and they had to—"

"Uh-huh. Now you say, sir, you came home one evening shortly after y'all moved in and you say you found your wife had been raped and beaten, right? Found her in the shower, you say?"

"Yes, sir."

"And of course, like any man would do who came home and found his wife had been beaten and raped and who found blood all over the place, you immediately got in touch with the sheriff to find the person who did it and to have him arrested and put him in jail, right?"

"No, sir."

Fleming put a hand to his ear. "What's that you say?"

"No, sir. I didn't. I didn't call the sheriff. Nellie told me—"

Fleming interrupted and faced the jury again. "And tell us, sir, what time the next morning, after you say you found out it was Lester Mayfield, Jr. who had attacked your wife and after you say he threatened you and hit you in the stomach, did you go to the justice of the peace and swear out an arrest warrant against him for what you say he did, sir?"

"I didn't go to one," Dewey answered.

"Even though you say, sir, he'd done these awful things to your wife and knocked you down?"

"Nellie said—"

"In fact, sir, you didn't tell anybody about that—not your in-laws, not your boss, not anybody, now did you, sir?"

"No, sir."

Fleming retrieved Dewey's confession from the court reporter and skimmed through it. "This says here," he said, slapping the document, "after you say Lester Junior told you to get off his place and left, you went on to work. Is that what you did?"

"Later that morning, yes, sir."

Fleming, his tongue against his cheek, glanced at Dewey's confession again. "And after Mr. Hammond had to let you go, you went looking for another job and for someplace else for you and your wife to live, isn't that right?"

"Yes, sir."

"And I believe you found another place and had made plans to move there?"

"Yes, sir. That's how come I had Mr. Hammond's truck that day."

"And the whole time you were doing these things—running your drink route, looking for and finding another place to live, hunting a new job, you left your wife all alone there at Lester Junior's place in Harpers' Joy, right? There at his hideaway."

"Yes, sir."

"After you say Mr. Mayfield came to your house that morning and told you what you said he did and supposedly hit you there in the stomach, you and your wife didn't immediately pack up your things and get the heck away from there, did you, sir?"

The jurors, like spectators at a tennis match, turned their heads as one toward Dewey, some straining to see around Fleming.

"No, sir. We couldn't. We didn't have us no place else we could go to."

"Is that right, sir?" Fleming asked, sneering and spinning around to confront Dewey. "Is that right? Where were you living before you moved to Harpers' Joy, sir?"

"At her daddy's. But Nellie didn't wanna move back there."

"How come?"

"She just didn't."

Fleming, his eyes wide and his mouth open, waited until most of the jurors copied his expression before he asked his next question. "Do you mean to tell this jury that you and your wife would rather live in a place owned by a man you say brutally raped your wife and beat you up than to live in a place where she would be surrounded by a loving father and mother? Is that what you are telling us, sir?"

Dewey appeared dazed. "I dunno, sir. I just know we couldn't move out right then."

"That's because your wife didn't want to move, isn't it, sir?"

"No, sir. I mean, yes, sir. Nellie—"

"And the reason, sir, is she was after Mr. Mayfield, wasn't she? She had a crush on him, I think the term is. And you found out about it, didn't you, sir, and you didn't like it?"

"No, sir."

"That's the reason you killed him, wasn't it, sir? You were jealous of him, weren't you?"

"No, sir."

"And the reason he ordered you and your wife off his place was because he didn't want a scandal, he didn't want some other man's wife chasing after him, isn't that right?"

"No, sir."

" 'No sir'? Do you mean to tell me and all these intelligent gentlemen here on this Semmes County jury and His Honor up there," Fleming said, sweeping his arms around and pointing, "that Lester Mayfield, Jr., a college graduate, a respected banker, a married man, a war hero who witnessed the surrender of the Japanese on board the Battleship Missouri, a man who came from one of the finest families in Semmes County—a respected community leader—wanted a scandal? Is that your testimony, sir?"

"I dunno what he wanted."

"Tell me, sir, if you can, what did such a man as Lester Mayfield, Jr. have to gain by becoming involved with a seventeen or eighteen-year-old girl, a girl who'd quit high school to marry a soft-drink salesman, a girl who was the wife of his tenant, his caretaker?"

"I dunno."

Candle groaned.

"But what did she have to gain, sir, if by some remote chance he had returned her affections like she wanted him to? Tell me that, sir?"

"She didn't have nothin' to gain."

"Nothing, sir? Is that your testimony?" Fleming's face was a picture of exaggerated disbelief. "I suggest, sir, she had everything in the world to gain had she succeeded. Why, if she had made him fall for her, she might could've gone from a house trailer to a mansion on a hilltop. And you knew that's what she was after and you just couldn't take it, could you, sir? You couldn't stand the thought of it, could you?"

Dewey did not answer but sat blinking his eyes.

"And that's why, sir, you followed him up to his hideaway and shot him down in cold blood, isn't it? You didn't want to risk that, did you, sir—him finally succumbing to her feminine wiles?"

"She wasn't wild. Nellie wasn't."

"And that's why, sir, a few days earlier you'd beaten and bloodied your wife up like you did, isn't that right? You thought she was running after him, didn't you and you were mad about it, weren't you?" Fleming was now screaming at Dewey.

"I didn't never hit her, Mr. Flemin'," Dewey said softly.

"Oh you didn't? Well, who's to say you didn't? Tell me that!"

"Nellie could tell you."

Fleming walked to the railing and pointed to the spectators seated in the courtroom. "But, sir, Nellie's not seated anywhere out there. She's not anywhere in the courthouse, is she?"

"No, sir."

"And that's because didn't neither you nor your lawyer saw fit to have her here, right, sir?"

Dewey offered no response but sat biting his trembling, lower lip.

Fleming glared at the jurors. "And tell me this, sir. How many extra days did you and your lawyer have to get her here? Wasn't it seven whole days?"

Dewey still did not say anything.

"So we're just supposed to take your word for what you say your wife would say were she here?" Fleming went to the clerk of court's desk and asked the clerk for the indictment. Standing less than a foot from the witness stand, Fleming unfolded the indictment and held it out toward Dewey, who ignored it. "Dewey Fletcher Coltraine, look at me."

Dewey raised his head but dropped it again to his chest.

"I say this, sir, and I say it right to your face, man to man," Fleming said, his voice low and authoritative. "I agree with the Semmes County Grand Jury—eighteen citizens—our neighbors and our friends—who, on their sacred oath, point their fingers at you and say that you shot, killed, and murdered with malice aforethought Lester Mayfield Jr. on November 22, 1946, with a shotgun."

Fleming laid the indictment back down on the clerk's desk. He straightened himself up and glowered at Dewey, who would not look back but continued to sit with his head bowed. Fleming bent forward, so close that his face was just inches away from Dewey's. "Look at me, Coltraine."

Dewey lifted his eyes, but not his head.

"You murdered Lester Junior for the same reason you attacked, assaulted, and beat your wife—out of pure jealousy."

"No, sir. That's not the reason."

"And this killing of Lester Mayfield, Jr., that wasn't some spur of the moment thing, now was it? You'd plan to kill him the first real chance you got, hadn't you?"

"No, sir. I didn't plan nothin' of the kind."

Candle did not like the defensive tone Dewey used in answering the solicitor's last question.

Fleming retreated to the front side of his counsel table. After a brief search of a file folder, he withdrew a piece of paper, glanced at it, and returned it to the folder. "Do you know a woman named Velma Creel?"

"Yes, sir. I know Miss Velma. She runs a store."

"Didn't you discuss with her the problem you were having with your wife? And didn't she tell you she thought you ought to exercise forgiveness?"

"I didn't tell Miss Velma nothin' special," he said in a weak voice.

"Well, we might just see about that after a while, sir."

Candle began a search of his own papers. He knew he had heard the name Velma Creel at some point in his talks with Dewey. Going to the notes of his first interview with his hapless client, Candle found the words "Miss Velma." They had been struck through. He tried to remember why they had been, but he could not.

Fleming walked around to the other side of his counsel table and stood behind it, facing the bench. "If it pleases the Court, I have no more questions of the defendant."

Candle, feeling ashamed either of his client or of himself—which one he could not be certain—announced there would be no further questions and told Dewey to come down from the witness stand.

Dewey sat in silence for a moment before he got up to leave. As he walked back to join Candle at their table, all the jurors watched him. Candle noticed not a single one of them manifested any pity for Dewey whatsoever. To a man, they seemed ready to announce their verdict then and there.

Candle stood, intending to say that he had no more witnesses. Before he could do so, however, and even before Dewey could find his seat, Judge Pryde announced that the court would take its lunch recess. Candle had lost track of the time. Events had moved at a fast pace that morning.

***

A deputy, Elbert "Sleep" Spangler, a tall, dimwitted giant of a man, came to remove Dewey from the courtroom. Candle, lost in thought about the collapse of his defense, failed to notice his coming. Spangler had handcuffed Dewey and was about to lead him away when Candle became aware of Spangler's presence. Indeed, it was Dewey's "see you after while, Mr. Reid" that reintroduced Candle to the present.

"What?" Candle asked, looking at Spangler, who now had Dewey by the elbow. "What do you call yourself doing, Sleep?"

Spangler's eyes widened. "Huh? I was just takin' him back to the jail so he could get him somethin' to eat, Mr. Reid. Don't you want him to eat?"

"I need to talk to him first. Come back here and sit down, Dewey," Candle said, motioning with his head. "You can leave the cuffs on him, Sleep. You just stand over there by the jury box until I get through talking with him, okay?"

Spangler obliged and made for the jury box where he sat down on the divider and began picking his teeth with a pocket knife.

"Dewey," Candle said, looking straight into the eyes of his doleful client, "there's still time to subpoena Colin Lucas, if you'll let me. Right now, I feel like his testimony is about the only thing that stands between you and the electric chair—and that's if he really would testify your wife killed Mayfield and not you and if the jury would believe him when he said it." Candle patted Dewey's cuffed hands. "What you say?"

Dewey sat for several seconds with his head bowed low. When he looked up, tears had filled his eyes. "Mr. Reid," he said at last, "I'm hungry."

Dewey's response shook Candle. "Dewey, is that a 'no' or a 'I'll think about it some during lunch time'? I've got to know. It might take some time to find Lucas."

"Don't try to go get him, Mr. Reid," he said trying to wipe his eyes with his shirt sleeves.

Candle sighed. "All right, Dewey. But I'll have to tell you—and I know I'm not much of a trial lawyer—I don't think you stand a dog's chance. Those men on the jury, they're going to find you guilty of murder and it's not going to take them more than five minutes to do it, either."

Dewey pushed back his chair and signaled the deputy to come get him by waving his cuffed hands back and forth. "Mr. Reid, sir. I've been knowin' that was gonna happen."

As Spangler walked toward them, Candle remembered Fleming's mention of Velma Creel during his cross-examination of Dewey. "Before you go get something to eat, what about this Creel woman? I had her name in the file, but I'd stricken through it. We must've talked about her at one time."

"She don't know anything, Mr. Reid."

"She doesn't? Well, the solicitor seems to think she does," Candle said. He glanced at his trial notes. "He asked you something about forgiveness. I missed the rest of it."

"We just talked one time—me and Miss Velma did—'bout Jesus and how He wanted us to forgive folks."

Feeling sympathy for Dewey, Candle watched Spangler lead him from the courtroom. He gathered up his papers and legal pad and left the courtroom by one of the back-hallway doors.

He needed a smoke. As he stood in the hallway behind the courtroom and lighted up, John Couick, a local lawyer, hailed Candle from down the hallway. "Hey, Candle, got a second?"

Couick, a few years younger than Candle and one whom everyone agreed was destined for great things as a lawyer and as a politician, had sat through all of Dewey's trial thus far. He rushed forward. "I'm glad I caught you."

"Yeah?" Candle said, turning around.

"Yeah. I've got a suggestion to make, but you've probably already thought of it."

Candle smiled. "What? I need all the help I can get."

"Ask Judge Pryde to charge manslaughter. That won't get your boy off, but it might save his life. There might be somebody on the jury that the Mayfields don't have in the bag, so to speak."

He searched Couick's face. Candle had focused so much on his "some-folks-just-need-killing" defense that he had given no more thought after his initial meetings with Dewey to the idea that his killing of Mayfield—if indeed it was Dewey, and Candle had some reason to doubt that it was—could be anything other than murder. "Manslaughter? How could what he did be manslaughter? Where's the sudden heat and passion?"

"You don't see it?" Couick said. "Coltraine comes back home, sees Mayfield out in his front yard, he knows what Mayfield has already done to his wife one time and figures he's come there to do it again and so he loses control, goes and gets himself a shotgun and comes back out and shoots him." Couick snapped his fingers. "Simple as that."

"I don't know, I still have trouble with the sudden heat and passion thing," Candle said. "Anyhow, you think he'd do it? The judge, I mean." He wiped his mouth with the back of his full-fingered hand. The other hand held his cigarette.

"Candle, tell me this. What have you got to lose? I mean, really?" Couick sounded more than a little aggravated.

***

When Candle announced to the court that the defense rested, Judge Pryde asked Solicitor Fleming if the State had any reply.

The solicitor stated he had one witness.

The announcement somewhat surprised Candle. Then he remembered Fleming's cross-examination of Dewey concerning Velma Creel.

Mrs. Creel settled into the witness chair after insisting her own Bible be used by the clerk of court to swear her as a witness. Holding the frayed, stuffed Bible in her lap, she smiled down at the jurors. She also smiled at Dewey once their eyes met.

Fleming began. "You're Velma Creel?"

"Yes, sir. Praise Jesus! Peace and grace, to all y'all."

Fleming smiled. "I understand you're an ordained minister of the Gospel?"

She held her Bible aloft and waved it. "Yes, sir. Praise the Lord! Ordained by the Lord His own self. He come to me one night in a vision and done it. I ain't been the same since. Praise Jesus!"

"The defendant sitting over there by Mr. Reid, you know him?" He turned and pointed.

A big grin covered her face. "That's Dewey Coltraine. He used to have

the Swizzle-Kola route one time. I run a store past Harpers' Joy, in Indian Town, close to the schoolhouse. He used to come there."

Fleming nodded. "All right, Mrs. Creel, I'm going to get right to the point." He glanced up toward the bench. Judge Pryde smiled and nodded also. "Now, directing your attention to November 19, 1946—that was a Tuesday—did the defendant come in your store that day?"

"You mean Mr. Coltraine? Yes, sir. He did. He was kinda hangdog lookin'."

"Did you have a conversation with him?"

"Yes, sir. I tried to find out what was botherin' him. He wouldn't say, so I guessed him and his wife must've had a fight of some kind." She held up her Bible. "I talked to him 'bout forgiveness, 'bout forgivin' his wife. You know, doin' what the good Lord wants all of us to do."

"What happened then?"

"He left."

"Did he say anything before he left?"

"Yes, sir. He said there was some things a man couldn't hardly forgive."

"Is that all he said?"

"No, sir. He said, 'A man's gotta do what he's gotta do,' sounded like."

" 'A man's gotta do what he's gotta do'?"

"Yes, sir. Sounded like."

Fleming turned toward Candle. "Witness with you, Mr. Reid, sir."

Candle whispered a question to Dewey and Dewey whispered back a reply.

"Mrs. Creel," Candle said, standing, his hand on his client's shoulder, "when Dewey here said, 'A man's gotta do what he's gotta do,' what did you think he meant by that?"

"Objection, Your Honor," Fleming said, halfway standing behind counsel table.

"Overruled," came a voice from behind and below the bench. Judge Pryde had disappeared, he had leaned back in his chair so far.

"Go ahead and answer, please, Mrs. Creel," Candle said.

"I thought he was talkin' 'bout forgivin' his wife."

"Thank you. That's all I have, Your Honor." Candle retook his seat.

Fleming got up from his chair. "Velma, you say you thought the defendant was talking about forgiving his wife when he said, 'A man's gotta do what he's gotta do,' is that right?"

"Yes, sir."

"You could be mistaken about that, couldn't you, Velma?"

"Yes, sir."

"When he said, 'A man's gotta do what he's gotta do,' he could have been talking about planning on killing a man he thought his wife was in love with, couldn't he?"

"I reckon he could."

"Couldn't he just as well have been talking about feeling like he had to kill somebody?"

"I sho' would hope not."

"And this was on Tuesday, November 19, three days before he shot Lester Mayfield, Jr. on Friday? Three whole days?" Fleming held up three fingers, waving them back and forth.

"Yes, sir."

"So, what we have here, then, is three days before the Friday he shot and killed Lester Mayfield, Jr., the defendant was already planning on what he was going to do. Right?"

"I dunno, Mr. Fleming. All I know is I thought he was talkin' 'bout forgiveness. But I could be wrong. If I am, I wished it had've been forgiveness he was talkin' 'bout, 'cause then maybe Mr. Mayfield, he'd still be alive and wouldn't none of us be in here today."

"Do you think, Mrs. Creel, if he had truly had forgiveness in his heart he would have gone out three days later and killed somebody?"

Velma closed her eyes and brought her hands together, as if in prayer. "No, sir. I don't reckon so," she whispered, opening her eyes.

"Tell me this and I'm through. Do you still believe, then, he had forgiveness in his heart when he left your store that day, knowing now what you do?"

Velma placed the Bible to her lips and peered over it with sad, watery eyes that she directed at Dewey. "No, sir. Not when you look at it like that, he didn't," she said, her mouth hidden by the black, golden-edged book.

Candle realized that, if there had been any question at all in the jury's mind regarding whether Dewey had acted with malice aforethought—the element that distinguished the offense of murder from manslaughter—the question had now been answered. Velma's testimony alone supplied sufficient evidence from which the jury could infer premeditation.

***

Before bringing the jury back into the courtroom, Judge Pryde inquired of both counsel whether either had any special instructions that he wanted given to the jury.

After Solicitor Fleming said he had none, Candle stood and requested a jury charge on manslaughter as a lesser-included offense of murder.

Judge Pryde sat for a moment, staring at Candle, not saying a word. He shook his head. "Your request is denied."

Candle glanced over toward the grand jury box where John Couick sat surrounded by several other lawyers and a sprinkling of law enforcement officers. Couick raised his hands in mock surrender.

Fleming waived opening argument, forcing Candle to go first. Candle's argument did not take much time because he had very little to argue. Rather than concentrate on what he had planned to argue, the "some-folks-just-need-killing" defense, Candle emphasized a defense that was the direct opposite—"some-folks-just-don't-need-killing." The word "folks" in the latter defense referred to Dewey Coltraine, whereas in the former it meant Lester Mayfield, Jr. Candle begged for Dewey's life.

During his entire summation, not a single juror would look Candle's way, no matter what he did to gain eye contact. If a juror was not studying a spot on the wall, the floor, the back of his hand, or a thread on his shirt or coat, he was staring past Candle. As he finished his argument, Candle knew he had succeeded in boring everyone almost to death. Even Dewey appeared relieved when at last Candle thanked the jurors for their attention—something every trial lawyer is expected to do whether the jurors paid attention to his case or not—and returned to his counsel table, defeated and resigned to his client's fate.

Fleming's argument, delivered in a spectacular, outrageous manner, reminded Candle of a fire-and-brimstone sermon he once heard an evangelist preach at a camp-meeting revival that his father made him attend one summer when he was a teenager. It brought the entire courtroom to life. The jurors in particular relished every shout, every whisper, every suggestion, every quote from scripture, every story, every wink, and every nod.

When Fleming, sometimes arguing facts outside the evidence, referenced Lester Junior's and the Mayfield family's contributions to their country and community and bemoaned Lester Junior's being the only child of one of Tekoa's leading citizens, a man who had helped many people through hard times with bank loans, many times given with little or no collateral, some jurors seemed on the verge of tears. Fleming concluded his argument by emphasizing the premeditated nature of the killing and by pointing to Dewey and telling the jurors, "If you don't convict this man, you might as well go ahead and tear this courthouse down brick by brick, use those bricks to build a wall around Semmes County, call it Hell, and blow it off the map."

Throughout the full hour or more that Solicitor Fleming spoke, Candle sat motionless at his counsel table, his chin resting on the knuckles of his good hand, his eyes downcast, his ears attuned to the savaging of his forlorn client.

Once or twice during the solicitor's argument, Candle felt he should look at Dewey to see how he was holding up. But he could not bring himself to do it. He never liked looking at dead people. And though Dewey then lived and breathed, he was as good as dead. Candle knew it and he suspected Dewey knew it too.

Much to Candle's surprise and, he surmised, to everyone else's, the jury stayed out for a little over four hours before returning with its verdict a few minutes before eight o'clock that evening. When the clerk of court published the jury's findings, however, there was no surprise. The verdict was what Candle understood it would be from the start. "Guilty," the back of the indictment read. The guilty verdict meant an automatic death sentence by electrocution.

As Candle learned several minutes after the trial, there had been one juror who had held out for Dewey's outright acquittal until the last vote. The juror, a down-on-his-luck insurance salesman who ran a debit route and coughed all the time, made no secret in the jury room about how much he despised the Mayfields and how he thought Dewey had done what any self-respecting man should have done under the circumstances. He had been brought around to the view held by the other eleven jurors only after they, to a man, told him they were prepared to stay in the jury room until Hell froze over. When he realized he could not outwait them, he capitulated.

Candle left the courthouse, went straight home, and went to bed. He was dead tired and cold sober when he fell asleep.

Bert Goolsby

Tuesday, April 15, 1947

Candle awoke to the sound of two bells jangling: one on his alarm clock and the other on his telephone. He reached for the telephone first. That proved to be a mistake. The alarm was so loud he could not make out the voice on the other end. "Just a minute, let me shut this alarm off," he mumbled into the mouthpiece. He laid the telephone down and picked up the alarm clock.

After turning off the alarm, he picked up the telephone again and apologized to the caller for the delay. He froze when he heard the caller's voice again and realized it was his wife.

"Candle, I read about your case in the paper this morning and I just wanted to tell you how sorry I am." Her voice was sweet, kind, and sympathetic.

For a moment, he didn't know quite how to respond. "Paula, my client confessed, you know. Plus, Lester Junior's wife caught him with the shotgun in his hand right after he did it. The case was hopeless from the start."

"From what I read in the paper and heard about on the radio, it sounded like it was."

A long silence ensued. Candle could not think of anything else to say. It had been weeks since he had last spoken to her and then only for a moment or two. The call both befuddled and unnerved him.

"Candle," Paula said, bringing the silence to an end, "I ran into Judy yesterday morning. Didn't she tell you?"

"No, huh-uh. I haven't hardly seen her to talk to her, I've been so busy with this case."

"She told me about how you hadn't had a drink in a week or more. I just wanted you to know that I'm proud of you. I've been praying for you every day. I really have."

That little bit of news startled him. "Praying for me?"

"Yes. The girls, too. They want their daddy well again."

Candle thought of his daughters and how very much he wanted to see them, to hold them, to talk to them. Being separated from them like he had been for the past seven months had made him realize what a blessing they both were and how much they meant to him. "Paula, I know this isn't a weekend I could visit with them, but do you reckon you could let me have the girls this Saturday? I need to get away from here. Go somewhere. Do something different. I've got to try and put this awful trial behind me. What do you say? Having them with me would help me a whole lot."

Paula paused before answering him. "Let me ask you this, Candle. After you got out of court yesterday and you went back to your apartment, did you have anything to drink?"

"No, I didn't," he said in a calm voice, though the question irritated him.

"You swear to me you didn't?"

"I swear," he replied, trying to sound convincing.

There was another pause. "Then yes, you can have them."

"Capital!" Candle exclaimed. "I'll come get them Saturday around lunch time, if that's all right with you—after I go by the Sheriff's Office and let them certify me."

"I don't think that's necessary."

"Well, I wouldn't want to give Judge Pryde the pleasure of throwing me in jail," Candle explained. "He'd love to do that, you know."

"Oh, Candle, that's just your imagination."

"And Paula?"

"Yes?"

"Can you also let me borrow our car?"

"Why, yes. Of course."

"And about ten dollars? I haven't closed a file in I don't know when."

Bert Goolsby

Thursday, June 17, 1948

Dewey Coltraine studied the troubled figure that sat opposite him in the visiting room. He figured this would be the last time he would see his lawyer. The United States Supreme Court had denied the petition to review his conviction, and the State Supreme Court had set the date for his execution. Not long afterward, the governor—in what some thought was unusual haste—had refused to commute his sentence. Dewey was scheduled to die the following evening at six o'clock.

"Mr. Reid, sir, I don't reckon I know how to say thank you for all you done for me, especially since you didn't get paid or nothin'. I hope you don't blame yourself for what's 'bout to happen to me. You did all you could and then some."

Candle did not look at Dewey. He sat with his head bent, a cigarette held between the only fingers of his left hand. "Dewey, I got something I don't think I ever told you before. But I'm the one who ought to be thanking you. Did you know that?"

"No, sir." The assertion surprised Dewey. Very few people in his life had ever thanked him for anything.

Dewey watched Candle raise his head and smile at him. "If it hadn't been for you, Dewey, I don't think I would have ever quit drinking and sobered up."

"Sir?"

"That's right. Do you know I haven't had a drink of liquor since right before your trial? Not a single drop." He flicked the burnt ashes off his cigarette and took another drag. "When my wife found out I'd quit drinking, she decided she'd stay in town and not take the kids and move to New York like she'd told me she was going to do. She said she didn't mind the girls seeing me as long as I was sober."

Dewey smiled. "That's real good, Mr. Reid. I'm proud for you."

"Maybe if you had gotten a new trial you could've helped me get rid of this habit too," Candle said, nodding at the cigarette.

"I bet you can still quit," Dewey replied, trying to be supportive of the only person he could call his friend, other than Nellie, whom he never heard from.

All that Candle had told him about Nellie was that she was still a patient at the State Mental Hospital. Her family refused to tell Candle anything about her condition and what progress, if any, she had made toward recovery.

Dewey's letters to Nellie at the hospital went unanswered as well. He wondered if she was allowed to read them or even if she was capable of reading them.

Candle's face grew very serious. "Dewey, you remember the first time we ever talked?"

"Yes, sir. I do."

"You remember my telling you that anything you told me as your lawyer would be held in strictest confidence? You remember my telling you that?"

"Yes, sir."

"I've got to know this, Dewey. I really got to—for my own mental health," Candle said, a frown on his narrow face.

"Know what, Mr. Reid?" Dewey replied.

Candle leaned back in his chair and snuffed out the cigarette in an ashtray on his side of the divider that separated them. "Was it you or was it Nellie who really killed Mayfield?"

"Mr. Reid, I done—"

Candle lifted his good hand. "Remember, Dewey, I'm not allowed to divulge confidences of a client."

Dewey lowered his eyes and dropped his head. "Like I always told you, Mr. Reid, it was me. It wasn't Nellie." He raised his head again and, blinking, stared into Candle's eyes. "Really, Mr. Reid. I'd tell you if it was otherwise. I really would."

Candle relaxed. "Dewey, one thing I've never understood is why Mayfield would have continued to stand there and yell and so forth after you got there, especially after you went inside and got the shotgun. Why wouldn't he have gotten back in his car and hurried away from there when he saw you with the shotgun?"

"I dunno. He just didn't. I guess he figured I really wouldn't shoot him since I didn't fight him back that time. You know, when he come—"

"Tell you what I've come to believe, Dewey. I think that Lucas fellow really did see what happened. I think he was there, like he said. He saw Nellie had the shotgun with her out in the yard and he saw her shoot Mayfield. All that happened before you got there and you're taking the blame for her."

"Like I done told you, Mr. Reid, he wasn't there, not out at the foldin' house, he wasn't. He's just storied when he told you that."

Candle reached down into his briefcase and brought up some documents. "I prepared the paper you wanted, where you leave your body to the medical college. And this other one is a change-of-beneficiary form for your G.I. insurance. This'll change it from your Aunt Ruth to Nellie, although, to tell you the truth, I don't know if she'll ever see a dime of the money, once the hospital or her family finds out she's got a little something coming in."

"I could name you, Mr. Reid. That way you'd be gettin' a little somethin' for all you done for me."

Candle smiled. "No thanks. I'm not going to profit from the lousy job I did representing you." He handed the papers across the divider to Dewey. A guard standing nearby came over and inspected the papers, although he had seen them earlier when Candle had entered the interview room and opened his briefcase to disclose its contents. Candle handed Dewey a fountain pen. "Just sign on the lines I've checked with a pencil."

Dewey signed the papers and returned them and the pen to Candle, who also signed them.

Candle placed the documents in his briefcase, closed it, and stood. He peered down at Dewey, who continued to sit. "Well, Dewey, I guess this is it. I guess we won't see each other anymore."

"Oh, I'll see you again someday, Mr. Reid, you and Nellie both. I'll be right up yonder, standin' by the gate, waitin' for both y'all."

As Dewey stood to leave, he rubbed away with his knuckles the tears that obscured his vision. "Mr. Reid, if you ever do see Nellie, would you tell her, please, sir, that I loved her a whole lot?"

"I won't have to tell her. All I have to do is tell her what you did for her."

Dewey smiled and extended his hand over the divider toward Candle. "Goodbye, Mr. Reid. And much obliged."

***

It was six o'clock when Candle returned to his office, exactly twenty-four hours before Dewey Coltraine would be strapped into the state's electric chair and put to death. Candle's imagination conjured up images that sickened him—so much so, that he contemplated dropping by Coe's Liquor Store and renewing old ties with Johnny Gray, notwithstanding he had been sober since the start of Dewey's trial months before. Candle knew of no one else who could help him through what lay just ahead.

Candle promised himself that, beginning Friday evening, he would make every effort to forget about Dewey Coltraine, Lester Mayfield, Jr., and everything that even reminded him of the terrible ordeal that his representation of Dewey Coltraine had been for him. He also promised himself he would never again undertake to represent a defendant in a capital murder case, even if that meant being held in contempt of court for refusing to do so. The pressure was just too great.

Candle searched the top of his desk for something to get his mind off Dewey and off Johnny Gray, at least for a little while. But that was not to be insofar as his thoughts related to Dewey Coltraine. Sitting atop everything was a large, garnet-colored file folder from the clerk of court's office. It contained the court record in the case of *The State versus Dewey Fletcher Coltraine*. A note from Jimmy Honeycutt, the clerk of court, asked Candle to review the materials inside and advise him about which documents in the folder could be discarded after Dewey's execution. Honeycutt complained about the lack of storage space within his office. He concluded his note saying, "Every little bit helps."

Candle thought the note insensitive; but then, Jimmy Honeycutt seldom showed sensitivity to anyone, especially lawyers.

Candle untied the string around the folder and opened it. Candle began thumbing through the items in the folder, intent on writing Honeycutt a note the next morning telling him to keep everything. He owed Honeycutt no favors and cared nothing for Honeycutt's space problems.

Candle lifted a small, capped bottle from the folder and jiggled it at his ear, listening as the object inside ricocheted within. He next removed the autopsy report and opened it. The document, which he had not read before, caused him several moments of discomfort during the trial as he fought to keep it out of evidence.

His eyes fell on the words typed below the heading "Wounds." Something didn't seem right. Candle reread the entry. Laying aside the autopsy report, he reached for the trial transcript. He flipped to Dr. Koutrakos' testimony and began reading it.

He jumped up from his chair. "How stupid of me! Why haven't I looked at this before?"

He opened the bottle and looked inside. "Oh, my God!" he cried.

He made a frantic search of his desk for the telephone book. Not finding it, he went to the outer office and got his secretary's. He ran a finger down the page of the listings that began with an "F." When he found the number he was searching for, he dialed the home telephone number of Solicitor J. Hopson Fleming.

A woman's voice answered. "Hello."

Candle responded, talking fast. "Mrs. Fleming, is the solicitor in? I need to talk with him. It's important."

"You say you're Mr. Porter?"

"No, ma'am. This is Candle Reid," he said, speaking a bit slower. "Could I please speak to your husband?"

"Wait just a minute."

When he thought the minute would never end, a familiar voice came on line. "Candle? What's up, ol' sport?"

"Solicitor, I'm sorry to bother you at home—"

"No bother. I'm always happy to hear from you. What can I do for you?"

"Do you mind if I drop by your house about thirty minutes from now? I've got something I need to show you. Something important."

"It can't wait until tomorrow?"

"No, Hop, it can't," Candle said. "It's about Dewey Coltraine."

"Coltraine? Now what?"

"It won't take up much of your time. I promise."

There was a long pause. "Anything to do with what's to happen tomorrow evening?"

"It might. That's why I need to talk to you tonight." Candle decided to hang up rather than give Fleming a chance to say no.

With Honeycutt's folder in hand, Candle left his office and headed straight for the sheriff's office. He knew Sheriff Madison kept late hours and seldom went home before eight o'clock. When he walked into the main lobby of the sheriff's office, Madison was leaning over the counter that divided the room, talking to an old black man. Candle waited by the door until the conversation ended.

The man turned and walked out of the office, bowing to Candle as he approached the door. "Lawyer Reid, sir," he said.

"Abraham," Candle replied, holding the door open as the old man walked past him.

"Sheriff, could you ride out to Solicitor Fleming's house with me?" Candle asked. "I've got something I want to show the two of you."

"Like what?"

"I'll show you when we get there." Candle strode to the door and opened it. "You coming or not?"

"I reckon so. But this better not be some kinda lawyer shenanigans."

***

When Candle and Madison arrived at Fleming's home, the front door opened before Candle could knock. "I heard y'all coming," said Mrs. Fleming, a tall, elegant woman with a sweet face. "Hop's out in his shop. He said for y'all to come on out there."

Madison led the way.

The shop served as Fleming's only known diversion. He was an expert craftsman in stained-glass. Many of his works graced churches and the homes of the rich and powerful throughout Semmes County and the surrounding area—each one a gift from Fleming. His best-known work, "Jacob Wrestling with God," provided the focal point for the sanctuary of the First Methodist Church.

Fleming greeted both men with a slight smile. After shaking hands, he motioned for them to sit as he continued to stand. "I didn't expect to see you, Sheriff. This is a surprise."

The sheriff glanced at Candle. "I'm surprised my own self. It wasn't my idea to come here."

Fleming leaned back against his work table. "Well now, Candle, what's so all-fired important that you'd drag the sheriff away from his office and me away from my stained-glass work?"

Candle dug into the clerk of court's file folder and removed the autopsy report. With a shaking hand, Candle handed it to Fleming.

Fleming examined the document front and back and looked at Candle, a studied look on his face. "What do you want me to do with this?"

"Open it and go to the page where Dr. Koutrakos discusses Lester's wounds."

Fleming found the page Candle wanted. "Now what?"

Candle pointed. "Read right there below where it says 'Wounds' what Dr. Koutrakos had to say about what he found. Read it out loud so Bo can hear you, if you will."

Fleming turned sideways and held the report up closer to the light that hung above his work table. " 'Shot penetrated brain—parenthesis—not retrieved but took a flattened piece of buckshot from between skull and scalp—parenthesis closed,' " he said, reading. "So?"

Candle smiled. He handed the solicitor the printed transcript of record on appeal. It contained the trial transcript. He had marked two places within the record with paper clips. "Now go to the first page I've got marked and read what Dr. Koutrakos testified to—just the part right there, beginning with line twenty, I think it is." he said, indicating.

" 'Answer: Only one wound—one shot—pierced the skull. The other one glanced off the skull and went beneath the skin. I removed a flattened piece of shot from between the skull and the scalp when I folded the scalp back.' "

"Read on," Candle said.

" 'Question: How about the other one? Did you recover it? Answer: No, sir. It had penetrated the brain and was deep inside the cranium. I didn't try to get it because I didn't want to bother with removing the scalp. Question: Was that shot, sir—the one you didn't take out, didn't remove—was it sufficient in and of itself to cause death? Answer: Yes, it was. Question: Doctor, what in your opinion caused the death of Lester Mayfield, Jr.? Answer: The shot that penetrated his skull and lodged in his brain. What did—' "

Candle interrupted. "That's enough."

Fleming laid the transcript down on his work table and eyed the piece he had been working on. "Where are we going with this, Candle? I don't catch on."

"Me, neither," the sheriff said.

"Look at the transcript again and read that other place I've marked."

Fleming lifted the transcript and turned to the other paper-clipped page. " 'Question: And what's that you're holding, Sheriff? Answer: Two empty shotgun shells. Winchester. Number Four shot. I personally removed them from the Daly. See? This is my mark there, on this one and on this one.' "

The sheriff jumped to his feet. "How could that've happened? I don't understand how come I didn't catch that!"

"And then there's this," Candle said, as he produced the bottle that held the object taken by Doctor Koutrakos from Mayfield's scalp. "Looks like buckshot to me. Too big to be anything else."

"What are y'all getting at?" the solicitor said, studying the faces of both men in his shop. I'm not sure I'm following all this."

"It's the shells, Solicitor" the sheriff said, his face drained of its color.

"What about them? You know I'm not a hunter."

"What Candle's sayin', Solicitor, is buckshot killed Lester Junior, not birdshot. Number Four shot is birdshot," the sheriff explained.

"Birdshot? Maybe the shells were mislabeled or something," the solicitor said, his face now drawn.

"Maybe, but I don't think so," Candle said.

"Well, could there be some other reason for the discrepancy?" Fleming asked.

"Another shotgun was used to kill Lester Junior," Candle said after a pause.

"But, Candle, Coltraine told me he done it," the sheriff said. "And he testified to it in court."

"Well, Bo, maybe he thought he was the one who did it. But if all Dewey fired was birdshot, then it couldn't have been him who killed Lester Junior, that's for sure. It had to have been somebody else. There's no other satisfactory way to explain the buckshot Dr. Koutrakos found in his scalp."

Fleming grunted. "Sheriff, I think maybe you better get in touch with the governor's office and tell them to hold off on executing Coltraine while we look into this."

The sheriff nodded agreement. "I'll do it soon as I get back to my office. How much of a reprieve should I ask for?"

"Just tell him to put it off for a month or so."

"And the reason?" the sheriff asked.

"So he can give the matter further consideration. He can say he's been too busy with other matters. Busy with the budget, recruiting industry—stuff such as that. He'll know what to say. He's the governor. You don't get to be governor without knowing how to say things that bamboozle the majority of the electorate."

Candle savored the moment. He had bought Dewey some more time. For the first time since his admission to the bar, Candle felt himself a lawyer worthy of the name. He only wished Mr. Blumberg had been alive to see what he had done for his client, and he had done it pretty much on his own. Mr. Blumberg would have been proud.

Sheriff Madison looked at Candle and then at Solicitor Fleming. "If Coltraine didn't shoot Mayfield, then who you reckon done it? Coltraine's wife? And if it wasn't her, the only other person it could have been would be Mayfield's wife. She was the only one up there besides them."

Candle had an answer for any suggestion that Georgia Ann Mayfield could have killed her husband. "No. I don't think it could have been Georgia Ann. When Dewey first saw her, remember, she was coming up the road, which would have been to Lester Junior's left. The shot that killed him hit him on the right side."

"Then, if it wasn't Coltraine and it wasn't Mayfield's wife, it had to be Coltraine's wife," the sheriff declared. "She could've reloaded the shotgun with birdshot."

Candle thought about Madison's statement for a moment. "Well, right, it could have been Nellie. And granted, she might could've reloaded the shotgun just like you said, Bo. First, she could've shot the buckshot at Lester Junior, killed him, and then shot up the car using birdshot. But I don't think that happened. Anyhow, y'all didn't find any other empty shotgun shells up there, now did you?" Candle paused and said in a reproachful voice. "And you did look, didn't you?"

Sheriff Madison's face flushed. "Well, yeah, we looked for things. Not for that particularly. But no, we didn't find no other empty shells. That doesn't mean, though, she couldn't've shot more than twice. And she and Coltraine, they had plenty of time to get rid of the shells, if she did."

Candle closed his eyes for a moment. "The reason I don't think it could be her is there was one other person up there that I know of. Somebody who thought he had a reason to kill Lester Junior."

"Who?" the sheriff asked. "Our investigation didn't show nobody else up there."

The solicitor picked up a piece of broken glass from off his work table and threw it into a small bucket. "He's talking about Colin Lucas."

Candle looked sideways at Fleming. "Mr. Mayfield told you about Lucas coming to my office and threatening me, didn't he?"

Before Fleming could answer, the sheriff asked, "What's this 'bout Lucas, Candle?"

"He came to my office the day the solicitor arraigned Dewey. He told me he was up at Lester Junior's place the day he got killed. Claims he saw what happened. That Dewey's wife was the one who'd shot Lester Junior," Candle responded. "I asked Dewey about what he said, but he kept insisting that he'd killed Lester Junior, not his wife."

"How'd Lucas happen to tell you that, Candle?" the sheriff asked, glancing at Fleming, his face registering disbelief.

"I represented the bank in a foreclosure suit which Lester Junior insisted on my bringing against Lucas. After Lester Junior got killed, Lucas came to my office and said he wanted me to tell old man

221

Mayfield that if the bank didn't drop the foreclosure suit, he would testify that Dewey's wife was the person who shot Lester Junior."

Candle paused. "I'll tell you both something. Once I got into this case good, I don't think I ever believed that Dewey really shot Lester Junior—not deep down, I didn't."

"Then how come you think he told us he was the one done it?" the sheriff asked. "I sure as heck didn't make him do it, I'll tell you that. And that's the truth, so help me."

"I think Dewey confessed because he thought his wife had shot him. He was afraid of what might happen to her—that she'd be arrested and sent off to prison and probably electrocuted. He loves her that much to do that, I believe," Candle explained.

Neither Fleming nor Madison said anything.

Candle continued. "I'll tell you something else, especially now that it looks—at least to me—like another shotgun was involved. I think Dewey's wife really was the one who shot up Lester Junior's car. That explains the two empty shells. I think she must've done it when he drove up and stopped in front of her house and honked or something. She probably came outside and, seeing it was Lester Junior, shot at him. I don't know. But if she did, she must've missed him because there is nothing in the autopsy report or the trial testimony to show any birdshot hit him."

"How 'bout the piece that's still in Mayfield's head? The piece the doctor didn't dig out? Couldn't it be birdshot?" the sheriff asked.

"The spread of the wounds shows you they both had to be buckshot; but that's just my opinion," Candle said. "Of course, if you've got some doubts, you could always get an order to exhume the body and get somebody to dig the shot out of his head. I don't have any doubt what you'll find."

Madison turned to Fleming. "I notice you ain't talkin', Solicitor."

"I've just been listening," Fleming said. "But after you call the governor's office, bring Lucas in and see what he's got to say."

The sheriff motioned to Candle. "Come on. I'll take you home before I go."

"No," Candle said, "I think I'll tag along, if you don't mind."

"Me too," Fleming said. "And Candle?"

"Yes?"

Harpers' Joy

Fleming laid a hand on Candle's shoulder, resting it there until Candle looked him straight in the eye. "I won't swear to it, but I really don't think I ever even read the autopsy report. But I'll say this, if I did read it, I didn't understand that ought-four shells weren't buckshot. To me, shotgun shells are shotgun shells."

Candle gave Fleming a slight nod. Although Fleming seemed sincere, Candle was not convinced he was. After all, Fleming was known to be a great pitchman. It was said of him that he could persuade an angel to trade its wings for a pair of roller skates. But since Fleming now seemed ready to assist, Candle chose to give him the benefit of the doubt.

"Solicitor," Candle said, "that makes three of us who didn't read it, and a man nearly died because we didn't."

***

"Is this where he lives now?" Candle asked as the sheriff drove up to the abandoned filling station.

"I don't reckon the fella had much of a choice after you and the bank saw fit to run him and his little girl off their place," the sheriff said.

Candle felt embarrassed, notwithstanding he had simply done what he had been employed to do and had operated solely within the law. He gazed at the front door of the building, wondering if he had made the right decision after all to accompany the sheriff and the solicitor to Lucas' place.

"'Course, the worst of it wasn't him losin' his farm." Madison shook his head. "No, it was his little girl gettin' real sick and dyin'."

"His little girl's dead?" Candle asked. "I hadn't heard anything about that."

"A few months ago—February, I think—she caught the pneumonia or somethin'," Madison said. "By the time he brought her in to see a doctor, it was too late, so I heard. Poor little ol' girl was weak anyway."

"Shall we get out, gentlemen?" Fleming asked.

"Let me blow the horn and see if he'll come outside," Madison said. "I'd rather do it that way. It'd seem less threatenin' to him than us goin' up there and knockin' on his door this late." He pressed down long and hard on the car horn.

In less than a minute, Candle saw a light come on inside the building and then move past the front window. A moment later, the front door opened, and Colin Lucas stood in the doorway, an oil lamp in one hand and a shotgun in the other. The sight of the gun frightened Candle. Now he was sure he should not have come.

Sheriff Madison stepped from the car and greeted Lucas. "Colin, sorry to bother you this time of the night. But me and the solicitor, we need to talk to you 'bout somethin'."

Lucas dipped low and peered into the car, moving his head from side to side. Candle saw Lucas' lips curl when their eyes met.

"Whatcha got that fella Reid with you fer, Sheriff?" Lucas asked, straightening up.

Madison slipped between Lucas and the car. "Candle? Oh, we just brought him along."

Lucas scowled and spat. "I don't like him, you know. Iffen it wasn't fer him, I wouldna lost my farm and Elsie, she wouldna got sick and up and died." He raised his shotgun one-handed and aimed it at Candle. "I ought to kill him right now fer what he done."

Madison pushed the barrel of the gun toward the ground. "That's enough of that now, Colin. Put it away. Better than that, hand it here."

Colin dropped the shotgun to his side.

"I said hand it here, Colin," Madison ordered, reaching out for the shotgun. "Don't make me have to take it from you."

Colin complied, but not without directing an angry look in Candle's direction.

Madison broke open the shotgun and removed its two shells. "Loaded with buckshot, I see."

"So what? I always keep it loaded with buckshot. There some law agin it?"

Madison gave Colin back his shotgun. "Mind if we go inside, Colin? What we need to talk to you about might take a little while."

Colin closed his upper arm around the stock of the shotgun. "I don't mind you and the solicitor, but I don't want him a'comin' in my place."

"I'm sorry, Colin, he comes in, too, or I'll have to take you on into town. Which is it gonna be?"

Lucas stood silent for a few seconds. "He can come in, I reckon."

Lucas turned and walked back into his home. When Madison reached the door, he motioned for Solicitor Fleming and Candle to exit the car and follow him inside.

The four men took seats around a table on which Lucas had placed the oil lamp.

Lucas, his arms folded, sat staring at Candle with hate-filled eyes. Candle tried not to look at him but was scared not to.

"Colin," Madison began, "I'll come directly to the point of why we're here. I know you were up at Mr. Mayfield's place there in Harpers' Joy the day he got himself killed."

Lucas dropped his arms and leaned across the table, his eyes burning Candle's. "Who says?"

Candle started to speak, but Madison put a hand on his arm. "Lucas, we know all 'bout you goin' to Mr. Reid's office here, threatenin' him, and tellin' him what you told him that day. We know you followed Mr. Mayfield out to the foldin' house trailer where Dewey Coltraine and his wife lived. We believe you have relevant information about the shooting and we want to know who really shot him. A man's life may depend on what you say. Understand?"

Lucas looked down. "Y'all probably wouldn't believe me even iffen I told y'all. Y'all'd think I was a'makin' it up." Lucas pointed to Candle. "He didn't believe me when I told him."

"Try us," Fleming said, removing a fountain pen from his shirt pocket.

"Okay then. Like I told him, it was Coltraine's wife what done it. She done shot him 'fore the boy got there."

"Colin," Madison said, "why didn't you say somethin' to me earlier 'bout this?"

Lucas squirmed around in his seat and pointed to Candle. "Well, like I say, I told him, but it didn't do no good, now did it? I knowed nobody'd believe me."

The sheriff smiled at Lucas. "I'm not askin' you about what you told some lawyer, Colin. I'm askin' you how come you didn't come tell me what you saw. I'm the law around here, not Candle Reid. And I've always shot square with you, haven't I?"

"Well, I reckon I jist didn't wanna git myself involved in nothin' what wasn't none of my business. I had 'nuff troubles of my own to tend to right then."

"You didn't wanna get involved and you knew an innocent man was about to be put on trial for his life for somethin' he didn't do, is that what you're tellin' me, Colin?" Madison said. "What kinda person are you anyway? I thought you were a better man than that."

Lucas remained quiet for a moment, taking deep breaths. "Well, I'm sorry. I reckon I shoulda done somethin' other. Is it too late now fer me now to try and help the boy some?"

Madison touched the back of Lucas' hand. "No, Colin, it's not too late to try and help him. That's why come we're here."

Madison drew his arm back and sat straight up in his chair. "But what I don't understand, Colin, is why you say Coltraine's wife shot Mr. Mayfield. That can't be true. Not from what I know about this case, it can't be."

Lucas' face went white and then red as he jumped up from his chair, knocking it to the floor in the process. "How come it can't? You a'callin' me a liar or somethin'? You listen to me, Sheriff, the reason I said it was her what shot him was 'cause I seen her shoot him my own self. Seen it with my own eyes, I did."

Madison glanced at Fleming, who busied himself writing on his notepad. "Where were you when this happened?"

Lucas lifted the chair from the floor, set it upright, and sat back down. "I was a'standin' kinda over to one side of the trailer house, over 'hind a tree there, kinda in a thicket like."

"Okay, so the only people there to start with were you, Mr. Mayfield, and Coltraine's wife, is that right? And Coltraine, he come up later?" Madison asked.

Lucas nodded. "Right. Jist the three of us there to begin with."

"Where was your daughter all this time, Colin? Who was looking after her?" the solicitor asked.

"I'd left her up there on the road in my truck. I'd locked the doors and told her not to open it up fer nobody."

Madison continued. "You're quite certain now that it was just the three of y'all?"

Lucas nodded but did not speak.

"Let me get clear about this. You're not tellin' me that Mr. Mayfield shot himself, are you?" Madison asked.

"'Course I ain't. Like I say, that girl shot him. I seen her do it. Then she fainted and Coltraine, he come up right after."

Madison nodded. "Did Coltraine have a shotgun with him?"

"Huh-uh," Lucas said, shaking his head. "He jist picked up the one his wife had. She dropped it when she fell down on the ground."

"Did his wife have another shotgun with her?" Madison asked.

"All she had was the one, the one what she shot at Mayfield with."

Madison looked at Candle and then at Fleming. "Colin," he said, shaking his head, "in that case I don't think Coltraine's wife could have been the one who killed Mr. Mayfield."

"How come you say that now?"

"Because she was usin' birdshot."

"So what? Birdshot can kill you."

"The reason the birdshot Coltraine's wife fired from her shotgun didn't kill Mayfield was because didn't none of it hit him."

Lucas angled his head. "Huh?"

"It was buckshot that the doctor found in Mr. Mayfield's head. How do you suppose that buckshot got there?"

Lucas did not answer but sat staring at the floor.

The sheriff reached toward Lucas and lifted his chin with his hand. "Look at me, Colin. We wanna take you up to the capital and let them give you a polygraph test."

Lucas brushed away the sheriff's hand. "What kinda test you a'talkin' about?"

"A polygraph test is what some folks called a lie detector test. Surely, you've heard of them. The folks up there, they can hook you up to one and it can tell them whether you're lyin' or not. We just wanna ask you one question and that's whether you killed Lester Mayfield, Jr. If you didn't do it, then you ain't got a thing in this world to worry about. So, whatcha say?"

Lucas sat in silence for a moment, his eyes closed. Then his body all of a sudden began shaking and he broke into tears.

"Colin, what's wrong?" Madison demanded.

Lucas wiped his nose on his shirt sleeve. "Sheriff, iffen it wasn't that girl what killed Mayfield, then I reckon it had to be me what done it."

"How could it have been you, Colin?"

"After you come out to my place that day and served 'em papers on me, I went and got my shotgun from over the mantel piece. Then me and my little girl, we drove into town. I was gonna try and catch Mayfield at the bank. I was gonna shoot him there. But then when I was a'gittin' outta my truck, I seen Mayfield drive by, a'lookin' like he was headed outta town. I got back in my truck and commenced to follow him. I aimed to shoot him first chance I got."

"Why'd you wanna do that, Colin?"

" 'Cause of what he was a'doin' to me and Elsie. I was real mad on account of him a'tryin' to git my land and home place and he wouldn't give me no 'nother chance to pay 'em back what I owed 'em."

"Your shotgun was loaded with buckshot?" Madison asked.

Lucas nodded.

"And you followed him out to Harpers' Joy?"

"Yes, sir. I seen Mayfield turn on what they call The Narrow Road. Then I seen him go through this here gate there. Soon as he done that, I stopped and got outta my truck and took off through the woods there."

"After you took off running through the woods, then what?"

"That's when I seen Mayfield'd stopped his car in fronta this here trailer house and'd got out. He was a'callin' fer this woman to come outside, a'sayin' he wanted to talk to her some. That's when I snuck up 'side the trailer house and got back of this big tree to see what was gonna happen. 'Bout that time, this real pretty lookin' girl, she come outta the house, a'carryin' a shotgun. I seen her shoot up Mayfield's car with it and when it looked to me like she was a'gittin' ready to shoot it up again, I come out from 'hind the tree, pointed my shotgun at Mayfield, and when she shot I shot at him too."

"Where were you when you shot?" Madison asked.

"Right there at the edge of the trailer, a few feet back from where she was a'standin'."

"Y'all fired right about the same time, you say?" Madison asked.

Harpers' Joy

"Pretty near. Then she passed out, the girl did, and fell down on the ground. And it was right after that when the boy come a'drivin' up and I run and got 'hind the tree again. I watched him git outta his truck and run over to where the girl was and seen him pick the shotgun up. That's when I took off a'runnin' out back through the woods. I figgered we both had killed him, but mainly I figgered it was her what done it 'cause she shot first and she was closer to him than I was and I might've missed him."

"What about Georgia Ann Mayfield? Did you see her there, Colin?" Candle asked.

"No, sir, Mr. Reid. I ain't seen her."

Candle felt like shouting but hid his elation. The feeling passed when he glimpsed a picture of Lucas' daughter on a nearby table. Seeing the picture made his stomach tighten.

"Lucas," Solicitor Fleming said, "I've tried to write down the essence of what you've told us just now on this notepad of mine. Let me read back to you what I've got written here. If I have it correct, I want you to sign it. Would you do that for me?"

Lucas wiped his eyes with his fingertips and nodded. "Yes, sir."

"And Candle?" Fleming said.

"Yes, Solicitor?"

"Soon as I can get to a telephone, I'll get in touch with the coroner and first thing tomorrow morning we'll ask the court for an order to exhume Lester Junior's body. Although, like you, I'm pretty certain we'll find buckshot in his skull, I want to be doubly sure. In the meantime, I'll consent to a writ of *habeas corpus* and an order for a new trial. Whether it was buckshot or birdshot, Dewey Coltraine did not kill Lester Junior. I'm convinced of that."

Candle felt a happiness that far exceeded any he had ever known before. Johnny Gray, even in his best moments, could not provide what Candle felt right then.

Bert Goolsby

Saturday, June 19, 1948

THE TEKOA NEW DEALER

Saturday, June 19, 1948

Death Row Inmate Released from Prison

    Tekoa (AP). Judge L. Malcolm Pryde yesterday afternoon signed a writ of habeas corpus that freed Dewey Coltraine, 21, from the state penitentiary after the body of a murder victim was exhumed and a piece of buckshot was removed from the victim's cranium. Another man, Colin Lucas, 42, of Cecelia, confessed Thursday night to the murder for which Coltraine had been convicted and given the death penalty. A Semmes County jury had convicted Coltraine last year of the murder of Lester Mayfield, Jr. near Harpers' Joy on November 22, 1946. The State Supreme Court, in a divided decision, later affirmed his conviction and sentence.
    Coltraine was to have died in the state's electric chair at 6 p.m. Friday. Papers filed at the Semmes County Court House show that District Solicitor J. Hopson Fleming consented to Coltraine's release. He also consented to an order both granting Coltraine a new trial and dismissing the murder charge against him. The solicitor's office said Solicitor Fleming was unavailable for comment.
    Although details remain sketchy, Coltraine's lawyer, Candle Reid of Tekoa, said Lucas' confession to having murdered Mayfield came about because Sheriff Bowden "Bo" Madison continued to investigate the case, notwithstanding Coltraine's conviction. He praised Madison for his dedication to the pursuit of justice and for maintaining an open mind about the case.
    When contacted after he regained his freedom, Coltraine told reporters a barber had shaved his head and he had ordered his last meal before word of his release reached him. Asked what he had ordered, Coltraine listed fried shrimp, fried catfish, french fries, baby-back ribs, and pecan pie topped with vanilla ice cream. "Right

now, though, a baloney sandwich and an ice-cold Swizzle would taste awfully good," he added.

Coltraine thanked Judge Pryde for ordering him freed immediately, Sheriff Madison for continuing his investigation, and Reid for his legal services. Reid had represented Coltraine by court appointment and received no fee for his services.

Sheriff Madison promised a full briefing later, saying, "I know all of you have lots of questions, but first I got to get all the answers."

Sunday, June 20, 1948

The head nurse escorted Dewey to a small waiting room not far from the nurses' station and told him it would be a few minutes. The few minutes stretched into well over an hour before Dewey heard sounds just outside the door.

Dewey stood as the door to the waiting room opened. He scarcely recognized the person in the drab, gray gown who stood at the door with the head nurse, her shoulders bent, her arms hanging by her side, slippers on her feet. The woman raised her head, brushed aside the strings of greasy hair that covered her face, and looked at Dewey with empty eyes.

"Nellie? Don't you know who I am?" He smiled, but not without tears inching down his cheeks.

The woman's head bobbed, and her eyes narrowed. "Are you somebody?"

He edged toward Nellie and reached for her hands. He took them into his own and kissed them. "It's me, Nellie. Dewey. I wanna try and help you get better."

"Dewey?" she whispered. "You're really Dewey?"

"Yes, sweetheart. Dewey."

"Dewey," she repeated. "I thought you were dead."

"I almost was," he said, pulling her close. "I almost was."

Harpers' Joy

Saturday, July 1, 1961

THE TEKOA NEW DEALER

Saturday, July 1, 1961

Candle Reid Sworn in as District Judge

Tekoa—Candle Reid, 47, of Tekoa took the oath of office as Judge of the Eighth Judicial District during a ceremony held yesterday afternoon at the Semmes County Courthouse. Retiring District Judge J. Woodrow Rhodes administered the oath as Reid's wife, the former Paula Gachet, held a Bible opened to the Eighty-second Psalm. Judge Reid's daughters, Rose Mary and Margaret Ann, helped their father don his robe for the first time. Following the swearing-in ceremony, the bar associations of Semmes and Lee Counties hosted a reception for Judge Reid at Ravenwood Country Club.

In prepared remarks, Judge Reid quoted *Philippians* 4:8, promising not only to think on "whatsoever things are honest" and "whatsoever things are just," but "to put those things into practice." He pledged to be "neither a plaintiff's judge nor a defendant's judge" but to be a judge committed to giving each litigant "his due." He asked for God's help in that endeavor. As he concluded, Judge Reid, an active AA member, credited both his wife and Dewey Coltraine, a former client, "with rescuing me from the deep." His voice cracked as he paraphrased the final words of an epitaph inscribed on a tombstone in a Harpers' Joy cemetery, "'Tis Candle Reid's joy."

Bert Goolsby

About the Author

Bert Goolsby grew up in Dothan, Alabama, and now lives with his wife the former Mary Ellen "Prue" Fraser in Columbia, South Carolina. He attended the University of Alabama before transferring to The Citadel where he earned his undergraduate degree. He also earned a law degree at the University of South Carolina and an advanced law degree at the University of Virginia. He is the former Chief Deputy Attorney General of South Carolina. His and Prue's son, Dr. Philip Lane Goolsby, practices family medicine in Green Bay, Wisconsin.

ALSO BY THE AUTHOR

FICTION

Troubles and Kuddles
Purple Yarn
Finding Roda Anne
The Mask No One Wanted
The Locusts of Padgett County
The Trials of Lawyer Pratt
Familiar Shadows
Five Stockings
Humanity, Darling
Her Own Law
The Box with the Green Bow and Ribbon
Sweet Potato Biscuits and Other Stories
On Grandma's Porch (anthology with other authors)
More Sweet Tea (anthology with other authors)

NONFICTION

Devotional Briefs (reprint of 90 Devotions for Lawyers & Judges and Those They Serve)
Lex Christi
The South Carolina Tort Claims Act: A Primer and Then Some

www.ingramcontent.com/pod-product-compliance
Lightning Source LLC
Chambersburg PA
CBHW021357210526
45463CB00001B/133